Conversations with Shōtetsu
(*Shōtetsu Monogatari*)

MICHIGAN MONOGRAPH SERIES IN JAPANESE STUDIES
NUMBER 7

CENTER FOR JAPANESE STUDIES
THE UNIVERSITY OF MICHIGAN

Conversations with Shōtetsu
(*Shōtetsu Monogatari*)

TRANSLATED BY ROBERT H. BROWER

WITH AN INTRODUCTION AND NOTES
BY STEVEN D. CARTER

Ann Arbor
Center for Japanese Studies
The University of Michigan
1992

Open access edition funded by the National Endowment for the Humanities/
Andrew W. Mellon Foundation Humanities Open Book Program.

The paper used in this publication meets the requirements of the ANSI Standard
Z39.48–1984 (Permanence of Paper).

Library of Congress Cataloging-in-Publication Data

Shōtetsu, 1381?–1459?
   [Shōtetsu monogatari. English]
   Conversations with Shōtetsu = Shōtetsu monogatari / translated by
Robert H. Brower ; with an introduction and notes by Steven D. Carter.
     p. cm. — (Michigan monograph series in Japanese studies : no. 7)
   Translation of: Shōtetsu monogatari.
   Includes bibliographical references and index.
   ISBN 978-0-939512-43-0
   I. Brower, Robert H., 1923–1988.   II. Carter, Steven D.
III. Title. IV. Series.
PL792.S55S4813   1992
895.6'124—dc20   90–2433
                                       CIP

A Note on the Type

This book is set in Garamond type. Jean Jannon designed it in
1615, but credit was mistakenly given to Claude Garamond (ca.
1480–1561), an early typeface designer and punch cutter, probably
because it resembles his work in refining early roman fonts. It is an
Old Style typeface, a group of typefaces first developed for printing
and characterized by their small x-height and oblique stress.

Composed by The Composing Room, Grand Rapids, Michigan
Book design by Lisa Jacobs

Printed and bound by CPI Group (UK) Ltd, Croydon, CR0 4YY

ISBN 978-0-939512-43-0 (hardcover)
ISBN 978-0-472-03815-2 (paper)
ISBN 978-0-472-12762-7 (ebook)
ISBN 978-0-472-90157-9 (open access)

CONTENTS

Contents

PREFACE

For a year or so before his untimely death in February of 1988, Robert Brower was working on a translation of the late medieval poetic miscellany, *Shōtetsu monogatari*, following upon his earlier translations of Fujiwara no Teika's *Maigetsushō* and Fujiwara no Tameie's *Eiga no ittei*. As was always his way, he labored diligently at his desk, even after illness made an already formidable project more onerous. Sadly, however, death took him before he was able to complete his task.

When he realized that he would not be able to finish the manuscript, Professor Brower, knowing that I had become well acquainted with Shōtetsu and his works through my own research, asked me to do it in his stead. I was happy to comply with his request, both because of my great affection and respect for him and because of my interest in Shōtetsu, whom I consider to be one of the finest of all classical Japanese poets.

This book, then, is a collaborative effort. The translation of *Shōtetsu monogatari* itself is largely Professor Brower's work, which I have modified only slightly, and then chiefly in the case of the poems. The notes, on the other hand, represent my contribution in the main; and the introduction, except for a few pages that Professor Brower had typed up in rough form, is also mine. For the sake of consistency, I have used Professor Brower's format for the translation of poems throughout the manuscript. Likewise, I have used his translations for titles and terms, relying upon his earlier works for reference. Needless to say, any mistakes that remain in the manuscript are solely my responsibility.

For editorial assistance I wish to thank Edward Peng and the managing editor of the Michigan Monograph Series in Japanese Studies, Bruce Willoughby.

Steven D. Carter
October, 1989

ABBREVIATIONS

GR   [*Shinkō*] *Gunsho ruijū*. Comp. Hanawa Hokinoichi. 2nd ed. 24 vols. Tokyo: Meichō Fūkyūkai, 1977–78.

GSIS   *Goshūishū*, in *SKT* 1.

GSS   *Gosenshū*, in *SKT* 1.

GYS   *Gyokuyōshū*, in *SKT* 1.

JCP   Robert H. Brower and Earl Miner. *Japanese Court Poetry*. Stanford: Stanford University Press, 1961.

KKS   *Kokinshū*, in *SKT* 1.

MYS   *Man'yōshū*, in *SKT* 2.

NKBT   *Nihon koten bungaku taikei*. 102 vols. Tokyo: Iwanami Shoten, 1958–68.

NKBZ   *Nihon koten bungaku zenshū*. 51 vols. Tokyo: Shōgakkan, 1970–76.

NKGT   *Nihon kagaku taikei*. Comp. Sasaki Nobutsuna and Kyūsojin Hitaku. 4th ed. 10 vols., 5 supplementary vols. Tokyo: Kazama Shobō, 1977–81.

NST   *Nihon shisō taikei.* Comp. Hayashiya Tatsusaburō et al. 67 vols. Tokyo: Iwanami Shoten, 1970–82.

SCSS   *Shinchokusenshū*, in *SKT* 1.

SG   *Shūi gusō*, in *SKT* 3.

SGSIS   *Shingoshūishū*, in *SKT* 1.

ShokuGSIS   *Shokugoshūishū*, in *SKT* 1.

ShokuGSS   *Shokugosenshū*, in *SKT* 1.

ShokuKKS   *Shokukokinshū*, in *SKT* 1.

SIS   *Shūishū*, in *SKT* 1.

SKS   *Shikashū*, in *SKT* 1.

SKKS   *Shinkokinshū*, in *SKT* 1.

SKT   *Shinpen kokkan taikan.* 5 vols. Tokyo: Kadokawa Shoten, 1983–86.

SM   *Shōtetsu monogatari.* Ed. Hisamatsu Sen'ichi, in *NKBT* 65.

SSZS   *Shinsenzaishū*, in *SKT* 1.

ST   *Shikashū taisei.* Comp. Wakashi Kenkyūkai. 8 vols. Tokyo: Meiji Shoin, 1973–76.

SZKKS   *Shinzokukokinshū*, in *SKT* 1.

SZS   *Senzaishū*, in *SKT* 1.

ZGR   *Zoku gunsho ruijū.* Comp. Hanawa Hokinoichi and Hanawa Tadatomi. 3rd rev. ed. 71 vols. Tokyo: Zoku Gunsho Ruijū Kansei-kai, 1974–1975.

Introduction

FOREWORD

For students of *waka*, the fifteenth through the eighteenth centuries have always been dismissed as a particularly dreary period. Nevertheless, even in the 1400 and 1500s, which the literary histories often characterize as "the age of *renga*," or linked verse,[1] the classical thirty-one syllable poem continued to be written on every conceivable occasion. Every major renga master was at the same time a waka poet; his knowledge and skill in the composition and poetics of linked verse were based upon a rigorous initial training in the ideals, techniques, conventions, and traditions of classical poetry. In this sense, it is not at all surprising that the supreme master of renga, the great Sōgi (1421–1502) himself, should have felt it necessary to undergo the "Initiation into the Secrets of the *Kokinshū*"[2] in order to

1. *Renga*, or "linked verse," began to be composed increasingly from the thirteenth century by court waka poets, who would often gather in a small group after a particularly tense and formal poetry contest (*uta-awase*) and compose a linked poem in a lighter, more relaxed frame of mind. What began as a kind of game, however, gradually developed into a serious art, almost on a level with traditional waka. This transformation was effected largely by the wholesale adaptation of waka conventions to the linked verse form. Also, the common lengths of chains of linked verse—particularly the form in one-hundred links, called the *hyakuin*—were derived from the waka sequences, especially the hundred-poem sequence or *hyakushu*, which had become extremely popular during the course of the twelfth century. For an account of the development of linked verse, see Carter 1987.

2. *Kokin denju*, the passing on from master to disciple of certain "secrets" concerning the reading or interpretation of the first and most influential of the twenty-one imperial anthologies, *Kokinshū* ("Collection of Ancient and Modern Times," 905) and other early works. The "secrets," a mixture of the most obvious facts with patent inanities (such as the names of the "three trees and three birds" and the like), were transmitted either orally or by means of slips of paper (*kirigami denju*). Modeled upon esoteric Buddhist and Shinto rituals of transmission, *kokin denju* was regarded with the utmost seriousness from the late fifteenth century on and became one of the chief ways to legitimate inherited family or school traditions of poetic authority and expertise.

3

give legitimacy to his status as an authority on literary matters and teacher of linked verse. Indeed, there is much to suggest that Sōgi's frustrated wish was to be a legitimate waka poet himself.[3]

This leaves the question of whether Sōgi and his cohorts saw something in the waka of their day that scholars since have not; and the answer would seem to be yes. For while many poets of that age were satisfied with vain repetitions of familiar lines, a few intrepid individuals still managed to approach the old form with vitality and artistic purpose. Among these, most prominent was Shōtetsu (1381–1459), author of the poetic miscellany *Shōtetsu monogatari*, or "Conversations with Shōtetsu," translated here.

Sōgi and his teacher Shinkei (1406–75) are very explicit in their praise for Shōtetsu, to whom they give credit not only for the excellence of his own poetry but also for the inspiration he gave to practitioners of their own genre of linked verse.[4] But, perhaps because he came at the very end of a tradition and thus appeared nowhere in the twenty-one imperial anthologies (*chokusenshū*) that have always been considered as the primary texts of court poetry, Shōtetsu was largely neglected in later years. Indeed, during the Edo period (1603–1868), when scholars busied themselves with the collation and analysis of virtually all of the other great texts of the court tradition, Shōtetsu's work, if considered at all, was generally dismissed as an aberration of interest only for its eccentricities and hardly a proper object for emulation. As one eighteenth-century pedant put it, "Secretary Shōtetsu's poems showed skill; but his style was bad."[5] One wonders whether this resistance came about partly because of the obstacle presented by his personal collection of poetry, *Sōkonshū*, "Grass Roots," which, containing over 11,000 poems, no doubt proved a daunting challenge to any scholar who wanted to study more than the works of one poet in a lifetime.[6] For whatever

---

3. See Carter 1983:39–40.
4. See for instance Shinkei's *Sasamegoto* ("Murmured Conversations," 1463, in *NKBT* 66:163–64), *Tokorodokoro hentō* ("Replies to Various Questions," in Kidō 1985:263–64), *Hitorigoto* ("Talking to Myself," 1468, in Kidō 1985:296–97), and *Oi no kurigoto* ("An Old Man's Mumblings," 1471, in Kidō 1985:378–79), in which the author specifically attributes the new seriousness of Sōzei (d. 1455) and Chiun (d. 1448) to Shōtetsu's influence—a conclusion with which Sōgi (*Azuma mondō* ["East Country Dialogues," 1470], in *NKBT* 66:208–9) concurs.
5. Inada 1978:7. The pedant is Karasumaru Mitsuhide (1669–1748).
6. *Sōkonshū* is a collection compiled by Shōtetsu and revised and supplemented by his disciple Shōkō (1412–94) of some 11,000 poems composed by the master between 1432 (age fifty-two), when a fire had destroyed Shōtetsu's quarters at Imakumano (for details see pp. 25–26 below), including, as he tells us in *Shōtetsu monogatari* (I, 104), thirty-six notebooks filled with some 20,000 poems composed before that time, and his death in 1459. (Please note that hereafter references to *Shōtetsu monogatari* will be made by citing first the part number, followed by the section number: thus I,

reason, Shōtetsu's work was noted only in passing references during the next four centuries.

Yet the poet's role in his own age, as attested by Sōgi and Shinkei and others, could not be denied even by his detractors; and this fact kept his name alive until eventually he was rediscovered by Japanese scholars of our own day, who have searched out his texts, documented the major events of his life, and created the foundation for further research. One outcome of this is the publication of several full texts of Sōkonshū; another is Inada Toshinori's massive study Shōtetsu no kenkyū: chūsei kajin kenkyū, which has done much to counteract the prejudices of the past toward a poet who is rapidly attracting the attention he deserves as one of the finest and most original artists of the entire medieval period. [7]

One thing that Inada's study clearly shows is that one cannot properly approach Shōtetsu without a firm understanding of the literature and literary history of his age—which means in essence of the entire period from the death in 1241 of Fujiwara no Teika, whom Shōtetsu worshipped as his one true god of poetry, to the late fourteenth century. For, however eccentric he may have appeared to some of his contemporaries, Shōtetsu was a man of his time as well, whose debt to the previous tradition is obvious in all of his writings. What follows, then, is an attempt to place Shōtetsu in his proper context, in order to in turn understand his unique contributions as a poet and critic.

104.) Consequently, most of the poems in Sōkonshū—the great bulk of Shōtetsu's surviving poems—date from about the last twenty-five years of his life. His complete oeuvre, if it existed today, would probably comprise over 31,000 poems.

7. Sōkonshū is found in several different versions. Most texts consist (or consisted originally) of fifteen books, with the poems arranged in sequence by date of composition, although some books are ordered by conventional topics (e.g., first day of spring, plum blossoms, spring snow, haze, cherry blossoms, etc.) and then by order of composition under these topics. Most texts contain a preface by the famous court noble and scholar Ichijō Kaneyoshi (1402–81). The best printed text today is said to be the one published in volume 5 (pp. 532–870) of Shikashū taisei. There is also a printed version of the so-called Kurokawa text of Sōkonshū in four volumes published by the Notre Dame Seishin Joshi Daigaku as part of their series Koten sōsho. It contains 10,643 poems grouped under twelve major rubrics (seasons, love, mixed topics, etc.) and then under detailed compound topics related to these.

In addition to these major collections of his "complete poems," there are a number of shorter collections of poems by Shōtetsu that contain a considerable number of verses not found in Sōkonshū. These are: Shōtetsu eiga (1433, in ST 5), in which 102 of the 206 poems are not found elsewhere; Shōtetsu eisō (1434, in ST 7), in which 436 poems of 781 are new; Eikyō kunen Shōtetsu eisō (1437, in ST 5), in which 97 of 116 poems are new, two of which are by poets other than Shōtetsu; Tsukikusa (1434–59, in ST 5), in which 149 poems of 325 are new; Kika jukkai waka (1448?, in Inada 1978:1185–94), in which all 152 poems are new; and Koi-uta ichijiku (in appendix to the Notre Dame Seishin Joshi Daigaku version of Sōkonshū noted above), in which 205 of 325 poems are new.

WAKA IN THE LATE MEDIEVAL PERIOD

The Shinkokin era—the era of Fujiwara no Shunzei (1114–1204) and his son Teika (1162–1241), of Lady Kunaikyō (precise dates unknown) and Lord Regent Yoshitsune (1169–1206), of Princess Shikishi (d. 1201) and Retired Emperor Go-Toba (1180–1239), and, most outstandingly, of *Shinkokinshū* ("New Collection of Ancient and Modern Times," 1206), the imperial anthology that immortalized those poets' achievements—was by any measure an age of innovation and experiment. Yet it is equally true that that vibrant era was followed by a period of mediocrity dominated by conservative men—including Nijō Tameuji (1222–86) and Tameyo (1250–1338), in particular—who were either too modest or too insecure to adopt the great poets of the previous generation as their models. The result was a series of imperial anthologies whose gray aspects serve to make the *Shinkokinshū* shine even brighter in contrast.[8]

For a brief period at the beginning of the next century a group of more venturesome poets, led by Retired Emperor Fushimi (1265–1317) and Teika's great-grandson Kyōgoku Tamekane (1254–1332), managed to produce a work of greater brilliance, entitled appropriately, "Collection of Jeweled Leaves," or *Gyokuyōshū* (1313). But the triumph of the innovators was short lived. Politics sent Tamekane into exile in 1316, and when the retired emperor died the next year, the court was once again left to men of less verve and talent. Then, against a background of succession disputes, the imperial court itself was divided from 1336 to 1392 into northern and southern branches, each supporting a different claimant to the throne, each with its own capital and bureaucracy.

By command of their respective emperors (often nudged by the shogun), imperial anthologies were compiled and promulgated by both courts. At the northern court, which remained in Kyoto except for a brief period and was considered the legitimate government by the great majority of the aristocracy, it was the heirs of Retired Emperor Fushimi who served as sovereigns. Still, poetic affairs were dominated by the Nijō family, the most conservative and politically powerful of the three family lines—the other two being the Kyōgoku and the Reizei—into which Teika's descendants had divided half a century before. Under their direction and with the

8. The five are *Shinchokusenshū* ("New Imperial Collection," 1234), *Shokugosenshū* ("Later Collection Continued," 1251), *Shokukokinshū* ("Collection of Ancient and Modern Times Continued," 1265), *Shokushūishū* ("Collection of Gleanings Continued," 1278), and *Shingosenshū* ("New Later Collection," 1303). For descriptions, see *JCP*:484–85.

sponsorship of the northern emperors, three of the four *chokusenshū* compiled during the era were partisan works showcasing Nijō poetry and Nijō poets.[9] Similarly, poetry contests were organized and judged by the stalwarts of the Nijō family themselves, then by their supporters like the regent Nijō Yoshimoto (1320–88) at court, and finally by Ton'a the Monk (1289–1372) and his progeny in the halls of the military aristocracy and the cloisters of the great Buddhist establishments of the capital at Kyoto. In the background were the Ashikaga shoguns, new caretakers of the state who quickly established themselves as crucial patrons of the arts as well.

Even in these unpropitious times a few of Kyōgoku Tamekane's comrades managed to keep alive some hope for a rejuvenation of the art, waiting for a chance to make their views known. Briefly, they, that is Retired Emperor Hanazono (1297–1348) and his salon, gained enough power to produce another anthology, the *Fūgashū* ("Collection of Elegance," 1346); but their real opportunity came in 1360, when Nijō Tamesada, heir of the conservative line, died, leaving only a young nephew of a junior line to conduct poetic affairs. This left the way open for Reizei Tamehide (1302?–72), a great-grandson of Teika, to assume a central place in the poetic circles of Kyoto. For although his family was by all accounts the least noteworthy of the three branches of the Mikohidari clan, he was himself a fine poet at the height of his powers, and one who had a great deal of experience to qualify him as an arbiter of poetic taste, including participation in the compilation of *Fūgashū* and years of activity both in the capital and in Kamakura, among the warrior clans of the east country that were now so important a force in cultural politics. Before long even poets of Nijō affiliations such as Ton'a and Nijō Yoshimoto were looking to Tamehide as a teacher. In 1364 he became tutor to the shogun Ashikaga Yoshiakira (1330–67) and remained a powerful figure until his death eight years later.[10]

Unfortunately for the Reizei line, Tamehide's heir Tamekuni had taken the tonsure as a lay monk, probably because of illness, just a year before his father's death. This allowed the Nijō to reclaim their former rights under Tameshige (1325–85) and Tametō (1341–81). If the Reizei had been unlucky, however, the Nijō line suffered

9. Since the Jimyō'in line stayed as the ruling house of the northern court, the liberals should have triumphed—and indeed did in compiling *Fūgashū* ("Collection of Elegance," 1346). But because the first Ashikaga shogun, Takauji (1305–58), was on good terms with Nijō Tamesada (1293–1360), the conservative side succeeded in dominating poetic affairs nonetheless. See Araki 1977:20.

10. Araki 1977:20–24 and Kawazoe 1964:37–42.

even more so in coming years, for Tametō turned out to be a thorough profligate whose time was spent more in drinking and philandering than composing poetry; and though Tameshige was a talented poet who seems to have taken his responsibilities more seriously, his life was brought to a premature end by a brigand in 1385. When his heir Tamemigi suffered the same fate in 1399, the Nijō line came to an abrupt end.[11] With both the Nijō and Kyōgoku lines now defunct, the heirs of Tamehide had the only legitimate claim to leadership by blood in a court society that valued lineage above almost everything else. They held to the claim tenaciously, not only gaining prominence at court for the rest of the classical age (until 1500) but also providing the court with poetic leadership down till the present.[12]

In the late fourteenth century, however, Tamehide's grandson Tamemasa (1361–1417), the heir of the family fortunes, still had reason to worry. For, while bloodline was of utmost significance at the imperial court, the Ashikaga shoguns were not always so punctilious about such matters; and Ashikaga Yoshimitsu (1358–1408) had around him a score of Nijō adherents at the time of Tamemigi's death—namely, Gyōjin, the grandson of Ton'a the Monk; another powerful courtier named Kōun (lay name Kazan'in Nagachika; d. 1429); and Asukai Masayori (1358–1428), the head of another court family that could trace its own poetic affiliation back to Teika himself, under whom the clan patriarch Asukai Masatsune (1170–1221) had studied several centuries before. The Asukai in particular figured to be formidable opponents since their family was of a rank equal to the Reizei themselves. Indeed, Masayori, the scion of the family at the time in question, held offices superior to Tamemasa's and was a close confidant of Ashikaga Yoshimitsu, who gave him special privileges.[13] What this meant was that Tamemasa needed more than his pedigree chart to triumph in his quest for poetic power; he needed an ally.

He got one from an unlikely quarter—the ranks of the military elite. The man's name was Imagawa Ryōshun (lay name Sadayo; 1326–1417?), an old student of Tamehide's who had recently returned to the capital after long residence in Kyushu and later in the East Country. A great warrior who had distinguished himself first in

11. Inoue 1984:31.
12. See Brower 1981 for a summary of the place of the Reizei family in later history.
13. For a brief sketch of Masayori's life and translations of a few of his poems, see Carter 1989:279–80.

battle against the southern court and later as chief officer of the *samuraidokoro* (Board of Retainers), Ryōshun was also a man of letters who had been a major figure in Tamehide's circle back in the 1450s and 60s. Indeed, had Ryōshun not been called as Commissioner of Chinzei (*kyūshū tandai*) in 1370, the course of poetic history in the capital might have been different. But he went, staying on for twenty-five years, during which time he remained active as a scholar and poet but one removed from the center of literary culture and thus of little help to the Reizei cause.

When Ryōshun came back to the capital in the autumn of 1395, it was not by choice: he had been recalled, and essentially relieved of duties, all due to attacks on his loyalty from a rival general.[14] For a time he returned to his family's traditional domains on the seacoast southwest of Kamakura (Tōtomi and Suruga), perhaps waiting to be appointed to another high post. But his hopes were dashed when Ashikaga Yoshimitsu, convinced that Ryōshun was in league with enemies of the central government, dispatched a shogunal force against him in the first month of 1400. Ryōshun capitulated, was pardoned, and, at age seventy-five, decided that he had had his fill of war and politics. He came back to Kyoto that autumn and took up poetry and Buddhist devotions as the occupation of his final years.

The loss to the shogunate—which at the time could have used Ryōshun's level head—was Reizei Tamemasa's gain. A brave, tenacious fighter, Ryōshun quickly put his military training to use in the poetic campaigns of the day. Moreover, he could make claims that no one else in 1400 could, having studied under Kyōgoku Tamekane's heir Tamemoto as well as Reizei Tamehide, and having sat in many poetic gatherings with Ton'a, Yoshida no Kenkō (b. 1283), and Nijō Yoshimoto, as well as in renga parties with Yoshimoto and the great master Gusai (d. 1376?). With the benefit of such experience, and his own indomitable spirit, he was the sort of man who could not be pushed aside, even by so powerful an adversary as Asukai Masayori. Ryōshun was convinced that Reizei Tamemasa, both by blood and talent, had greater claim to primacy in poetic affairs at court than any of the latter's rivals, and he immediately set about making his views known.

He chose as his weapon the polemical treatise, turning out six of them between 1403 and 1412. In each he championed the liberal

14. The rival was Ōuchi Yoshihiro (1356–1400). See Kawazoe 1964:221–30.

cause against Nijō adherents, complaining that such interlopers could not properly serve as the heirs to Shunzei and Teika—a position that only Tamemasa, whose grandfather had after all been teacher to the grandfathers of the current Nijō ilk, could rightly hold. In the process Ryōshun made it clear that he saw Ton'a's heirs, in particular, as upstarts who had no right to usurp Tamemasa's position at court. But he also made it clear that his devotion to Tamemasa was not simply a matter of partisan politics. He liked the man's spirit, which had about it the directness of Tamekane's: for Ryōshun still took as perhaps the best direction that could be given to a poet Tamekane's advice to rely not solely on convention but rather on experience "as it is" (*ari no mama*).[15] The poems of the conservative school, on the other hand, he saw as too limited in style, too narrow in range of sentiment, too fastidious in diction, too lacking in vibrancy and verve. For an old warrior, Tamemasa was therefore "a bright mirror for our time" whose poems always sounded "fresh and new," and always came "from deep within his own heart."[16]

This insistence on originality and on the poet's individual heart as the only proper source of poetic inspiration was the hallmark of Reizei poetics, as Ryōshun had learned from Tamehide years before.

> He [Tamehide] taught that to tend toward only one style was to constrict the Way. Tameyo's teaching allowed only for poems of gentility, and Tamekane's instruction was to maintain a lofty tone, use a lot of words without discrimination, and write any way you like. Tamesuke, however, taught that no matter what the style, a poet had to first establish his own poetic manner, and consider his own talents. From the past to the present, the poems of disciples have been unlike the style of their masters, and the poems of sons have been unlike the poems of fathers. This is why one must follow one's own strengths.[17]

15. *Ben'yōshō* ("Notes on the Fundamentals of Poetry," alternatively titled *Ryōshun isshiden*, "Ryōshun's Testament to His Heir," 1409, in *NKGT* 5:180). Araki Hisashi traces the source of this dictum to Abutsu the Nun (d. 1283), mother of Tamesuke, founder of the Reizei line. See Araki 1977:50–59, 332–33 and *JCP*:359–60.

16. *Rakusho roken* ("Anonymous Document Revealed," ca. 1412), in *NKGT* 5:191.

17. *Shisetsu jikenshū* ("The Master's Teachings and My Personal Opinions," 1408?), in *NKGT* 5:215.

To twentieth-century readers living in a culture that values the ideal of individualism, a statement of this sort may seem innocent enough. But in order to understand it fully one must remember that Nijō poets ever since Tameuji and Tameyo had been taught that there was only one proper ideal for poetic practice—the ideal of *ushin*, or "deep feeling," a rather vague term that came in practice to mean an insistence on courtly diction and highly refined and usually melancholy sentiment, all presented via simple rhetorical forms—in a word, "gentility." To those committed to so exclusive a standard, Ryōshun's statements must have sounded disturbingly liberal. What he was doing was insisting that style should be partly a matter of personal inclination, and not simply convention, and that the question of which style to use might be a question of circumstance. And the argument was made more threatening because it also involved an unmistakable appeal to the father of their tradition, Teika, who had said something similar long before:

> With respect to the ten styles I have mentioned above, they should be taught with an eye to the temperament of the pupil. For both the gifted and the untalented have an individual style that is congenial to them . . . It would result in terrible damage to the Art of Poetry to insist that a person who has no disposition for it compose in a certain style that the teacher prefers simply because he happens to find it personally congenial to himself. A given style should be taught to a pupil only after careful study of the particular style of poem he tends to compose. For with every style it is essential to keep in mind that it must be honest and right. [18]

In the opinion of Nijō poets, the other nine styles Teika alluded to in this quotation—including perhaps most prominently *yūgen tei*, or the style of mystery and depth, and *hito fushi aru tei*, or the style of originality [19]—were best forgotten. For Ryōshun to bring them up was no doubt considered an affront to courtly taste, at the least, and an outright attack, at the most.

This was particularly so since Ryōshun's young ward Tamemasa was able to display in his own poems a facility with a number of different approaches to poetic expression, as a few poems from

18. *Maigetsushō* ("Monthly Notes," 1219?), in *NKBT* 65:135; Brower 1985:420–21.
19. For Teika's treatment of the "ten styles" (*jittei*), see Brower 1985:410–12.

Tamemasa senshu ("Tamemasa's Thousand-Poem Sequence," 1415)
will demonstrate.

"Autumn Rain"

Yamamoto no	Below the mountain,
Usuki yūhi ni	In the thin light of evening,
Mozu nakite	A shrike is calling;
Kozue ni haruru	And clearing in the treetops—
Aki no murasame.	A passing autumn shower.[20]

"Moon in a Grove of Trees"

Tsuki sayuru	From the treetops
Mori no kozue ni	Of a grove chilled by the moon
Kikoyu nari	I hear a sound:
Yuki no shita naru	Beneath the snow falling down—
Yogarasu no koe.	The call of a crow in the night.[21]

"Haze on the Fields"

Usumidori	Faint green in hue,
Sue no kasumi	The haze off at the far edge
Todaeshite	Breaks and scatters—
Mada moeyaranu	Showing no new growth as yet
Ogi no yakehara.	On a burnt-over field of reeds.[22]

"Snow in the Fields"

Chigusa saku	Not a dewdrop remains
Nobe no omokage	To remind me of the wild flowers
Tsuyu mo nashi	Blooming in the fields.
Yuki no hitoiro no	Now there is only one color—
Akebono no sora.	Of snow beneath the dawn sky.[23]

"Love and the Sea"

Tanomazu yo	I trust you no more—
Hito no kokoro wa	Leaving your heart to the whims
Ōumi no	Of passing winds
Kata yuku fune no	That carry a boat on its way
Kaze ni makasete.	Over the breadth of the sea.[24]

"Grasses around a Mountain Home"

Sabishi ya na	How lonesome I am!
Noki no shitakusa	When the wind bends the grasses

20. *Tamemasa senshu* 394, in *SKT* 4.
21. Ibid., 410.
22. Ibid., 21.
23. Ibid., 563.
24. Ibid., 641.

Uchinabiki　　　　　Beneath my eaves,
Matsu hodo kaze no　But makes no sound in passing
Oto wa nakeredo.　　Up higher, in the pines.[25]

"Fireflies Resembling Jewels"
　　Kusa no ito ni　　　　On threads of grass—
　　Tama nuku tsuyu no　Dewdrops like a string of jewels
　　Kazu soete　　　　　In countless numbers—
　　Hotaru mo sugaru　　Where fireflies too are clinging now
　　Nobe no yūyami.　　　In the evening gloom on the fields.[26]

"Love and Gate"
　　Aware ta ga　　　　　Who might that man be—
　　Shizumaru hodo o　　Too anxious to keep waiting
　　Machikanete　　　　Until all is still,
　　Katamenu kado ni　　Standing by an unwatched gate,
　　Tachishinoburan.　　Yearning to meet with his love?[27]

"Love and Pine Crickets"
　　Kikiwabinu　　　　　How forlorn it seems
　　Tsuraki chigiri no　　To listen now that your vows
　　Kakikurete　　　　　Fade into darkness—
　　Nokiba shigururu　　With the voices of pine crickets
　　Matsumushi no koe.　Showering down near my eaves.[28]

The first two of these poems would have won praise from Tamekane himself for their directness of expression and "impressionistic realism." The next four, on the other hand, evince the more restrained and melancholy lyricism of Ton'a in ways that the Nijō tradition could generally accept. But the last three, which employ more complex syntactical structures and more unconventional metaphors than the previous five, recall not so much the poets of Tamemasa's own day as the poems of the young Teika—the Teika that the heirs of Ton'a and the Asukai were wont to forget. More important than any individual qualities, however, is the variety of styles these poems represent, showing Tamemasa to be a master of his poetic tradition as a whole rather than the prisoner of one style.

Partly because of Ryōshun's persistence as a polemicist and partly because of his own proficiency as a poet, Tamemasa was remarkably successful in restoring the hopes of his house. Invited to

25. Ibid., 886.
26. Ibid., 284.
27. Ibid., 662.
28. Ibid., 745.

court to serve in the capacity of contest judge and imperial lector, and in other such offices for poetry gatherings at the palace, he increased in reputation rapidly. In 1402 he was advanced to the office of Middle Counselor; then in the spring of 1408 he was even made *minbukyō*, or Minister of Popular Affairs, a title that had traditionally been given to the senior poet of the Mikohidari line since Teika had held the position two centuries before, and one that because of the Nijō house had been denied Tamekane and Tamehide. In a final triumph, Tamemasa was granted the honor of choosing topics and acting as imperial lector for a grand formal poetry meeting held by Ashikaga Yoshimitsu on the event of an imperial visit to his villa in the Northern Hills of the capital in the spring of the same year. Yoshimitsu died just two months later—with rumors circulating that he had been struck down by the gods for his vain ambitions, which seem to have included wanting to play the part of retired emperor to his subjects. But the Ashikaga heir, Yoshimochi (1386–1428), was already a Reizei supporter in some ways; and Tamemasa took advantage of the situation, missing no opportunity to show his talent as he trained his own heirs to carry on the family name. At last, after decades of chagrin, the Reizei had assumed their proper place in poetic history.[29]

SHŌTETSU

Although Ryōshun's contributions to Tamemasa's successes were of course crucial, the older man rarely took part in public events, content instead to play the role of shadow warrior. Since his was not a poetic house in the way of the Asukai, Reizei, or Jōkō'in (the name of the temple in Ninnaji where Ton'a's descendants resided), poetry was for him less a business than a pleasure. Yet we know that he still went on occasional outings to see the blossoms with literary friends and spent a good deal of time studying old texts and copying out documents for his library. The way we know this, however, is not from his own writings but from those of a young man who had by this time become his student—Sonmyōmaru, later to be known as Shōtetsu.

Exactly when Shōtetsu had first met the man who would later become his teacher is not certain, but a section from *Shōtetsu monogatari* indicates the circumstances in which the first meeting took place.

29. Inoue 1984:47–56.

. . . before I had actually studied how to write verse, I used to attend formal poetry gatherings and practice composition with no thought to the shame I might bring upon myself. My house was at Sanjō and Higashi no Tōin. Across the street, at the house of the commissioner from the Bureau of Civil Administration, there were monthly poetry gatherings attended by more than thirty persons, including Tamemasa and Tamekuni of the Reizei family, the former shogunal deputy Ryōshun, and others closely associated with them.

A certain preceptor of the Ontoku'in once said to me, "If you want to compose poetry, I will take you with me to the civil administrator's house across the way." At that period of my life, I was still wearing my hair long in the manner of young children, and I felt embarrassed about my extreme youth, but nevertheless I went with the preceptor to the civil administrator's house. He was at the time a lay priest of impressive appearance, more than eighty years old, with white hair. But he came out to meet me and said, "These days, not one of the children studies poetry any more, although when I, Zen'on, was in the prime of youth, I used to hear of such things. It is an elegant and tasteful thing for you to do. We have a monthly poetry gathering here on the twenty-fifth of every month. You are most welcome to attend. The topics for this month are thus and so." So saying, he wrote them down for me with his own hand . . .

This conversation took place toward the beginning of the eighth month. Then, when I arrived at the poetry meeting itself on the twenty-fifth, the highest places on the one side were occupied by Reizei Tamemasa and Tamekuni, and on the other side by the former shogunal deputy . . . [who] was at that time a lay priest of more than eighty years. He was dressed in a habit without the black overskirt and had a sash with a long fringe around his waist . . .

After this occasion, I just kept going again and again to those meetings and thus gained experience in poetic composition. I was fourteen years old at the time.[30]

As many scholars have pointed out, there is much in this passage that is obscure, including the identities of the "civil

30. *SM* I, 104.

administrator" (*jibu*) and the "preceptor of the Ontoku'in," as well as the precise year during which the meeting described took place.[31] Even if Shōtetsu's memory was somewhat muddled when he wrote down his story half a century later, however, there can be little doubt that he met both Ryōshun and Reizei Tamemasa in just such a setting. Monthly poetry meetings—*tsukinamikai*—were held at many temples and residences at the time, and provided just the sort of opportunity a young man interested in poetry could be expected to seek out.

About Sonmyōmaru's life before this incident we know even less. Traditional biographies record that he was born in a small castle town in Bitchū Province (modern Okayama), the son of a samurai named Komatsu Yasukiyo—a contention that reliable sources would seem to support. It was probably there that he was raised as well, with the given name of Masakiyo. Other statements indicate that the family moved to Kyoto when he was about ten years old, living for a time in a house near the intersection of Sanjō and Higashi no Tōin avenues, but why the move was made or what his father did in the capital is also unknown.[32]

What little we can learn about Shōtetsu's early years is thus easily summarized: that he came from a middle-class warrior family in the provinces, that he went up to the capital with his parents while still a child, and that in his mid-teens, probably around 1395, he met Ryōshun and Tamemasa. *Shōtetsu monogatari* also records, however, that he left Kyoto the very next year to enter a temple in Nara, the ancient capital of Japan that now was a religious center— and not a major center for poets, which may have been why his father sent him there.[33] In any case, he was placed in a prominent *monzeki*, or princely cloister, there, and spent the next five years preparing for a life in the Buddhist world that left little time for composing verses.[34]

Thus Sonmyōmaru seemed destined for life as a cleric. But it appears that the young man was a born poet whose talent would not

31. For a rehearsal of the problems, see Inada 1978:162–64. The chief point of contention involves a discrepancy in the ages Shōtetsu gives for himself and Ryōshun, which suggests that the disciple may be confusing separate meetings with Ryōshun and Tamemasa on separate occasions some years apart.
32. Inada 1978:20–33. Inada's sources indicate that Shōtetsu was more likely Yasukiyo's brother, both being the sons of Hidekiyo.
33. Inada 1978:31.
34. Traditionally the cloister has been identified as the Ichijō'in, one of the governing temples of Kōfukuji, but there is no real evidence to support this contention. See Inada 1978:36–38.

be denied, for not many months after his father's death in 1400 he returned to the capital and sought out Ryōshun. It was at this time that he became a disciple to the old warrior. For its time the relationship was a conventional one. Masakiyo—as he was still called—no doubt submitted work for his teacher's criticism, and a number of documents show that around this time Ryōshun was lending his student important texts for study, and even lecturing him on *Genji monogatari* ("The Tale of Genji") and other court classics. The young man proved to be a fast learner, and before long he was winning praise from the old warrior.[35] At the same time he also had contact with other prominent poets, most notably Tamemasa and the renga poet Asayama Bontō (1349–1417).[36] But it was clearly to Ryōshun that he looked for constant instruction. It was an exciting time, when Ryōshun was writing some of his most powerful essays in support of the Reizei cause, to which Masakiyo himself became a devout convert. A diligent student, Masakiyo also spent a good deal of time copying out famous texts, the colophons of which provide information about his life not found elsewhere.[37]

According to notations in *Sōkonshū*, in 1406 the young poet made a journey to eastern Japan, crossing Mount Utsu in present day Shizuoka Prefecture and skirting Mount Fuji. Thereafter, he was again in the capital, living for a time in Shōmyō Temple in the Eastern Hills,[38] where he styled himself the hermit Shōjō—the

35. In *SM* I, 18, Shōtetsu describes how at a poetry contest at which the participants decided winners by discussion, with the authorship of entries concealed until after debate, he held out stubbornly in defense of a poem that later turned out to be by Tamemasa—thus impressing Ryōshun greatly.

36. In his travel journal, *Nagusamegusa* ("Consolations"), written in 1418, Shōtetsu reveals (p. 119) that he had studied linked verse under Asayama Bontō (d. 1417) in his youth.

37. The information gathered from such sources is incorporated into Inada's chronology (pp. 1205–72). One implication of Shōtetsu's lifelong work as a copyist is that he undertook much of that kind of work for fees paid by patrons anxious to have access to the "secrets" of the poetic tradition. It should be noted also that the same sources tell us a good deal about what the poet concentrated on in his own study and sometimes about his relationships with men of his day. Texts in his own hand and in the hand of later poets copying from his manuscripts show that he studied the personal anthologies of Shunzei, Teika, and Ietaka, in particular, and that he also spent much time copying out texts of *Tsurezuregusa* ("Essays in Idleness"), *Genji monogatari* ("The Tale of Genji"), and *Ise monogatari* ("Tales of Ise")—the latter two from original copies owned by the Reizei family. The colophon of one work also indicates that in his younger years he had access to a number of important texts, including forgeries like *Kirihioke* ("The Paulownia Brazier") and major treatises such as *Eiga taigai* ("An Outline for Composing Uta," ca. 1222) and *Kindai shūka* ("Superior Poems of Our Time," 1209) through Imagawa Ryōshun. See Inada 1978:170–80.

38. Inoue 1984:77. The temple was evidently located not far from Kiyomizu Temple in an area called Raisan.

Sino-Japanese reading of the characters for his lay name of Masakiyo. But in the third month of 1414, in the thirty-fourth year of his life, he took the tonsure under the Buddhist name Shōtetsu and was admitted to the great Rinzai Zen temple, Tōfukuji, located in the southeastern area of Kyoto. His reasons for doing this were probably of the most ordinary sort: he needed a way to make a living while establishing himself as a poet. Once again it was Ryōshun who seems to have paved the way for him, using his close relationship with the temple as an entree for his student.[39] Shōtetsu had not been long at Tōfukuji before he had been assigned the duties of secretary or scribe. He evidently threw himself into his new tasks with considerable enthusiasm, for he was soon known all over Kyoto as "Shōtetsu the Scribe" (Tesshoki, a name consisting of the second character of Shōtetsu and the word *shoki*, "scribe"), an appellation that stuck to him for a good part of the remainder of his life.[40]

During these years Shōtetsu was still active in poetic events, composing poems and participating in many gatherings and contests. Ryōshun, now in his nineties, had left the capital to spend his final years in Tōtomi; but Tamemasa was more active than ever, and the Reizei cause was thriving at court. In the spring of 1415 Tamemasa was made Major Counselor, the first time anyone from his line had been granted such an honor. And, at the request of Ashikaga Yoshimochi, he presented a thousand-poem sequence (*senshu*) of his poems for shogunal review, in response to which the government returned to Reizei control the rights to two estates long held by the Nijō house and then powerful military families. Even after this, the family could not claim total victory in its quest for recognition, since the Asukai and Gyōkō (1391–1455) were still highly favored at poetic gatherings as well. Nevertheless, Tamemasa could no longer complain of ill treatment.

As the Reizei family prospered, so did Shōtetsu, who was proving adept at composing poems in the realistic style most favored by Tamemasa, such as this one written on the topic "Travel" in 1414.

| Yamabito no | Surely mountain folk |
| Hirou tsumagi ni | Will come to collect them later |

---

39. Inada 1978:45; Miura 1976:264–65; Araki 1977:19; Kawazoe 1964:49–50. Ryōshun had studied Zen under Bukkai Zenji (d. 1349), eighteenth abbot of Tōfukuji, in earlier years and retained a close relationship with the temple thereafter.

40. In addition, he was known as Shōgetsu, a name that he probably received from Ryōshun (see Inada 1978:176–77). Shōtetsu's home was referred to as Shōgetsu-An even after his death, when it became the residence of his chief disciple.

Narinu beshi	As wood for the fire—
Koyoi orishiku	These boughs of scrub oak I spread
Mine no shiishiba.	For a night spent on the peaks.[41]

The topic was an old one, and the treatment hardly original. But the somber beauty of Shōtetsu's imagery no doubt impressed his teachers. If the poem evokes the loneliness of travel, it does so with great subtlety—showing experience "as it is," rather than conveying it through abstractions.

One undeniable sign that Shōtetsu was indeed attracting attention in the capital came in the late summer of 1416, when he submitted fifty verses to Tamemasa and Sōga (the Buddhist name of Asukai Masayori) for formal judgment. Predictably, Tamemasa gave his student high marks, singling out twenty-three of the fifty poems for praise. Among them was the following, which, in its witty conception, shows that Shōtetsu was no mere imitator but one who sought to follow Tamehide's edict to use a variety of styles.

"Blossoms in the Garden"

Nokori naku	Gone without a trace
Ame wa haretsuru	Is the rainstorm that left puddles
Niwatazumi	Here in my garden—
Nao kumo utsusu	Where still clouds cast their shadows
Hana no shitakage.	Beneath boughs of blossoming trees.[42]

Comparing blossoms to clouds was nothing new, but to present those "clouds" as reflected in the puddles left after a passing shower revealed an originality of conception that came less from instruction than from inborn imagination. The same quality is evident in another poem on the topic, "Searching out Calling Insects."

Ayaniku ni	Ah, what a pity
Kusamuragoto no	That when I push my way through
Mushi no ne mo	Clumps of grass,
Wakereba kiyuru	The insect voices too should vanish
Nobe no yūtsuyu.	With the dusk dew on the fields.[43]

This poem even Sōga had to praise for its creative handling of its topic. A more conventional approach would have perhaps hit on the idea of having the insects cease their song when the speaker drew

41. *Sōkonshū* 56; written in 1414. (Here and elsewhere numbers refer to those of *Shikashū taisei* text of *Sōkonshū*).
42. *Sōkonshū* 70.
43. *Sōkonshū* 82.

near, but to combine the disappearance of the insects with the vanishing of dewdrops shaken loose from their lodging on leaves of grass was something new. Furthermore, the poem had what the Nijō school always demanded—intensity of feeling, clearly expressed. With such talent Shōtetsu's future seemed as secure as the fortunes of the Reizei family.

Fate intervened, however, when Tamemasa, at the height of his powers, died suddenly in the first month of 1417. And when Ryōshun too passed away around the same time,[44] Shōtetsu had even greater reason to mourn. Now in his thirty-seventh year, he was well established as a poet, and on good terms with Tamemasa's young heir, Tameyuki (d. 1439). But to lose both of those who had been his teachers for the past twenty years was hard. Furthermore, he must have been conscious that the absence of his two supporters could only make his life as a poet more trying. Above all he knew that he could play the part of neither Tamemasa nor Ryōshun, having neither the social status nor the artistic stature to act as a leader in poetic affairs. For had not Ryōshun himself attacked the priestly Gyōkō and his supporters—men of Shōtetsu's own class—as upstarts?

For a year or so after Tamemasa's death Shōtetsu stayed in the capital, pursuing his art. But in the spring of 1418 he set out on the road for what would be, so far as records tell us, the only major journey of his life. The excursion was a short one that kept him away from Kyoto for only several months, but fortunately for us he saw fit to record it for posterity in the form of a travel journal titled Nagusamekusa, "Consolations," that reveals a great deal about his state of mind at the time.

He had of course read the great travel records of the past, from Tosa nikki ("A Tosa Journal," 935) of Ki no Tsurayuki (872?–945) to Izayoi nikki ("Diary of the Waning Moon," 1279–80) of Abutsu the Nun (d. 1283); and his own record begins conventionally enough, with a listing of the famous places (utamakura) the poet passed as he traveled northeast from Kyoto along the shore of Lake Biwa and then east to Kuroda in Owari Province. Even in these first few pages, however, he hints that his purpose was not simply to record the usual observations and sentiments of the travel diarist.

---

44. Traditionally scholars have taken 1420 as the year of Ryōshun's death, but recent discoveries make it appear likely that he died in 1417—a contention that is supported by Shōtetsu's Nagusamegusa (1418), which refers to Ryōshun as "the late lay-priest and Governor of Iyo" (p. 120). See Araki 1977:9–11.

Passing a place called Ono, I recalled how the late Middle Counselor Tamemasa, an Elder of the Way of Poetry who had lived in an age of decline when the Way had been largely abandoned, was asked to present a thousand-poem sequence to the Palace Minister, among which was the following lament:

Ika ni sen	What am I to do?
Ono no yamashiba	At Ono the groves of scrub oak
Koto taete	Have disappeared,
Nao tatekanuru	Leaving the homes with no fires
Yado no keburi o.	To raise a trail of smoke.[45]

Now, Ono Estate in Ōmi and Hosokawa Estate in Harima had been in the control of the Bureau of Poetry since the time of Gojō of the Third Rank [Shunzei] without a break, until, as the Way declined, they had fallen into the hands of warrior houses; this poem was meant to express how the Mikohidari house was wasting away. The winter of that same year, the Hosokawa Estate was returned, and soon it was announced that the Ono Estate would be returned too—actions that showed the goodwill of the shogun, for which the family was truly grateful . . . And then Lord Tamemasa was elevated to Major Counselor of Third Rank, and it looked as if the Way of Poetry would flourish once more. But that next spring, he departed as if in a dream, before the flowers had blossomed, vanishing like clouds, lost in the mists. I grieved much then, and even now as I take a moment to jot down these words tears of remembrance mingle with the ink of my brush.[46]

The next few pages of the record recount how Shōtetsu continued from Ono to Kuroda in Mino Province, where he stayed for some days before going to worship at Ise Shrine to the south—a trip that took ten days but which is related in a few sentences. While he writes nothing of his experience at the shrine of the Sun Goddess, he does, however, record much about his days in Kuroda and nearby Kiyosu, where he took up residence in a hermitage named Bamboo Shade for the remainder of the summer at the invitation of an old friend met quite by chance on a visit to one of the temples in the area. At this point, in other words, Shōtetsu's record becomes less a

45. *Tamemasa senshu* 926 (Lament).
46. *Nagusamegusa*: 112–13.

travel journal than a rambling essay in which he describes his surroundings and details his pastimes, in the process creating an image
of himself as a literatus in the tradition of Yoshida no Kenkō, author
of the essays and anecdotes collected under the title *Tsurezuregusa*
("Essays in Idleness").

[The hermitage was] a place where men in their cast-off
robes would congregate to encourage each other in their Zen
devotions. But perhaps because it was the middle of summer,
none of that sort were present, leaving just my old friend and
a few others to occupy the place. So there I sat, with no care
for my appearance, using the desk where I should have studied
Zen texts as a place to spread out works of poetry, and lying
down to peruse pillow books on the mat where I should have
been sitting in meditation.[47]

In such idle pursuits, then, Shōtetsu spent his time—
reading, composing poems, drinking wine, and enjoying the summer nights and the company of his friends and fellow travelers who
happened to stop at nearby inns. To one such group he even agreed
to lecture informally on *Genji monogatari*. But even in this he could
not avoid concentrating on his own past, remembering how for ten
years he had studied the tale under the direction of the late
Ryōshun.[48] In everything he saw reason for lamentation. Even when
discussing linked verse, a genre that in later writings he seldom paid
any attention to at all, he spoke in wistful tones, recalling the age of
the masters who have now all died, leaving the Way to decline into
downright "wickedness" (*yokoshima*).[49] The pattern of his thought
was clear: more and more he found himself drifting away from the
present, yearning more and more for the past. The way behind was
bright with the soft light of memory, both directly experienced and
acquired through study; the way ahead was dim.

47. Ibid., 118. Here Shōtetsu alludes to section 13 of *Tsurezuregusa*, where Kenkō opines that
    "the pleasantest of all diversions is to sit alone under the lamp, a book spread out
    before you" (*NKBZ* 27:103 and Keene 1967:12). Earlier, he also uses the words
    tsurezure naru mama ni ("with nothing better to do"), the phrase with which Kenkō
    begins his book.
48. *Nagusamegusa*:120.
49. *Nagusamegusa*:119. This may also explain why Shōtetsu, unlike almost every other waka
    poet of his time, did not compose linked verse, the "revival" of which—supported by
    his own students Shinkei, Sōzei, and Chiun—did not begin until he was already well
    advanced in years and no longer interested in experimenting with a different genre of
    poetry.

He was able to take some comfort, however, in the friends with whom he had discussed *Genji*, and for whom, he says in his last sentences, he wrote his journal in the early autumn of 1418, while still in Kiyosu. The tone of his statements makes it seem that he was in love with one of the young men. Appropriately, he revealed his sentiments indirectly in a poem.

Ikite yo ni	Had I lived on
Meguriawazuba	And never met you on the way,
Iku aki ka	How many autumns
Munashiki sora no	Might I have made my complaints
Tsuki ni ureen.	To the moon in an empty sky?[50]

Needless to say, he could not take his young friends with him when he returned to the capital. His poem provides a fitting conclusion to a melancholy work that reveals a mind more and more withdrawn into itself.

One thing that he was able to take back to the capital was a new-found dedication to his art, which he now embraced with a fervor that decided him against any further attempts to make a priestly reputation for himself at Tōfukuji.[51] For although our records for the next ten years of his life are scanty, it is apparent from what we can piece together that he was more active in poetic affairs than ever before. By 1424 he was no longer living at Tōfukuji but at a hut of his own on Rokkaku in the northern part of the capital, which would serve better as a base of operations for an aspiring poet. From there he was frequently summoned to meetings at the Reizei household and at the city estates of the great military families—the Hosokawa, the Yamana, and the Hatakeyama, and even at the palace of the shogun Ashikaga Yoshimochi himself. That he was gaining a name for himself is also evident from the appearance in records from around the same time of a number of students, most notably his foremost disciple, Shōkō (1412–94).

His known connections with Ryōshun and the Reizei family made it certain that he would also be involved in poetic disputes, from which he did not shy away. But Yoshimochi was, for a potentate, an even-tempered man, and poetry of all sorts flourished

50. *Nagusamegusa*:125.
51. In *Nagusamegusa* (p. 120) he notes that after going to Tōfukuji he had put aside his study of *Genji Monogatari* out of concern for what his fellow monks might think of such frivolous hobbies—indicating that for a time, at least, he had been resolved to act the role of the priest conventionally. His activities after his journey, however, make it clear that from 1418 on he made the decision to make poetry his Way.

during his reign. It was at this time, for instance, that Shōtetsu had an open dispute with Kōun over the interpretation of a poem by Teika.[52] But neither man suffered as a result, and it was thus a peaceful time in all, which gave Shōtetsu the leisure to continue his studies of classical texts and compose a great deal of poetry. Asukai Masayori died in 1428, and Kōun the next year. As the years progressed, the disciple of Ryōshun and Tamemasa gained status as a senior figure in the *buke kadan*, or poetic world of the military elite, with patrons in the most important houses who kept him busy attending their monthly poetry gatherings, writing works on commission to be presented at temples and shrines as votive offerings, and providing instruction for a host of students.

In the early summer of 1429 Shōtetsu moved to a hermitage in Imakumano, located in the Eastern Hills outside the capital, where for a time he was in retreat, perhaps because of illness. For whatever reason, he did not stay in seclusion. Nearly fifty years old, he was a mature poet with a style his own, who was not afraid to take chances. Once again, a poem makes his boldness clear.

"Winter Moon"

Saetsukusu	In unto itself
Shimo ya kōri o	The moon gathers the freezing cold
Tsuki no uchi ni	Of frost and ice
Atsumete yomo ni	To shower down on all quarters
Kudasu kage kana.	In the light of its rays.[53]

Such "surrealistic" treatment no doubt gave ammunition to his rivals, but if so, he seems still to have had many friends and patrons. A paraphrase of the headnotes of poems composed during the first two months of 1432, for instance, shows that he was not being avoided by those who valued the art of poetry.[54]

1.1   Composed first poem of new year at Imakumano hut

1.2   Wrote poem about cuckoo in the bamboo around his home

1.6   Made a trip into the city

1.7   Made pilgrimage to Kitano Shrine

1.18   Composed poem at house of Yamana Hirotaka

---

52. *SM* I, 89.
53. *Sōkonshū* 367.
54. Taken from chronology in Inada 1978:213.

1.26 Visited rooms of Archbishop Kōkyō at
      Kai'inji
2.2   Composed poem in fondness for his mother
2.13 Visitors came to his house, composed poems
2.15 Composed poems at home of Jissō the Monk
2.16 Received visit from Fujiwara Motoyasu
2.19 Composed poem at house of Yamana Hirotaka
2.22 Attended monthly poetry meeting (*tsukinami*) at
      house of Hatakeyama Yoshitada
2.25 Attended monthly poetry meeting at house of
      Hatakeyama Mochizumi
2.29 Visited mountain residence of Archbishop Kōkyō

Although we know very little about some of the people mentioned here, some of them, like Archbishop Kōkyō (d. 1433), were high-ranking clerics, while others—most notably Yamana Hirotaka (d. 1441), Hatakeyama Yoshitada (d. 1463), and Hatakeyama Mochizumi—were prominent members of the military elite.[55] And other entries demonstrate that contact with such people was the rule and not the exception for Shōtetsu at the time. His circle of acquaintances encompassed some of the most powerful patrons of the age, and his life was busy and prosperous.

Then disaster struck in a way it had done seldom in the whole history of Japanese poetry. He describes the calamity in his personal poetry collection under the second day of the fourth month of that same year, 1432:

> On the night of the second, I stayed over at the house of the Chief of Central Affairs and awakened to a report that my hut at Imakumano had burned in a fire in the neighborhood in the middle of the night—a report that was to no avail, for the damage was already done, with all of the poems I had composed since my twentieth year, all 27,000 or so of them, in more than thirty volumes, gone up in smoke, not a single one escaping—and this along with all my books and hand-copied treasures.[56]

Thus, at the age of fifty-two, after more than thirty years of toil as a poet, the fruits of his long labor vanished as he slept.

55. See Inada 1978:115–18.
56. From headnote to *Sōkonshū* 1734; quoted in Inada 1978:65–66.

Friends rallied around, some probably bringing gifts to assist him in starting over. Understandably, he at first thought of giving up the art and capitulating to what must have seemed like a cruel fate. But, with friends and students—which included at the time major figures such as Takayama Sōzei (d. 1455), Chiun (d. 1448), and Shinkei—persuading him to use poetry at least as a consolation in his declining years, he found a new residence back in the city, at Sanjō-bōmon and Nishinotō'in. On the twenty-eighth day of the fourth month he held his first monthly poetry meeting at his new home and made a fresh start. Although the memory of his loss would remain with him the rest of his life, he appears never again to have faltered in his resolve. In the future he took precautions, which saved his work from two other fires that destroyed his dwellings later.[57]

The remaining months of 1432 saw him as active as before, attending monthly meetings at the homes of his warrior patrons, studying old texts, and tutoring a host of disciples. During the next few years he moved from place to place in the northern district of the capital. According to one disciple, at least one of his "huts" was a substantial dwelling with a guest room, a main meeting area that could accommodate ten men for poetry gatherings, and a small garden that adds to our impression of the poet's rising stature in the literary community.[58]

If he was popular in some quarters, however, he was not so in all, particularly in those of the new shogun Ashikaga Yoshinori (1394–1441), who had assumed that high title upon the premature death of his elder brother Yoshimochi in 1428. What the new shogun had against Shōtetsu is not known, but records of the time reveal that Yoshinori was an unstable and excitable man, given to violent outbursts of temper. Moreover, he was a firm supporter of the Asukai family, relying on Masayori's son Masayo (1390–1452) to function as the leader of the shogunal salon and even taking him along on his trips to Ise and the East Country.[59] By contrast, the new shogun, no doubt encouraged by Masayo, did everything in his power to make the Reizei and their cohorts miserable.

But in the case of Shōtetsu more than partisan politics seems to have been involved in Yoshinori's dislike. Some early biographies

57. Inada 1978:64–66. Shōtetsu's dwellings burned again in 1448 and 1457, but this time he appears to have stored copies of his poems elsewhere.
58. Inada 1978:83.
59. Inoue 1984:104–5.

of Shōtetsu claim that the poet so offended Yoshinori—although how, we can only guess—that the latter actually put the poet in house arrest for a time, a contention supported, circumstantially at least, by unexplained gaps in his poetry collection in the mid-1430s.[60] And it is certain that at some point Yoshinori confiscated the incomes of the Oda Estate in Bitchū, which had been perhaps his only source of income outside the fees and gifts he received from students and patrons. In all of this, though, Shōtetsu still retained some alliances that allowed him to survive as an artist. Even while living in relative seclusion, he remained active as a poet.

While Shōtetsu had much reason to grieve, he also had one major reason for rejoicing: the announcement in 1433 that the court was about to compile a new imperial anthology of *uta* after a long hiatus of fifty years. It would be the twenty-first such collection—and the last, although no one could know it at the time. Ever wanting to imitate his father Yoshimitsu, who had sponsored the last imperial collection in 1383, Yoshinori was the power behind the project—encouraged, of course, by the Asukai family. But poets of all persuasions celebrated the announcement. Even eccentrics agreed that to be included among those represented in an imperial anthology was deemed the highest honor available to a poet.

The first order of business in the matter was the appointment of a chief compiler, a distinction that fell to Asukai Masayo. However, no other compilers were designated, which was of course a blow to the Reizei family, who were furious to learn that their status as direct descendants of Teika did not earn them some participation in the project. But with the shogun as the sponsor, the Asukai had their way, and the project was begun. As part of the routine established for such ventures, the imperial house commissioned hundred-poem sequences from prominent literary men in the autumn of 1433. Included were the names of the retired emperor, the reigning emperor, the former regent Ichijō Kaneyoshi (1402–81), most of the high-ranking ministers and counselors of the court, the abbots of the most powerful temples, and the representatives of the poetic houses, the Asukai and the Reizei. Lastly, Gyōkō, the heir of Ton'a's Jōkō'in, was asked to submit his work, in addition being called to the post of librarian to assist Asukai Masayo. Probably because he was not of appropriate social rank to be considered along with court nobles, Shōtetsu was not among the fortunate few selected for this singular

60. Inoue 1984:129–33; Inada 1978:1223–25.

honor. But a poem written at the monthly poetry meeting of one of his patrons shows that he still had hope of being represented in the anthology, if only by a few poems:

Shikishima no   Even travelers
Michiyuku hito mo   On the Way of the Many Islands
Tamaboko no   Have hope in this reign—
Tama migaku beki   That the gems on their jeweled spears
Tanomi aru yo zo.   Will shine forth in times to come.[61]

Such was Shōtetsu's hope as he spent his time in relative seclusion, waiting with others for the completion of the project.

While he waited, the years went by. In the past the process of compilation had usually taken several years, with the compilers adhering to a long list of precedents and rituals in the process of choosing poems. In this case, however, a number of problems impeded progress. First was the death of Retired Emperor Go-Komatsu in the early winter of 1433, just days after the news of the project had been announced. Then, after the mourning period was over, squabbling between the Asukai and the Reizei, who held in their storehouses a number of documents important to the venture's success, kept the project bogged down almost indefinitely. Yoshinori did what he could to mollify the Reizei, and then resorted to confiscating one of their estates when they failed to respond.[62] But they were adamant.

In the end, it was only after six years, in the summer of 1439, that the collection was finally revealed to the world. Reizei Tameyuki had taken ill while waiting, succumbing to a cancer early in that very year—and just as well, since only two of his poems appeared in the anthology, which was dominated almost totally by the friends of the shogun, most notably the Asukai and the late leaders of the Nijō line. Reizei Mochitame (1401–54) was excluded altogether, a fate shared, sadly, by Shōtetsu himself. Whether it was the Asukai themselves who conspired to give him the ultimate snub or Yoshinori, still smarting over some imagined injury, will never be known.

As it turned out, the *Shinzokukokinshū*, or "New Collection of Ancient and Modern Times Continued," as the book was called, did not please everybody else either. Yoshinori was greatly displeased

61. *Sōkonshū* 2012.
62. Inoue 1984:114–16. Inoue 1984:520 argues that there may be a connection between the confiscation of the Reizei estates and that of Shōtetsu's noted earlier.

with it because it contained too many poems from military men who were friendly with the Asukai. In retaliation, he did not allow it to be publicly displayed for a time.[63] Yet it was still clear that the Reizei family and Shōtetsu had been intentionally rebuffed. And they knew from recent history that there would not be another imperial collection compiled for years to come.

Forced to hear around him the joy of all those whose names found their way into the pages of the new book—Masayo with eighteen poems, Gyōkō with seven poems, and even his patron Hatakeyama Yoshitada with one—Shōtetsu stayed in his hut, recording only a handful of poems in his collection for the next few years. In his sixties, he may have been suffering already from the asthma that would plague his last years, but it is just as possible that he withdrew out of depression, occupying his time with leisurely pursuits while leaving the poetic affairs of the capital to Ashikaga Yoshinori and his lackeys.

Fortunately for Shōtetsu, as well as the court, Yoshinori's high-handed ways did not continue for long. Fed up with his lord's capriciousness and cruelty, one of Yoshinori's own generals at last took the shogun's head in the summer of 1441—an act for which the perpetrator was made to pay with his own life, but one over which no one could pretend to be truly surprised. Few men grieved the assassinated tyrant. The senior generals of the great houses acted maturely in the event, appointing a young man as shogun and making every effort to restore stability to the capital. As a result, those who had been under censure were welcomed back to society, among them Shōtetsu.

If the last decade had been a lean one for the poet, the next one was healthy and full. Within a year of Yoshinori's death he was returning to his place of prominence in the capital, attending poetic gatherings, writing poems on commission, and teaching his disciples.

In 1443 Shōtetsu participated in an event that signaled a renaissance for the aristocracy in general and for those who had been ill-treated by Yoshinori in particular. A grand poetry contest in the old style held at the home of Ichijō Kaneyoshi, who had become a new champion of the Reizei family, the event reversed the trend of

63. Yoshinori's reactions are recorded in the court diary *Kennaiki* (see Eikyō 11 [1439]:6.27–29). *Dai Nihon kokiroku, Kennaiki II.* Inoue 1984:516 explains that a number of the anonymous poems in the collection are actually by those out of Yoshinori's good graces. But Shōtetsu, probably because of the prejudices of the Asukai, was not even allowed such "anonymous" recognition.

the past decade by involving none of the leaders of the Asukai family, who asked to be excused from participation. Instead, the contest was dominated by Kaneyoshi himself, members of his family, Reizei Mochitame, and Shōtetsu. Gyōkō, no doubt feeling rather forlorn as the only confirmed conservative in the group, could not easily turn his invitation down and attended as a representative of the opposition. The gathering occurred in the second month of the year, with invitations having been sent out some time before. Although limited in his ability to finance a contest in the style of his ancestors, Kaneyoshi did everything in his power to make the event one to be remembered.

Unfortunately for students of late medieval *uta*, few of the many poetry contests of these years were recorded for posterity, probably because many of them were rather informal affairs not worthy of such attention but also because of the expense involved in doing things in a style that would make such an occasion worth preserving. But the 1443 contest was done in conscious imitation of the great contests of earlier eras. Kaneyoshi therefore had the poems and judgments recorded, adding his own summaries of the discussions that led to decisions, which were arrived at by *shūgihan*, or debate and voting. His efforts led to a text known in later generations as *Saki no sesshō-ke uta-awase*, "The Poem Contest at the Home of the Former Regent."

As might be expected, the record reveals that Reizei Mochitame carried the day. But Shōtetsu too fared well in the voting, gaining praise for a number of his contributions, among which the following, from early in the competition, stands out.

Hanazakari	Blossoms at their height!
Kasumi no mio mo	And deep as the dark of night
Fukaki yo no	Is the misty channel
Haru no monaka ni	Where the very midpoint of spring
Niou tsukikage.	Glows in the light of the moon.[64]

Aptly, the participants praised this poem by describing it with the old word, *en*—"charmingly beautiful," a word that echoes Teika's famous ideal of *yōen*, or "ethereal beauty"—and awarded it the win. True to his affiliations, however, Shōtetsu showed his versatility by producing a much less dreamy but equally interesting poem in round 117:

---

64. *Saki no sesshō-ke uta-awase* 48 (Round 24, Spring), in *SKT* 5.

Katami to ya	As a parting gift,
Ko no ha katsu some	It turns over to the frost
Oku tsuyu o	Leaves on the trees
Shimo ni makasete	Already dyed by its dews—
Aki no yukuran.	So does autumn, going away.[65]

This poem earned him only a draw, but still his place at the contest was secure. In other rounds he produced some controversy by offering unusual conceptions and "inelegant" diction. But the very words used to criticize him—*mezuraka*, "unusual," and so on—were to him titles of praise. Whatever the cost to him in the competition, such comments made him seem unique, and every indication is that his eccentricities endeared him all the more to Kaneyoshi, who was an independent spirit himself. If not a total victory, then, the contest was nevertheless for Shōtetsu no defeat. He emerged with both his reputation for originality and his crucial alliances still intact.

In coming years Shōtetsu gained place as the grand old man of the liberal cause, acting as contest judge, critic, and lecturer. For the first time he was invited into the homes of aristocrats such as Kaneyoshi, with whom he developed a relatively close relationship despite the great gap between them in status.[66] Eventually, in 1452, he would even be invited to lecture on *Genji monogatari* before the young shogun, Ashikaga Yoshimasa (1435–90). The lectures continued on until 1455, and the next year, in gratitude, Yoshimasa restored to Shōtetsu the income from the Oda Estate that had been appropriated by Yoshinori several decades before.[67]

It is worth noting, however, that when the estate rights were returned Shōtetsu immediately made them over to his disciple and heir Shōkō, indicating that by this time the older poet had little need for such support himself.[68] And a glance at the headnotes to his personal collection for these years—and there are hundreds of them, in contrast to the years 1433–44—shows why. For not only was he lecturing to the shogun in his palace, but he was also in favor with numerous political figures, including again prominent members of the Hosokawa, Hatakeyama, Yamana, Shiba, Isshiki, Takeda, Akamatsu, Ogasawara, Sugiwara, and other military families, as well as priests at prominent temples such as Miidera,

65. *Saki no sesshō-ke uta-awase* 231 (Round 117, Autumn), in *SKT* 5.
66. Inada 1978:273–74.
67. Inada 1978:85–86.
68. Ibid.

Ninnaji, and Sanbō'in. A short excerpt from the summer of 1449 illustrates the pattern of his days.[69]

6.6   Attended monthly poetry meeting at house of
      Yamana Noritoyo
6.11 Attended monthly poetry meeting at house of
      Fujiwara [Saitō] Toshinaga
6.13 Attended monthly poetry meeting held by lay monk
      Sochin
6.26 Composed poem for first visit to house of Akamatsu
      Norisada
6.27 Composed poem by request for Kanbe Yukimoto
7.7   Composed poem at residence of Chōsan at Butsuji'in
7.?   Composed poem on topic requested by Isshiki
      Norichika, sent from Miidera
7.9   Attended first monthly meeting at house of Yamana
      Noriyuki
7.11 Attended monthly poetry meeting
7.18 Attended monthly poetry meeting at house of
      Takeda Shinken
7.19 Composed poem at house of Hatakeyama Kenryō
      [Yoshitada]
7.22 Had visit from Tō no Tsuneyori at inn near Myōkōji
7.23 Attended monthly poetry meeting of Isshiki
      Norichika
7.25 Attended monthly poetry meeting at house of
      Yamana Noritoyo
7.26 Had visit from Tō no Tsuneyori at inn in Horikawa
7.29 Attended monthly poetry meeting of lay monk
      Sochin

Of the dozen or so men mentioned here, eight—Yamana Noritoyo (a son of Yamana Sōzen, 1404–73), Saitō Toshinaga (d. 1465), Akamatsu Norisada, Isshiki Norichika (d. 1451), Yamana Noriyuki (d. 1473), Takeda Shinken (1420–71), Hatakeyama Yoshitada, and Tō no Tsuneyori (1401–84)—served at one time or another as provincial governors or shogunal constables (*shugo*). And other passages from his collection could make the list longer, revealing the names of the most powerful men of elite military society as patrons. Even the former shogunal deputy (*kanrei*) Hosokawa Katsumoto

69. Taken from Inada 1978:1230.

(1430–73) asked to become his disciple in 1450, a request that Shōtetsu first declined out of modesty but later was obliged to accept. With such patrons he was able to live his chosen life, not as rich as some later poets, but well enough off to want for little.[70]

Thus Shōtetsu's life in the 1440s and 1450s seemed to regain the vitality of the 1420s, when he had been a rising talent. In one way, however, his life in the post-Yoshinori era was profoundly different, namely, that it involved much less contact with the Reizei family, and less activity in support of the Reizei political cause. The reasons were no doubt numerous, the most obvious one being that the current Reizei heir, Mochitame, displayed meager talents. But numerous witnesses attest that another reason was that Shōtetsu was simply tired of partisan politics, which were more a source of annoyance than inspiration. As he confided privately to a disciple, he was tired of being perceived in the context of the age-old rivalry between the Nijō and the Reizei as "the last leaf on the Reizei tree."

> Both factions are tiresome. I myself have no respect for those degenerate houses. I study only the essence of Shunzei and Teika.[71]

This was a radical sentiment for a man of the age, though perhaps understandable when one takes into account the long years of rejection he had suffered earlier because of his dedication to Ryōshun's memory—years that seem to have led him to an overwhelming question: Why not cast the inferior models of the present aside and return to the acknowledged source of the tradition itself, to Teika? For a man of over sixty years, with confidence in his art, the conclusion must have seemed obvious, although his response to it was largely responsible for the reputation of eccentricity that was to stigmatize him for centuries to come. Even he admitted that his admiration for Teika may have seemed excessive when he confessed that on awaking from sleep he would often think of one of Teika's poems "and feel as if I were about to lose my mind" (II, 67).

This confession notwithstanding, the old master never disavowed his obsession and proceeded to hang a portrait of Teika in his guest room and to put most of his books in storage except for an old text of famous poems by Teika and Ietaka (1158–1237). Furthermore, he revealed to his disciples, perhaps with not enough tact,

70. See Inada 1978:84–86.
71. From *Tokorodokoro bentō*, in Kidō 1985:273–74.

that he was now a self-proclaimed "worshipper" of the poet who had founded the medieval tradition.[72]

The warrior-poet Tō no Tsuneyori, a sometime student of Shōtetsu during these years, records one occasion in which Shōtetsu made his feelings known.

On the evening of the eighteenth day of the ninth month of Hōtoku 1 [1449], the lay monk [Tō no Ujikazu; d. 1471] and the governor of Awa [Hatakeyama Mochizumi] went to Shōgetsu's [Shōtetsu's] hut, with Tsuneyori also accompanying. The governor of Awa offered these three poems and, noting that they were of course all very fine, asked Shōgetsu which of the three he would choose if forced to do so.

Omoikane
Imogariyukeba
Fuyu no yo no
Kawakaze samumi
Chidori naku nari.

As pressed by love
I go to hunt her in my yearning,
The wind blows cold
Through winter darkness on the river,
Where on the banks plovers cry.

[Ki no Tsurayuki]

Yū sareba
Shiokaze koete
Michinoku no
Noda no tamakawa
Chidori naku nari.

As evening falls
The sea breeze blows from afar—
And at Tamakawa
In Noda, in the land of Michinoku,
I hear the plovers crying.

[Nōin the Monk]

Hamachidori
Tsumadou tsuki no
Kage samushi
Ashi no kareba no
Yuki no shitakaze.

When shore-plovers cry
In yearning, then how cold are the rays
Cast by the moon!
Over withered leaves on the reeds—
A low wind beneath the snow.

[Teika]

72. In his *Tōyashū kikigaki* ("Memoirs of Lord Tō," 1456?, in *NKGT* 5:348), Shōtetsu's sometime student Tō no Tsuneyori (1402–84) notes that his teacher had a copy of a portrait of Teika by Emperor Juntoku in the alcove of his guestroom. The story that he put away all of his books save the *Teika-Karyū* [*Ietaka*] *Ryōkyō Senka-awase*—a mock poem contest between the two poets put together by Retired Emperor Go-Toba (1180–1239)—is recorded by Shinkei's disciple, the renga master Kensai (1452–1510) in his *Kensai zōdan* ("Kensai's Notes About This and That," late fifteenth century, in *NKGT* 5:396).

In reply Shōgetsu said, "Since I will be of the Teika sect to the end, I would have to choose *Hamachidori* . . . although the styles are about the same."[73]

This of course did not mean that his rivals in the poetic world of the time would forget his affiliations with the Reizei house; nor could Shōtetsu have been unaware that to opt for Teika as a model was itself a "liberal" act. And that Tō no Tsuneyori, who was strictly speaking a disciple of Gyōkō, still saw Shōtetsu as a member of the liberal camp is apparent from another quote following almost immediately on the above anecdote.

A poem said to be by Shōgetsu:

Nushi shiranu	Owner unknown:
Irie no yūbe	At evening, by an inlet,
Hito nakute	With no one around—
Mino to sao to zo	Just a raincloak and a pole
Fune ni nokoreru.	Left behind in a boat.

Truly a poem I cannot admire . . . This is what is meant "by the voice of a violent age."[74]

"The voice of a violent age" is a direct reference to a condemnation of unorthodox verse in the introduction to the Chinese *Shih ching* ("The Book of Odes") that no educated man of Tsuneyori's time would have missed.[75] And just as clearly it is the unadorned realism of Shōtetsu's expression—a style that he had learned at great expense from Ryōshun and Tamemasa decades before—that a more orthodox poet such as Tsuneyori found unsettling.

Nevertheless, there are developments in Shōtetsu's work at this time that betray a bold attempt to move beyond the Reizei style and adopt Teika as his model. For clearly it is Teika and not his old teachers who are at the center of attention in his one work of critical prose, *Shōtetsu Monogatari*, which was probably written just prior to

73. *Tōyashū kikigaki*, in *NKGT* 5:336. Tsurayuki's poem is recorded in *SIS* 224, Nōin's in *SKKS* 643 (line 2 reading *shiokaze koshite*), and Teika's in *SG* 2443 (*SKT* 3).
74. *Tōyashū kikigaki*, in *NKGT* 5:340–41.
75. In fact, Tsuneyori quotes the introduction in relation to an anecdote concerning Retired Emperor Go-Komatsu in the section immediately preceding the one noting Shōtetsu's poem. See *NKGT* 5:340.

the time of Tsuneyori's criticism, most likely in the spring and summer of 1448.

A more detailed treatment of this work will be offered below in the introduction to the translation. However, a few things deserve mention here as evidence for the change in attitude that Shōtetsu was experiencing in the twilight of his life. First is the unequivocal declaration with which he begins his task:

> In this art of poetry, those who speak ill of Teika should be denied the protection of the gods and Buddhas and condemned to the punishments of hell.[76]

Not even Ryōshun had adopted a more strident tone in his tirades against the conservative camp. And the rest of the work, although more gently, elaborates Shōtetsu's thesis statement by quoting Teika's critical works, providing commentary and exegesis for some of Teika's poems, and in general using Teika as the ultimate authority in all matters connected to the way of poetry.

To be fair to Ryōshun and Tamemasa, it must also be said that the aging Shōtetsu remembers them with anecdotes that show his respect and affection, and that he draws on Ryōshun's critical works frequently.[77] Also there are words of praise for Ryōshun's teacher, Tamehide. But there is not a word of support anywhere in *Shōtetsu monogatari* for Kyōgoku Tamekane, nor is there much mention of the more recent members of the Reizei family. Instead, Shōtetsu focuses almost entirely on the poets of the early Kamakura period, the Shinkokin age—the era of Teika's youth, whose poets he extols continuously. For those later adherents of the Nijō school, Ton'a and his descendants and the Asukai, on the other hand, he has only a few words, which are civil but no more. The only exception in the last case is Yoshida no Kenkō—and, significantly, not for his poetry but for his *Tsurezuregusa*.[78]

And this is not all: those of his own poems he quotes for comment or exegesis show the rhetorical complexity and tonal resonance that only Teika and the other Shinkokin poets could have

---

76. *SM* I, 1.
77. See notes to translation of *Shōtetsu monogatari*, which contains over a dozen references to Ryōshun's critical works.
78. Readers of the late medieval age generally knew Kenkō for *Tsurezuregusa* and not for his poems, although in his own time he had been known primarily as a poet. See Carter 1989:174–75.

taught him. One example with Shōtetsu's own commentary will suffice.

Yūmagure	In the dim twilight,
Sore ka to mieshi	I glimpsed her as in a vision
Omokage no	Scarcely seen at all:
Kasumu zo katami	An image brought back by spring haze
Ariake no tsuki.	Against the moon in the dawning sky.

The idea of the poem is that at twilight, when the spring haze spreads over all, he catches a faint glimpse of someone, and thinking it may be the woman he loves, he cherishes the image carefully in his heart. Then the sight of the moon in the sky at dawn reminds him of that vision and thus becomes a fragile keepsake of her. The imagery of thin clouds wreathing the moon and haze trailing across the cherry blossoms is not expressed in the poem in so many words but instead is left to the atmosphere of mystery and depth and gentle elegance. Such things lie outside the words of the poem.[79]

The interpretation speaks for itself. One must only add that by using the word *yūgen* ("mystery and depth")—a poetic ideal abjured by conservative poets—he makes a clear statement about his goals as a poet. No doubt Gyōkō and the Asukai would have complained that the poem was too misty, too obscure, too dreamy, not understanding that according to his own aesthetic, that was precisely the effect Shōtetsu was aiming for.

Despite his reputation as an eccentric, Shōtetsu's reputation grew through the last decade of his life, thanks partly to the support of men like Ichijō Kaneyoshi, it must be admitted, but also due to his own undeniable experience and irrepressible talent. His forementioned invitation to lecture on *Genji monogatari* before Yoshimasa in 1452 was a crowning honor, but not a solitary one. In the *buke kadan*, at least, he held a conspicuous place. *Sōkonshū* shows constant contact with his old patrons, and a few new ones as well, including the courtier Hino Katsumitsu (1429–76), brother-in-law of the young shogun and one of the most powerful men in the city.

The last five years of Shōtetsu's life were difficult ones for the capital, with peasant riots and constant conflicts in the shogunal

79. *SM* I, 69.

house and those of its daimyo captains. And for Shōtetsu it was a time of personal loss. His disciple Chiun had already died in 1448, and Reizei Mochitame died in 1454. Then came his student Sōzei who, after leaving the capital with Yamana Sōzen in disgrace the year before, died in 1455. When Gyōkō succumbed in 1455 it must have seemed that soon he would have no one, friend or foe, from the old days to chat with. His calendar became crowded with memorial services. And Shōtetsu himself was suffering more numerous and more intense bouts of his chronic asthma. In the first months of 1454 he was kept bedridden much of the time; in the late autumn of 1456 he was down again. Then, in the second month of 1457, he was stricken and nearly died. Now in his seventies, his body was weak and no longer had the resilience to promise complete recovery.

He finally passed away in 1459, after a brief respite that allowed him to attend poetic gatherings at the homes of the linked-verse poet Senjun (1411–76) and his old patron Hatakeyama Yoshitada. Virtually his last act, so far as we know, was to copy out the first chapter of *Genji monogatari*, perhaps hoping that fate would allow him time to finish the remaining fifty-three chapters as well.

To sum up so long a life—he was in his seventy-ninth year at the time of his death—is no easy matter. One monkish friend described him as a gentle, sensitive man, a judgment with which any reader of his poetry can concur.[80] But the record also indicates that he was a strong-willed and self-confident artist who maintained his artistic integrity in a world that was more wont to reward the sycophant than the rebel. Among his friends, and especially his many disciples, he was not soon forgotten. As first disciple, Shōkō inherited his master's hermitage and properties and went on to make a distinguished career for himself, although never achieving anything to compare with the accomplishments of his master. By necessity, he did something Shōtetsu seldom did—he traveled, seeking patrons among the war barons of the provinces, as did his contemporary, the renga master Sōgi.[81]

One thing we have Shōkō to thank for is his labor in compiling Shōtetsu's poems, creating the book we know now as *Sōkonshū*. The title, "Grass Roots Collection"—intended no doubt to communicate the lasting quality of his work, which could stand the cold blasts of winter and still emerge green in spring—was probably chosen by Shōtetsu himself, who had evidently put some effort into

80. Inada 1978:91.
81. See Inada 1978:129–61 for a treatment of Shōkō's life and works.

organizing his own magnum opus before his death.[82] But it was Shōkō who did most of the work, and it was Shōkō who went to Nara during the dark days of the Ōnin War (1467–77) to ask Ichijō Kaneyoshi to write a preface for the work in memory of his old friend. Appending Kaneyoshi's prestigious name to anything gave it a greater chance of circulation and survival. No doubt Shōkō rejoiced in Kaneyoshi's willingness to secure the reputation of his master into the future—not knowing, of course, that it would be centuries later before the name Shōtetsu would be of interest to scholars and poets again.

SHŌTETSU MONOGATARI

As the ample evidence of *Sōkonshū* shows, Shōtetsu was above all a creative artist who spent his life perfecting his craft through private study and practice, participation in poetry contests, and meetings both formal and informal. He was not a scholar-critic in the sense that earlier poets such as his mentor Teika had been, but one who believed that rather than spend his time on gaining "learning and knowledge" (*saigaku*) a poet should concentrate on gaining "a clear understanding and grasp of the nature of poetry" (I, 25). What scholarly work he undertook was all for the sake of his practice of the art. In the process of long years of activity in the poetic world, however, he quite naturally developed ideas and opinions that were conveyed to students in various forms. These, such as we have of them in written form, have become part of his legacy.

He was not alone in this, as any student of medieval Japanese poetry knows. Most semiprofessional poets of the previous ages, from Ton'a to Tamemasa, had been active as contest judges, and many, like Ryōshun, had left critical writings, often cast in the format of "teachings" given in response to questions by students. Such writings, passed down in handwritten copies from teacher to student for generations to come, typically consisted of lists of anecdotes and records of "secret" lore, some exegesis and interpretation, and, occasionally, more extended theoretical expositions. As a whole, they therefore strike the modern reader as being discursive in nature—often frustratingly so. But for the patient student they provide not only a good deal of insight into the theoretical assumptions of their authors but also a great deal of practical knowledge about the poetic institutions, preoccupations, and ideals of their times.

82. Inada 1978:267–98.

This is as true of *Shōtetsu monogatari*, the poet's only critical work, as of any other text of the late medieval period. In its pages we find documentation of Shōtetsu's own attitudes and beliefs about the nature of his art, his conception of poetic history, his frustration with the factionalism of the poetic world, his dedication to Teika and the Shinkokin age, his teachings about how aspiring poets should approach their art, and, finally, a host of notes that reveal a great deal about poetic customs and his everyday life as a poet. In short, his critical work reads like a concrete extension of his profession.

As might be expected given the context in which they were produced, many medieval critical works have complex textual histories that can be traced to their source in "secret" documents passed on from master to disciple. In the case of *Shōtetsu monogatari*, we in fact are not even certain about the precise date of the work or whether the actual writing was done by Shōtetsu himself or by a disciple. Even the title of the work is subject to debate. Thus the earliest extant manuscript of the work, made from a manuscript in the hand of Tō no Sosan (nephew of the poet-scholar Tō no Tsuneyori) bears the title *Shōtetsu nikki*, or "Shōtetsu's Diary." According to Hisamatsu Sen'ichi, editor of the *Nihon koten bungaku taikei* edition of the work that uses this earliest version as a primary source, Tō no Sosan's text is of late Muromachi or early Edo date, and has the following colophon: "This preceding volume is a copy by Tō no Sosan of the manuscript in the author's hand." The text shows signs of having been carefully examined by an anonymous scholar or scholars, and some passages show suggested emendations, with a thin line drawn through the original text so that it can still be easily read. Unfortunately, the manuscript is in very poor condition, with much insect damage, and cannot be relied upon alone.

From where then does the accepted title, *Shōtetsu monogatari*, derive? Predictably, from the second most important surviving manuscript copy, the so-called Eishō text, which bears that title and ends with the following words:

> The text says that this work was copied by Tō no Sosan from a manuscript in the imperial handwriting. Dated the fourteenth year of Eishō [1517], intercalary tenth month, twenty-third day.

In other words, this copy was made from a copy of Tō no Sosan's manuscript (i.e., the *Shōtetsu nikki* described above). It too was used by Professor Hisamatsu in preparing the edition for the *Nihon koten bungaku taikei* text, which serves as the basis for the translation below.

Of the other surviving manuscripts, dating from the late Muromachi through the Edo periods, some consist of the whole text with the title *Shōtetsu monogatari*, whereas others consist of the first part of the work only, with the title *Tesshoki monogatari*, "Tales of Secretary Shōtetsu." One manuscript in the imperial library has the long inscription on its cover, *Shōgetsu seigan wakasho, ichimyō Shōtetsu monogatari, edosha* ("Notes on Classical Poetry by Shōgetsu Seigan, Also Known As Conversations with Shōtetsu, Edo-Period Copy"). Nevertheless, this manuscript, too, consists of only the first part of the work. In the printed edition published in *Gunsho ruijū*, Part I appears under the title *Tesshoki monogatari* ("Conversations with Shōtetsu the Secretary"), whereas Part II is printed in *Zoku Gunsho ruijū* under the title *Seigan chawa* (also pronounced *Seigan sawa*: "Tea Talk by the Verdant Cliff, or Tea Talk with Seigan"). This second part of *Shōtetsu monogatari* was traditionally held to have been written down from Shōtetsu's comments by his disciple Chiun, and to be considerably later in date than the first part—although recent scholarship debates the latter point.[83] Late in the eighteenth century, first in the Tenmei era (1781–89) and again in the Kansei era (1789–1801), *Tesshoki monogatari* was combined and issued in a woodblock-printed edition together with *Seigan chawa* under the overall title *Shōtetsu monogatari*.

As Hisamatsu points out, there are some difficulties in accepting Chiun as the "author" of the second part of the work. But it should also be borne in mind that there is no guarantee that the first part was actually written by Shōtetsu, either. For while the first part is written mostly in the first person, this could simply mean that the writer was taking down more or less verbatim what Shōtetsu was saying. Since some manuscripts bear the title *Shōkō nikki*, or "Shōkō's Diary," it is even possible that it was Shōkō, as Shōtetsu's foremost disciple, who recorded what he chose to from recollections of his talks with his teacher.

Much of the history of Shōtetsu's one work of poetic criticism thus remains unclear. Modern scholars, however, judge it to be an authentic work, recorded perhaps by Shōtetsu himself, in part, or by a close disciple. And although the date of the work has also been a subject of debate, it now appears certain that it was first written

83. See Hosoya 1976:354–81. Hosoya concludes that both parts of the work were written in 1448.

between 1448 and 1450, when Shōtetsu was well into the final phase of his career, which was, it will be remembered, characterized by the strident "Teika worship" expressed in the opening sentence of the work. This means that it was produced while the poet was still living; and it may not be going too far to suggest that, whether actually recorded by a disciple or not, the master knew the work was being done and sanctioned its contents.

The work is made up of 210 sections, arranged in no particular order,[84] whose contents themselves may be roughly divided up into several broad, nonmutually exclusive categories: (1) anecdotes concerning poets of the present and past; (2) special knowledge or lore, more or less esoteric; (3) notes of instruction and advice to students concerning everything from technique to proper modes of study and practice; (4) interpretation and commentary on Shōtetsu's own poems or on the poems of others, ranging from the ancient age to the present, sometimes with some attention to poetic ideals; and (5) a few short essays on aesthetics per se. Each of these categories deserves separate attention.

ANECDOTES

It is from the anecdotes that we of course learn a good deal about Shōtetsu's own life. In part I, section 104, for instance, Shōtetsu explains how he first encountered Ryōshun and Tamemasa, as already indicated above. Other anecdotes document an excursion to see the spring blossoms with Ryōshun, Tamemasa, Tamekuni, and others in 1402 and participation in a poetry contest with the same basic company, showing that even as a young man Shōtetsu was accepted as part of the Reizei circle. And there are stories from later years, too, involving Gyōkō and Kōun. Although not numerous, such anecdotes give us a glimpse into the patterns of Shōtetsu's alliances and rivalries over the years.

Not all of the stories Shōtetsu relates are about the present, however; some go back as far as the period of Teika. From these stories we learn how Archbishop Jichin (1155–1225) replied to his brother's suggestions that dedication to poetry was unseemly in a high-ranking cleric (II, 88); how Nijō Yoshimoto instructed Ryōshun about the proper approach to keiko, or composition practice

---

84. Although some sections of similar content do seem to be grouped together in series (I, 29–33 all dealing with dai, or conventional topics; II, 12–14 all treating questions relating to proper etiquette in poetry meetings), there is no organizing structure for the whole work.

(I, 59); how Ton'a tutored his son Kyōken (II, 11); how Fujiwara no Tameie (1198–1275) gave his son Tameuji practical advice about a poem to be entered in competition (I, 93); and so on. These stories, gathered from a variety of sources, range in length from several lines to a page or more, dealing with various persons and periods and revealing attitudes and habits of interest to the student of medieval poetic history. A few even strike a humorous note, as in the case of II, 101, in which the son of Ietaka laments his meager talents.

Having heard that Teika had said of him, "When Takasuke was young his poetry was not a bit inferior to that of his lordship his father, and I was quite confident of his future. But as he grew older, his poetry deteriorated badly," Takasuke is said to have retorted angrily, "Very well then, never mind about the poetry of my older age. Why doesn't he pick some poems of my youth for his imperial anthology?"

More often than not, however, Shōtetsu's stories have a more serious point, often a partisan one showing the narrow-mindedness of poets of the Nijō school or, by contrast, the wisdom of Ryōshun. Some stories, particularly the ones involving Shōtetsu himself, have clearly been included to establish his credentials as a poet or his own knowledge, sensitivity, and skill. An example appears in I, 16, where the poet explains how participants at a poetry gathering mistook a poem of his as an allusion to *Genji monogatari*:

Everyone . . . asked each other whether there was some allusion to *Genji monogatari*. I had not given the slightest thought to *Genji* in composing the poem. . . . What a terrible age we live in when people can no longer even understand something as simple as this!

Surely Shōtetsu was not so derogatory toward his cohorts in the gathering itself. Nevertheless, the motive of recording the occasion is transparent, lending the story a purpose greater than mere amusement. He could have little respect for those who knew the greatest of court classics only through synopses and a few poems.

LORE

If Shōtetsu's anecdotes are often motivated by partisan ideals or personal beliefs, his presentation of "special knowledge" about poets and poetry seem to aspire to greater objectivity. Indeed, many passages simply present what now would be found in a dictionary, as in the examples that follow:

I, 66: *Moshio* means "seaweed steeped in salt." Therefore, *moshio* may also be used in poems on the topic of "Love and Seaweed."

I, 77: The birch cherry (*kabazakura*) is a single-flowering cherry.

II, 19: The word *mashimizu* is the same as just *shimizu*, "pure water." It means "true pure water."

This is also true of his forays into the the realm of literary history, where he records for his students—who, in an age before printing and public libraries, could of course receive much of their information about such matters only from such a source—a few facts like the following:

I, 12: With regard to Ton'a: Tameakira was the compiler of *Shinshūishū*, but he died while compiling it and before submitting the completed draft. Because Ton'a carried on the task of compilation beginning with the miscellaneous or love poems, he must have possessed the requisite documents and materials.

I, 46: Lord Tsurudono was the son of Lord Kōmyō-buji. He is the ancestor of the present Tsukinowa family. Lord Tsurudono was one of the compilers of *Shokukokinshū*.

II, 41: The anniversary of Hitomaro's death is kept secret, so that few people anywhere know the date. It is the eighteenth day of the third month. Poetry gatherings in commemoration of Hitomaro have not been held on this date. The commemorative poetry gathering sponsored by Akisue of the Rokujō house took place in summer, in the sixth month.

From what sources Shōtetsu himself gleaned such information is not always clear, but most of it probably came from his teachers,

Ryōshun and Tamemasa, or from documents in his private possession. This would explain why he is often mistaken in such matters
(the second example above being one instance[85])—a fact that is
worth noting if only as a way to remind us that lore passed on from
teacher to disciple orally or through private texts tended to perpetu-
ate errors. As we shall see later, this was also true even in the case of
very widely distributed poetic treatises.

Thus the historical information in *Shōtetsu monogatari* is not
always reliable because the poet often based his statements on incomplete or incorrect information. Moreover, a careful look at some
of the "special knowledge" Shōtetsu records also reveals ulterior
motives at work even in his seemingly "historical" notes. A
few examples dealing with Asukai Masatsune make those motives
apparent.

I, 3: Masatsune had a fondness for striking phrases, which
may explain why his poems sometimes have serious faults.
Also—no doubt unaware that many similar phrases already
existed—he seems to have taken phrases from many other
people and incorporated them into his own poems.

I, 11: Although Masatsune was included among the five compilers of *Shinkokinshū*, he was but a youth at the time and was
merely listed as a compiler. His family could hardly have
possessed any valuable poetic documents or materials.

The first of these passages does little more than repeat a criticism
initially offered by an earlier poet of Masatsune's own day,[86] making
Shōtetsu's own statements seem more like history than dogma. But,
given his documented rivalry with the Asukai family, Shōtetsu's
purpose in including it in his writings is obvious. And this is even
more apparent in the second quotation, which attempts to contest
the authority and competence of the Asukai to undertake official
poetic duties at court—duties that, despite the precedent established by the compilation of *Shinzokukokinshū*, Shōtetsu of course
wanted to reserve for the Reizei, whose possession of documents was
unquestioned. In both cases, Shōtetsu's partisanship could not be
more blatant. History was to him perceived in the context of the
great rivalry that dominated poetic politics throughout the late

85. See nn. 149 and 150 in the translation below.
86. See n. 18 in the translation below.

medieval age, after all; to expect him to write with disinterest would be to ignore everything we know about the nature of literary work in his age.

INSTRUCTION TO STUDENTS

One of the lessons of *Shōtetsu monogatari*, therefore, is that, like all poets of his time, Shōtetsu was engaged in philosophical struggles all of his life, even after he tried to rise above them. No aloof scholar or otherworldly hermit, he was an active competitor in the poetic arena whose practice and theory were dictated to a great extent by a tradition over which he had little control. This is particularly obvious in the third category of material represented in *Shōtetsu monogatari*, namely notes he left to his students about the proper practice of their art. Many of these deal with technical matters ranging from the proper employment of allusion to the proper handling of poetic *dai*, or "poetic topics"—precisely the sorts of questions that a young poet would be asking of his instructor in an age when nearly every facet of composition was dependent on the law of precedent.

> II, 54: For the topic "A Fire in the Brazier," one may treat either buried embers or a burning fire, but for the topic "Buried Embers," one may not treat a fire in the brazier.

> II, 71: The topic "Love: Seducing a Man's Wife" means that the speaker seduces another man's wife. Women like Utsusemi and Ukifune in *Genji monogatari* would be suitable for this situation.

Statements like these may make for dry reading today, when most students read treatises like Shōtetsu's in order to understand the poetry of his day, but for students faced almost daily with the task of composing poems in the presence of competitors and patrons, such instruction was doubtless exactly what was most wanted from a teacher. That *Shōtetsu monogatari* is so dominated by exactly such material thus becomes understandable if we take his writings as being meant primarily for students eager for advice about how to proceed in an art that was undertaken almost always in a social setting, where originality was only deemed acceptable when defined by proper etiquette and knowledge of convention. With this in mind we can comprehend the significance of even the most formalistic statements:

II, 13: Stacking the poems at a poetry gathering is a matter of the utmost importance. It is very difficult because they must be collected and stacked in sequence according to the participants' court rank and family standing. The stacking procedure is easy at a gathering attended solely by court nobles because their official titles and court ranks are in an established order. The procedure is difficult when the party consists of both court nobles and members of the military aristocracy.

This is the voice of experience talking, providing guidance to students, most notably Shōkō and others like him, who would face the challenge of accommodating important patrons of various classes all of their artistic lives. To such men in such circumstances, knowledge of social convention would indeed have been "of the utmost importance."

EXEMPLARY POEMS

In the final analysis, however, Shōtetsu doubtless realized that knowledge of convention was not enough in itself to make a poet, and he therefore dedicated a great part of his "conversations" to the presentation and analysis of poems, usually exemplary ones. Not surprisingly, it is in these passages that his writing proves of greatest interest to a modern reader. It is here, for example, that Shōtetsu's own tastes become most obvious—here, for example, that he reveals his pronounced bias for the poems of the Shinkokin era, especially Teika's. A chart listing the number of poems quoted by respective poets of the past and present shows the pattern.

Poets of the Kokin Age

Ki no Tsurayuki	2
Sosei the Monk	2
Archbishop Henjō	1
Ariwara no Narihira	1
Total:	6

Poets of the Shinkokin Age

Fujiwara no Teika	13
Fujiwara no Ietaka	5
Archbishop Jien	4
Shunzei's Daughter	3

Fujiwara no Shunzei	3
Princess Shikishi	2
Emperor Juntoku	2
Lady Kunaikyō	1
Fujiwara no Takanobu	1
Total:	34

Poets of Later Ages

Ton'a	3
Genka	3
Nijō Tameshige	2
Nijō Tameuji	1
Asukai Masaari	1
Kyōgoku Tameko	1
Nijō Tamesada	1
Keiun	1
Reizei Tamehide	1
Reizei Tamemasa	1
Keikō	1
Total:	16

Poets of the present

Shōtetsu	48
Total:	48

Beyond this, the only thing necessary to make Shōtetsu's biases clear is to note that Nijō Tameyo, Kyōgoku Tamekane, Ryōshun, Asukai Masayori, and Gyōkō are noticeably absent from these lists and that the poems by Ton'a are quoted in anecdotes, as are the ones by Tameuji, Tameshige, Tamehide, Tamemasa, and Keikō, whereas those by Teika and other poets of the Shinkokin age are presented, usually with some analysis, as exemplary works. The conclusion that he looked to Teika as a mentor is inescapable. Indeed, judging from quantity alone, it would appear that the only poet besides Teika that Shōtetsu could recommend enthusiastically was himself.

Why he favors the poetry of the Shinkokin era—or his own, modeled upon it—is also apparent in these sections. I, 86, which presents an analysis of a poem by Teika (SG 858; Love), is one example.

Kaze araki　　　　　A bitter wind
Motoara no kohagi　　Blows through tangles of bush clover
Sode ni mite　　　　Mirrored in my sleeves,
Fukeyuku tsuki ni　　That in the light of the sinking moon
Omoru shiratsuyu.　　Grow heavy with drops of white dew.

In this poem, Teika has so completely entered into the heart of the topic that even though he does not actually say it, the idea of waiting is felt implicitly. On a first hearing, one would not understand the poem at all, perhaps thinking the poet is making some sort of joke. Nevertheless, because the poet has conceived the poem after thoroughly assimilating himself to the situation of the speaker, it beautifully expresses the very essence of the topic. Gazing out upon the garden, where the bush clover are blooming in profusion, the lady waits for her lover. The wind blows roughly through the tangles of bush clover, breaking off beads of dew and dashing them to the ground. These seem to be the very tears upon her sleeve, and as the moon sinks in the advancing night, ever more tears fall upon her sleeve, which grows heavy under their weight. Thus the poet conceives the idea of the tears vying with the dew on the bush clover and imbues the poem with a profound sense of what it is for the woman to wait for her lover. One may even imagine from the style of the poem that she goes out to the edge of the veranda and sits there sadly, gazing at the garden. Truly, the effect of her experience as she sits waiting all night long in misery is conveyed in a style of gentle and evocative elegance.

In passing, it should be said that such lengthy and impassioned exegesis is a rare thing in the annals of medieval poetry. And such passages also explain why Shōtetsu says elsewhere (I, 67) that he has little use for "the kind of treatises that go into all sorts of pretentious details" but fail to provide meaningful interpretation and appreciation. But the other thing this section reveals is Shōtetsu's fondness for rhetorically complex poems—precisely the sort of poems for which the poets of the Nijō school had so many reservations. The critical term he uses to refer to such effects is *omoshiroshi*, a word with a long history that is frequently encountered in the writings of Shunzei and Teika, where it is applied to poems that treat their topics with particular ingenuity and intellectual flare. Shōtetsu uses it in the same way, finding its effects evident particularly in the poems of the era of *Shinkokinshū*, which are the ones he not coincidentally quotes more often than any others. His conclusion (from I, 75) is forthright:

> Whatever it may be about, a poem by a skilled poet will display some special element of treatment to hold one's interest [*hito fushi no kyō arite, omoshiroki nari*].

This emphasis on intriguing and often complicated conceptions expressed in difficult language of course put off the Asukai and Gyōkō. But to them his reply (from I, 22) was equally blunt: "Let such critics look at the collected poems of Teika. There is not a single flat verse to be found among them."

AESTHETICS

Yet, true to his education in Reizei ideals, Shōtetsu did not emphasize one quality to the detriment of others. His conception of poetic beauty embraced all of the heritage of Teika, not just part of it:

> II, 84: So long as a person composes his poems with intense seriousness [*kyokushin*, the equivalent of *ushin*[87]], his art will not deviate from the Way. Nevertheless, that is but one of the styles to be found in the imperial anthologies. It may be difficult for a man to be called a skilled poet if he deviates from it, but this sort of thing only came about after the division into poetic factions. Throughout his life Tamekane preferred poetry of so eccentric a kind that in the end no one ventured to follow him. At the same time, Tameyo composed primarily in the style of intense seriousness, and as a result Ton'a, Keiun, Jōben, Kenkō, and all the other important poets adopted the style of his house. Thus everyone composed in this style of intense seriousness, believing it alone to be the epitome of the art, and from this period on poetry began to suffer. Prior to this division into poetic schools, all three generations seem to have written poems in many different styles.

Practically speaking, this meant that Shōtetsu had praise for a number of different styles—including the "pathetic style"

---

87. Judging from his attribution of the style to Tameyo, Ton'a, and later Nijō poets, it would appear that by "the style of intense seriousness" [*kyokushin no tei*] he means *ushin*.

(*mono aware tei*) of Shunzei and others (II, 17, 23, 68), the "withered style" of Emperor Fushimi (I, 7; II, 1),[88] the style of "vigor and strength" (*futō takumashiki tei*) of Ietaka (II, 7), the simple style of Tamekane's sister Tameko (I, 22),[89] a particularly "clever" (*omoshiroshi*) poem by Asukai Masaari (I, 38), and so on. In the section quoted above (I, 75) in which he champions "special elements of treatment," he even warns younger poets away from striving for such things too early in their training:

> While still a novice, a person should simply sit down with his fellows and compose verse that is straightforward and easy to understand.

That elsewhere he repeats the same thing, advising his students that it is in an "easy, gentle style one ought to train oneself to compose" (II, 45), shows that he is sincere. In certain circumstances, the *ushin* style was exactly what was demanded; what he rejected was the favoring of that style to the exclusion of all others.

Nevertheless, it is clear that Shōtetsu did attach greater value to some styles than others. In particular, he seems to have favored poems of complex conception, as the evidence of his own poetry amply shows. And there can be little doubt that his highest praise went to poems that he described with the term *yūgen*, or "mystery and depth."

Predictably, this term is one borrowed directly from earlier texts, chiefly those of Shunzei and Teika; and, just as predictably, Shōtetsu uses it chiefly to characterize poems by himself and poets of the Shinkokin era. But, fortunately, he also presents his own definition of the term in two rather lengthy passages.

> I, 82: The style of mystery and depth can perhaps be only understood by those who have actually reached that level of accomplishment. What most people seem to understand by mystery and depth is simply the style of overtones [*yojō tei*], which is not mystery and depth at all. Some people call the style of the sad beauty of things [*mono aware tei*] mystery and depth, and so on. But the style of overtones and the style of mystery and depth are completely different from each other even though everyone thinks they are the same. Lord Teika

---

88. The reference in this case is to the emperor's calligraphy and not to his poetry, but it shows an awareness of the style nevertheless.

89. His comment is that Tameko's poem "works well" (*yoku kikoetaru*).

wrote, "The poet Tsurayuki, in ancient times, composed in a style of strength, but he did not compose in the ultimate style of mystery and depth." The style of the sad beauty of things is favored by poets.

II, 100: How can one define the style of mystery and depth? It is not something that can be described exactly, either in words or in terms of what one feels in one's heart so as to say, "This is the style of mystery and depth." Because the styles of moving clouds and swirling snow are also known by this name, perhaps the poetic effect of clouds trailing in the sky or of snow floating on the wind may be called the style of mystery and depth.

In the work known as *Guhi{shō}* ("Secrets of a Fool"), or something of the sort, written by Teika, it says, "If the style of mystery and depth were to be defined by means of a comparison, in China there once lived a sovereign called King Hsiang. Taking his midday nap one day, he had dropped off to sleep, when a divine maiden came down from heaven and, in such a way that he could not tell whether it was dream or reality, gave herself to him with a pledge of love. Loath to part from her, King Hsiang begged her to remain, but the divine creature said, 'I am a heavenly maiden from the world above. Because of a bond from a previous life, I have come here at this time and given myself to you in love. But I cannot remain in this land.' So saying, she was about to fly away, when the king, overcome with longing, said, 'Then at least leave me some keepsake.' The divine maiden replied, 'Let this be a keepsake of me: there is a mountain near the royal palace called Mount Wu. Gaze out upon the clouds that trail away from this Mount Wu in the morning and the rain that falls on it in the evening.' And she disappeared. After this, filled with love and longing for the divine maiden, King Hsiang could gaze out upon the clouds that trailed away from Mount Wu in the morning and the rain that fell in the evening as a reminder of her. His attitude in gazing at the morning clouds and the evening rain may be called the style of mystery and depth."

So it is written. But here, too, just where the mystery is to be found depends upon the inner feelings of each individual. No doubt it is something that cannot possibly be explained in words or distinguished clearly in the mind.

To begin a statement of aesthetic theory by saying that one's term is not something that can properly be described in words may seem to be admitting defeat from the start. But in the first passage Shōtetsu at least says clearly what *yūgen* is not: not simply the style of overtones, or *yojō*; not the style of "pathetic beauty," or *mono aware*; and not the style of the famous early Heian poet, Ki no Tsurayuki. If he is not quite sure what the term *is*, then, he is clear about what it *is not*.

But there is a problem with these items, particularly the last one, which is not a correct quotation of what Teika actually said in his treatise *Kindai shūka* ("Superior Poems of Our Time," 1209). And it is here, ironically, that Shōtetsu's definition begins to become clear. In his version of Teika's comment he has substituted the phrase "the ultimate style of mystery and depth" for the actual text, which reads instead, *yojō yōen no tei*, "the style of overtones and ethereal charm." It would appear that for Shōtetsu, the term *yūgen* meant something close to what his great mentor had called *yōen*.[90] The source of this discrepancy is apparent at the very beginning of the other passage quoted above, which refers for its authority on the proper meaning of *yūgen* to a work titled *Guhishō*, or "Secrets of a Fool"—a work that Shōtetsu accepted as by Teika but which in fact was one of a group of forged texts falsely attributed to was one of a group of forged texts falsely attributed to Teika by partisans who wanted to gain an audience for their own beliefs.[91]

Not all medieval poets accepted these texts—a list which included *Guhishō*, *Sangoki* ("Record of Thrice Five Nights"), *Gukenshō* ("Notes on My Foolish Views"), *Kirihioke* ("The Paulownia Brazier"), and *Miraiki* ("Record of the Future")—without question, but even those who had doubts about their authenticity seem to have accepted much of the contents of the treatises as representing Teika's views.[92] The resulting distortion of the old master's original intentions can be seen in the writings of Shōtetsu as much as in those of any other critic of his time, thus making him seem a fool—a devotee of a false god. There can be no doubting, however, that his belief in the writings was complete, as the above quotations make embarrassingly clear. "The style of moving clouds and swirling snow"

90. Fukuda 1976:107–8.
91. Ibid.:103–21. For a description of how these works came into being, see Brower 1981:450–51 and *JCP*:350–52.
92. Tō no Tsuneyori for instance notes in his *Tōyashū kikigaki* (*NKGT* 5:369) that *Sangoki* is not actually by Teika, but that there are "still many of the master's words in the book."

(*kōun kaisetsu tei*) is a product not of Teika's own work, but of those who evoked his name in their own defense.[93]

This seems a cruel fate for so dedicated a disciple. But in Shōtetsu's defense one must add that many Nijō poets were equally as dependent on forgeries for their understanding of terms such as *ushin*. Furthermore, Shōtetsu quotes liberally not only from the forgeries but also from authentic texts such as *Maigetsushō* ("Monthly Notes") as well, making it clear that his image of Teika was not totally a product of spurious texts. In fact, one can even argue that in the end his confusion of *yūgen* with Teika's *yōen* may have resulted in a more complete understanding of Teika's achievement, since it is clearly the latter ideal that is the chief contribution of Teika to the development of the court tradition. *Yūgen* was largely Shunzei's term, which Teika saw as representing a rhetorically and conceptually simple surface structure made resonant with suggestions of symbolism underneath, as in a famous poem by Minamoto no Toshiyori (1055–1129) quoted in *Kindai shūka*:

Furusato wa	My former home
Chiru momijiba ni	Lies buried under crimson leaves
Uzumorete	Fallen in the garden,
Noki no shinobu ni	And in the sedge grass on the eaves,
Akikaze zo fuku.	The melancholy autumn wind.[94]

This is an exquisite poem, to be sure, and Teika himself wrote a number like it. His most original poems, however, are in the style of *yōen*, as Shōtetsu—regardless of what critical texts may have influenced him—was perceptive enough to see. Hence the latter's praise for poems in passages like the following (I, 90):

Yasurai ni	When you left my side,
Idenishi mama no	You seemed so hesitant to leave—
Tsuki no kage	But then you were gone.
Waga namida nomi	And now the moonlight and my tears
Sode ni matedomo.	Wait in vain upon my sleeve.

This poem of Teika's is the epitome of his style of mystery and depth, like his

| Shirotae no | As we parted, |
| Sode no wakare ni | The dew on our white hempen sleeves |

93. See n. 535 in the translation below.
94. See Brower 1985:410, n. 25.

Tsuyu ochite   Mingled with our tears,
Mi ni shimu iro no   While the autumn wind struck my heart
Akikaze zo fuku.   With a tinge of greater cold to come.

Such poems are difficult to understand on a quick
reading.

As Shōtetsu concludes, poems of this sort are indeed difficult
to understand without considerable effort, as is the case with many
of Teika's poems in the *yōen* style, by which he meant poems of depth
and resonance in the manner of *yūgen* and with the sorts of subtle
overtones prized by Shunzei but presented in a dreamy atmosphere
and with the greater rhetorical ingenuity communicated by Shōtetsu's other vital ideal, *omoshiroshi*. Not surprisingly, both poems are
on the topic of love, a theme conceived by the courtly sensibility as
the most psychologically complex of human states of mind, which in
the opinion of Teika seem to have called for complex modes of
expression. No wonder, then, that throughout *Shōtetsu monogatari*
Teika's disciple concentrates so on his mentor's love poems, arguing
that "It is in his love poetry that Teika has no peer" (I, 89).

In this way the nature of Shōtetsu's debt to Teika becomes
more clear. Regardless of how erroneous his conception of Teika's use
of the term *yūgen* may have been, he comprehended the special
beauties of Teika's poems supremely well. One further quotation (II,
77) is necessary, however, to expand the point to its proper limits.
Again it involves Shōtetsu's analysis of a particular poem, but this
time one of his own.

Sakeba chiru   No sooner do they bloom,
Yo no ma no hana no   Than the cherry blossoms scatter—
Yume no uchi ni   The fleeting dream
Yagate magirenu   Of a night that takes away all doubt
Mine no shirakumo.   About the white clouds on the peak.

This is a poem in the style of mystery and depth. Mystery and
depth is something that is in the heart but is not expressed in
words. The moon veiled in thin clouds, or the bright foliage
on the mountains concealed by autumn mists—such poetic
conceptions are regarded as having the effect of mystery and
depth. But if one asks in which particular feature the mystery
and depth are to be found, it is difficult to specify exactly. A
person who failed to comprehend this fact would argue that
the moon is at its most enchanting when it is glittering

brightly in a clear sky with not a cloud in sight. But with
mystery and depth it is impossible to say just what it is that is
enchanting or lovely.

This poem establishes that love was not the only topic Shōtetsu associated with his *yūgen*. And if elsewhere he quotes forged texts
by Teika, here he definitely hearkens back to an earlier source,
namely the poet-essayist Kamo no Chōmei (1155–1216), who in his
Mumyōshō ("Nameless Notes," 1211?) had given one of the earliest
and most complete definitions of *yūgen* in the tradition.

Every poetic style is difficult to master. . . . This is all
the more true of the style of mystery and depth, whose very
name is enough to confound one. Since I do not understand it
at all well myself, I am at a loss as to how to describe it in any
satisfactory manner, but according to the views of those who
have developed the skills necessary to penetrate its mysteries,
the qualities deemed essential to the style are overtones (*yojō*)
that do not appear in the words alone and an atmosphere that
is not visible in the configuration of the poem. When both
conception and diction are full of charm, these other virtues
will be present of themselves. On an autumn evening, for
example, there is no color in the sky nor any sound, yet
although we cannot give any definite reason for it, we are
somehow moved to tears. . . . Again, when one gazes upon
the autumn hills half-concealed by a curtain of mist, what one
sees is veiled yet profoundly beautiful; such a shadowy scene,
which permits free exercise of the imagination in picturing
how lovely the whole panoply of scarlet leaves must be, is far
better than to see them spread with dazzling clarity before our
eyes.[95]

Reading this, one sees that Shōtetsu's understanding of *yūgen* is not
as dependent on forgeries as other quotations lead one to believe.
The term is, like so many critical terms, a rather elastic one in the
final analysis. The important thing in all late medieval treatments of
it is precisely what Chōmei says: that the poem should leave room
for the imagination. As Shōtetsu concludes in his own work, "The
best poems are those that leave something unsaid" (I, 19).[96]

95. *NKBT* 65:87–88. Translation from *JCP*:269.
96. See also I, 2, 38; II, 24, 37, 68, 77.

As the record of Shōtetsu's life reveals, most poets of his day, including even many liberals, did not agree with his high evaluation of *yūgen*. The concept was too imposing for less versatile minds. As he notes (I, 74) when quoting Yoshida no Kenkō's famous lines "Are we to look at cherry blossoms only in full bloom, the moon only when it is cloudless?" (lines that probably influenced Shōtetsu's conceptions as much as any others, it should be added[97]), "a person with this kind of sensibility is hardly to be found in the world." The result was artistic loneliness that he expresses in a statement that sums up his life more aptly than any outsider could hope to do.

II, 65: In poetry there are many vexations. Winding up loose ends and thinking of the future—things never turn out as one had intended. If one continues to compose poems of the sort that everyone else considers good, one must remain forever at that ordinary level. On the other hand, when one writes poems whose essence is profound and difficult, others fail to understand them, and this is frustrating. No doubt what is generally called good would seem to be good enough, I suppose.

There is probably some contempt in that final "good enough," since to follow the trends of the day was never good enough for Shōtetsu himself—who was nothing if not stubborn, even in the face of the humiliation he endured in his middle years. But even his early poems show an adventurous spirit that he must have been born with. Beyond that, one can call on the final words of *Shōtetsu monogatari* itself (II, 103), which express the same religious dedication to poetry that begin the book:

Above all there is nothing more precious and essential than dedication to the Art. . . . So long as a man is truly devoted to this Art, how can the time of enlightenment fail to come for him?

Both Shunzei and Teika had shown this same kind of dedication, as is testified by a section of Shōtetsu's record telling the story of how both men underwent religious conversion to the way of poetry (I, 58). Whether Shōtetsu himself experienced something

---

97. See n. 212 to the translation below.

similar is not known, but it is clear at least that he followed
Ryōshun's advice to not bow before the trends of his own day.[98] And
the witness of his poetry and of his teachings is enough to allow him
the same distinction as a Master of the Way.

98. In *Rakusho roken* (NKGT 5:190–91) Ryōshun praises both Tamehide and Tamemasa for
their courage against popular opinion. It should be noted, however, that Araki
(1977:130–48) argues that one of Ryōshun's essays was probably meant to encourage
the young Tamemasa not to give in to Nijō criticism, indicating that the young man
may have been sorely tempted to mimic the bland style of his opponents in order to
win a place for himself at court.

Translation:
Conversations with Shōtetsu
(*Shōtetsu monogatari*)

PART 1: CONVERSATIONS WITH
SHŌTETSU THE SECRETARY
(Tesshoki monogatari)

1. In this art of poetry, those who speak ill of Teika[1] should be denied the protection of the gods and Buddhas and condemned to the punishments of hell.[2]

Teika's descendants split into the two factions of Nijō and Reizei, and these with Tamekane's faction make up three schools,[3] like the three eyes of the demon king Maheśvara.[4] Since they sometimes express admiration and praise for each other, and sometimes censure

1. Fujiwara no Teika (1162–1241).
2. Here Shōtetsu repeats the common analogy between poetry and Buddhism: both the religious and artistic practices are "ways," each with its own secret formulae, conventions, and levels of expertise conveyed secretly from master to disciple. Shōtetsu's particular point is his invocation of a curse upon anyone who might dare question Teika's authority in the slightest degree, and the sentence is the expression *par excellence* of the "Teika worship" (*Teika sūhai*) for which Shōtetsu is famous.
3. That is, the three branches into which the squabbling Mikohidari poetic family divided on the death of the Teika's heir Tameie (1198–1275). They were: the senior Nijō branch descended from Tameie's oldest son, Tameuji (1222–1286); the Kyōgoku branch descended from Tameie's second son (actually third, depending on whether his actual second son, being a priest named Genshō, is counted or not), Tamenori (1227–79), and particularly Tamenori's own son, the lively Tamekane (1254–1332); and the Reizei branch descended from Tamesuke (1263–1328), the elder of two sons Tameie sired in his old age by his second wife, Lady Anka Mon'in no Shijō, or as she is usually called, Abutsu the Nun (d. 1283). See the introduction (pp. 6–7) for more details.
4. Makeishura in Japanese. The Indian deity that resides in the Shokkyuko heaven at the summit of our world of desire. He is guarded by sixty divine warriors and surrounded by 100,000 divine women. He is usually represented with three eyes and eight arms, wearing a crown and seated on a white ox. He holds a trident. In older Brahmanism, Maheśvara was an epithet of Shiva, the great creator of all things. In Buddhism, he was sometimes represented as an enemy of the dharma, but usually as an attendant and guardian of the Thousand-armed Kannon. In the present instance, Shōtetsu uses Maheśvara's fierce three-eyed countenance to represent the division and enmity between the Nijō, Kyōgoku, and Reizei branches of the Mikohidari family.

and blame, how is it possible to accept one faction and reject the others? Each of these schools has succeeded in mastering only a single poetic style and is constantly disputing with its rivals.[5]

It is my opinion that a person should pay no attention whatever to these schools. Instead, he ought to cherish the style and spirit[6] of Teika and strive to emulate him even though he may never succeed. Some will say that this is the path of perfection to which the ordinary mind cannot hope to aspire, and that instead a person should take as his standard the poetic styles of Teika's descendants. However, as the saying goes, "Emulate the highest art to achieve the mediocre."[7] So, even if a person cannot attain to it, he should still emulate the highest artistic standard, for then even in failure he may still achieve something of reasonable quality. In the ascetic practices of Buddhism as well, a man is expected to perform with the goal of attaining Buddhahood. Surely he is not supposed to discipline himself with the idea of aspiring weakly to the Three Vehicles[8] and no more. At the same time, to speak of emulating the style of the Master and then merely to imitate his diction and cadences would be deplorable. Instead, one should constantly emulate his style and spirit and cast of mind.

The twentieth day of the eighth month is the anniversary of Teika's death.[9] When I was a child, people used to commemorate this day by composing poems at the Bureau of Poetry.[10] Each participant would take a successive syllable of the following poem by Teika and place it at the beginning of his own verse:

5. See the introduction (pp. 10–13). The accusation that the Nijō poets employed only one style figures prominently in the writings of Shōtetsu's teacher Imagawa Ryōshun (1326–1417?); see for instance his *Shisetsu jikenshū* ("The Master's Teachings and My Personal Opinions," 1408?, in *NKGT* 5:215). Shōtetsu himself extended the accusation to the Reizei, his erstwhile patrons. A clearer statement of Shōtetsu's contention is recorded by Tō no Tsuneyori (1401–84). See *Tōyashū kikigaki* ("Memoirs of Lord Tō," 1456?, in *NKGT* 5:346) and Carter 1989:xxi–xxii.

6. *Fūkotsu*, a compound referring literally to "manner" or "style" (*fū*) and "spirit" (*kotsu*).

7. Source unknown. Shōtetsu's "middle way" may contain a veiled reference to the "middle stage" of Tendai Buddhism's dialectical doctrine of three stages: *kū*, "the stage of emptiness," *ke*, "the stage of phenomena," and *chū*, "the middle stage"—the latter being a middle ground where transcending opposites can find harmony.

8. *Sanjō*. The three "vehicles" of enlightenment in the Buddhist faith. The first, *shravaka* (J *shōmon*) describes one who is a hearer of the law, whose goal is to become an arhat. The second is *pratyeka* (J *engaku*), or one who practices his religion alone without announcing his truths to the world. Lastly comes the *bodhisattva* (J *bosatsu*) who, after achieving enlightenment, goes out into the world to save others. Traditionally the first two are together referred to as the Lesser Vehicle (*hinayana*) and the last the Greater Vehicle (*mahayana*).

9. Teika died on that date in 1241.

10. *Wakadokoro*, an abbreviation of *sen wakadokoro*, the court office responsible for the gathering and preservation of poetic documents and for providing the resources necessary for the compilation of imperial anthologies (*chokusenshū*) of poetry. In the early days of the court, those assigned to such tasks had offices within the palace compound, but

Akeba mata	With the coming dawn,
Aki no nakaba mo	Once more the middle point of autumn
Suginubeshi	Will have passed by.
Katabuku tsuki no	Must one only feel regret
Oshiki nomi ka wa.	For the setting of the moon?[11]

This was possible because the poem does not have the syllables *ra*, *ri*, *ru*, or *re*, which is why they used it.[12]

2. Ietaka[13] wrote with great rhetorical skill, producing poems of grace and elegance. Teika was evidently quite partial to him, for he included so many of his poems in *Shinchokusenshū*[14] that it is like Ietaka's personal collection. Yet, at the same time, Teika feared him, saying that his style had something about it that presaged the extinction of his house—a poetic manner that indicated his descendants would not long endure.[15]

3. Masatsune[16] had a fondness for striking phrases,[17] which may explain why his poems sometimes have serious faults. Also—no

from the late thirteenth century onward compilers generally undertook their work in their own home libraries. Late medieval documents indicate that both the Nijō and Reizei families had collections of documents and artifacts. Given his affiliation with the Reizei family, it is likely that the *wakadokoro* referred to here by Shōtetsu as the place where memorial services for Teika were held was located in the Reizei library. Moreover, in section 11 below Shōtetsu notes that the Asukai family—the chief bastion of the conservative faction since the dying out of the Nijō family line in the late fourteenth century—probably had no poetic documents, which would have left the Reizei as the only legitimate authority on such matters. This fact is borne out by the conflicts that arose between Asukai Masayo (1390–1452) and the Reizei family when the latter refused to turn over documents to Masayo in preparation for compilation of the last imperial anthology, the *Shinzokukokinshū* ("New Collection of Ancient and Modern Times Continued," 1439)—a purely partisan work that excluded almost totally the Reizei poets and their supporters, Shōtetsu among them. For details, see Inoue 1984:109–24 and Araki 1977:135–42.

11. *SCSS* 261. Headnote: "Written for a fifty-poem sequence on 'the moon' when the Go-Kyōgoku regent was still Captain of the Left."
12. There are no native Japanese words that begin with these syllables.
13. Fujiwara no Ietaka (1158–1237), a cousin of Teika who was likewise selected as one of the compilers of *Shinkokinshū* ("New Collection of Ancient and Modern Times," 1206) by Retired Emperor Go-Toba (1180–1239; r. 1183–98), a fine poet himself and the major patron of the Shinkokin age.
14. Forty-three of the 1,374 poems of the work are Ietaka's, a number greater than any other poet's.
15. "A style . . . that presaged the extinction of his house" translates *bōshitsu no tei*. Just what quality in Ietaka's personal style evoked this characterization is unclear. The term *bōshitsu no tei* is found as early as *Fukurō sōshi* ("Commonplace Book," ca. 1157–60) of Fujiwara no Kiyosuke (1104–77). Shōtetsu's source, however, was doubtless *Guhishō* ("Secrets of a Fool," precise date unknown), one of the apocryphal Cormorant/Heron texts of the late Kamakura period, which has this to say about Ietaka (*NKGT* 4:296): "Lord Ietaka always produced verses of splendid effect, and he had an unusually fine poetic manner. Nevertheless, from time to time are found in his verse elements of a style presaging the extinction of his house, which makes one want to keep his distance."
16. Asukai Masatsune (1170–1221), a favorite of Retired Emperor Go-Toba whose descendants later became standard-bearers for the Nijō cause.
17. "Striking phrases" translates *shūku*, meaning "fancy" poems overladen with wordplay and complicated rhetorical flourishes.

doubt unaware that many similar phrases already existed—he seems
to have taken phrases from many other people and incorporated
them into his own poems.[18]

4. *Gen'yōshū*[19] was, I believe, an unofficial collection of noteworthy verses. It is said that all of the poetic families have such
collections, called "Things Heard," in which they have gathered
together the verses of the day.[20]

5. Tamesuke[21] was the son of Lady Ankamon'in no Shijō.[22]
His mother was in the service of Retired Empress Ankamon,[23] and
during that time she was known as Ankamon'in no Shijō. Tamemori[24] was also the son of this lady. After taking Buddhist vows,
Ankamon'in no Shijō was called Abutsu the Nun.

6. Priest Gyōgetsu[25] is said to have belonged to the Pure Land
sect.[26] His lay name was Reizei Tamemori.

7. The handwriting of Retired Emperor Fushimi[27] is like a
withered tree, with no outward beauty at all.[28] Since he took no

---

18. In *Yakumo mishō* ("Imperial Notes on the Art of the Eightfold Clouds," ca. 1234, in
    NKGT, supplementary volume 3:430), a poetic treatise written by Retired Emperor
    Juntoku (1197–1242), this criticism is attributed to Go-Kyōgoku Yoshitsune
    (1169–1206), another prominent poet of the age of *Shinkokinshū*.
19. An anthology compiled by Teika's grandson Tameuji sometime between 1278 and 1286.
    Although the work is not extant, references in treatises and essays indicate that it
    contained twenty books of poems, most of them by adherents of the Nijō cause. The
    first half of a later work entitled *Shoku gen'yōshū* ("*Gen'yōshū* Continued," 1323)
    compiled by Tameuji's son Tameyo (1250–1338) has survived. Text available in *GR* 7
    (item 155).
20. *Uchigiki*, or private anthologies, generally containing the poems of a poetic family and its
    supporters, as opposed to *shikashū*, or "personal collections" containing the poems of
    only one poet. Such works, no doubt meant as future source books for those compil-
    ing imperial anthologies, are mentioned as early as the twelfth century.
21. Reizei Tamesuke. Founder of the Reizei family. For a brief sketch of his life and transla-
    tions of a few of his poems, see Carter 1989:85–91.
22. Commonly known as Abutsu Ni (Abutsu the Nun). Wife to Fujiwara no Tameie in his
    later years. For a brief sketch of her life and translations of a few of her poems, see
    Carter 1989:78–84.
23. Ankamon (1207–86). Consort of Retired Emperor Go-Horikawa (1212–34; r. 1221–32).
24. Reizei Tamemori (1265–1328). A younger brother of Tamesuke, also by Abutsu the Nun.
    After beginning a career at court, he took the tonsure as Gyōgetsu, not the same man
    as the renga poet Kyōgetsu, with whom he is sometimes confused.
25. See n. 24 above.
26. Jōdo Shū. First of the faith sects of Buddhism, founded by the priest Hōnen (1133–1212).
27. Retired Emperor Fushimi (1265–1317; r. 1287–1298). Prominent poet and patron
    of the arts who sponsored a lively salon at court, which among other things pro-
    duced the fourteenth imperial waka anthology, *Gyokuyōshū* ("Collection of Jeweled
    Leaves," 1313), compiled by Kyōgoku Tamekane. As indicated here, Fushimi was
    also known as a calligrapher in his day, and his reputation has only increased with
    time.
28. Although this characterization of Fushimi's style may seem rather negative at first glance,
    later comments (II, 1 below) make it clear that Shōtetsu admired the retired em-
    peror's style. What Shōtetsu is stressing here, then, is that Fushimi's calligraphy,

trouble at all over his calligraphy, his style should not be imitated by ordinary people.

[8.²⁹ Wooden images of the poet Hitomaro³⁰ can be found in the provinces of Iwami and Yamato. The one in Iwami is located in Takatsu.³¹ There is an inlet from the sea on the western side of this place, and to the rear it is encircled by the Takatsu mountains. The image was enshrined in a square-shaped chapel out in the fields. It held in one hand a writing brush and in the other a piece of paper. It was made of wood.

One year, when there were heavy rains, the area was flooded along with the rest of the countryside; the tide came in and the sea covered it up; and the chapel was swept away by tide or waves and disappeared, no one knew where. Then after the waters had subsided, a peasant was digging with shovel and hoe in order to make an arable field, when it sounded as if his tool had struck something. He dug it up, and there it was, the image of Hitomaro. It had been buried under the seaweed and still had the writing brush safely in its hand. Believing this to be no ordinary occurrence, the people quickly repainted the image, rebuilt the chapel as it had originally been, and enshrined it there. The story spread abroad and people from two or three provinces around all flocked to see it. I heard this story from someone who gave me a full account of the incident.

Takatsu was the place where Hitomaro used to live. It was there that he composed the poem in *Man'yōshū*³² that goes:

> which may be taken as an articulation of the medieval ideal of *hie sabi*, or withered, forlorn beauty, should not be imitated by beginners—a view that is consistent with the same sort of distinction between novice and master that Shōtetsu insists upon throughout his treatise. As support for his stance, Shōtetsu may have had in mind a comment by Fujiwara no Shunzei (1114–1204) concerning a poem by Saigyō (1118–90): "This poem is not in the style of outward beauty . . . and if those not already far along the way should try to compose a poem like this, they will not be up to it." See *Mimosusogawa uta-awase* 13 ("The Mimosuso River Poetry Contest," 1189, in *SKT* 5).

29. Hisamatsu notes that sections 8, 9, 10, here placed in brackets, are probably additions to the original text, although they were inserted at a fairly early date in the manuscript's history. The *NKGT* text (vol. 5) doesn't include them.

30. Kakinomoto no Hitomaro (fl. ca. 690–710), the great Man'yō-period poet who was revered as a kind of patron saint by poets.

31. The precise location of Takatsu remains a mystery, but some scholars suggest the area around Takatsunoyama in modern Tsunozu, Gōtsu City, Shimane Prefecture.

32. The first great anthology of Japanese poetry, put together from materials in earlier collections some time around 759 by Ōtomo no Yakamochi (718–85). Although not compiled upon imperial command, it was revered by later poets as the first great accomplishment of the court tradition.

Iwamino ya	There in Iwami,
Takatsu no yama no	Between the branches of the trees
Ko no ma yori	On Takatsu's hills,
Waga furu sode o	Did my beloved see me wave
Imo mitsuran ka.	My sleeves in fond farewell?[33]

It is also said that he died there. The first three lines of his deathbed poem are the same as in this one:

Iwamino ya	Here in Iwami,
Takatsu no yama no	Between the branches of the trees
Ko no ma yori	On Takatsu's hills,
Kono yo no tsuki o	I have gazed for the final time
Mihatetsuru kana.	Upon the moonlight of this world.[34]

There are other traditions about Hitomaro. They say that if Japanese poetry is in danger of dying out, he will without fail come back to the world of men and pass on the art as before.[35] He has also manifested himself numerous times as a god.

9. A person should not keep refusing when asked to contribute the first poem for one of the books of seasonal poems in an anthology.[36] Such reluctance is proper only when the poetic topic concerns the beginning of spring. The leading poem for an extemporaneous set of a hundred poems[37] should be deferred to the person of

33. This poem is the second *hanka* (envoy) to MYS 131–33, a *chōka*, or "long poem," by Hitomaro. For a complete translation, see Levy 1981:98–99.

34. Hisamatsu notes that the last two lines of this poem—the source of which is unknown— are not in the MYS style, indicating that the poem is probably not by Hitomaro. Another deathbed poem is recorded in MYS (223).

35. The source of this belief is unknown.

36. To have one's poem chosen as the first of any section of any collection was of course deemed an honor, but Shōtetsu here cautions that making a show of humility in such cases is uncalled for, except perhaps in the case of the first poem in a spring book, the composition of which was usually granted to someone of the highest court rank. Implicit in his statement (and explicit in the ones that follow it) is the fact that he is speaking primarily of the small, informal anthologies that were produced at the poetic gatherings of his day, and not of imperial anthologies, only one of which was compiled during his active life as a poet.

37. *Hyakushu*, a set of one-hundred poems; here referring to *hyakushu no tsugiuta*, a genre involving a number of poets in the composition of a one-hundred-poem collection on prescribed topics. At such activities, poets would generally choose topics from a pile of topics placed on a stand, with each poet composing his poems extemporaneously. The completed poems would then be collected and arranged in the prescribed order of topics—spring, summer, autumn, winter, love, miscellaneous—to make a full hundred-poem sequence. Often, the same procedure was used to make smaller anthologies of thirty, forty, or fifty poems as well. Diaries and personal anthologies, including Shōtetsu's *Sōkonshū*, make it clear that this was probably the most common form of poetic composition in his day.

appropriate status—the master of the house, or the most accomplished poet. However, when choosing by lot[38] the topics for a set of twenty or thirty poems on the seasons, the leading poem may be composed by anyone.

10. I heard some lectures on a part of *Man'yōshū* at the Daikyō'in.[39] But after the notes I took at the time were burned in the fire at Imakumano,[40] I gave up the whole business and made no further attempt to practice reading *Man'yōshū*.[41] Yet I do still remember something of what I heard. For *Man'yōshū* there is the commentary produced by Sengaku,[42] *Shirin saiyōshū* by the monk Amidabutsu,[43] and also Sengaku's new commentary.[44] If only one possesses these three works, one can read *Man'yōshū* aloud before others. This so-called "new commentary" is a great treasure for *Man'yōshū* studies. Only two *Man'yō* poems are passed on in the ritual of secret transmission.[45] I too have received this transmission. I have one commentary on *Man'yōshū* that is of no particular value.]

11. Although Masatsune was included among the five compilers of *Shinkokinshū*,[46] he was but a youth at the time and was

38. "Choosing by lot" translates *dai o saguru*, referring once again to the practice of choosing topics at random for extemporaneous composition.
39. A temple affiliated with the Ninnaji, on the western outskirts of Kyoto.
40. The fire occurred on the night of the second day of the fourth lunar month, in 1432. See the introduction (pp. 25–26) for details.
41. Because it was written in *man'yōgana*, an early form of writing used to record Japanese with Chinese characters (before the development of the *kana* syllabary), most people of later times could not read *Man'yōshū* aloud in its original form without extensive instruction in the proper readings of the ancient script.
42. A priest (b. 1203) of the Tendai sect who continued the work of Minamoto no Chikayuki (ca. 1188–1275?) in collating the texts of *Man'yōshū*, finishing with the work of providing diacritical marks that would allow the Chinese of the text to be read as Japanese. His commentary on the work, *Man'yōshū chūshaku*, appeared in 1269.
43. A reference to Yūa (1291–1375), a monk of the Shōjōkōji Temple in Sagami Province (modern Kanagawa Prefecture).
44. Not extant.
45. *Denju*. Tightly guarded secret teachings of all sorts—concerning everything from pronunciation of old names to proper reading and interpretation of old poems—were passed down from master to disciple in the poetic families and their various offshoots, often in ways that mimicked similar customs regarding the esoteric rites and formulas of Shingon and Tendai Buddhism. Eventually, this custom developed into the so-called *kokin denju*, or "secret teachings on the *Kokinshū*," which played a major part in poetic history during the fifteenth and sixteenth centuries in particular. Shōtetsu most likely received his "transmission" from some member of the Reizei family.
46. The other compilers—there were six altogether and not five, as Shōtetsu mistakenly notes—were Jakuren (d. 1202), Teika, Ietaka, Fujiwara no Ariie (1155–1216), Minamoto no Michitomo (1171–1227). Shōtetsu may have omitted Jakuren because he died before the task of compilation was complete.

merely listed as a compiler.[47] His family could hardly have possessed any valuable poetic documents or materials.[48]

12. With regard to Ton'a[49]: Tameakira[50] was the compiler of *Shinshūishū*,[51] but he died while compiling it and before submitting the completed draft.[52] Because Ton'a carried on the task of compilation beginning with the miscellaneous poems or love poems, he must have possessed the requisite documents and materials.

13. Masatsune had the status of a poetic disciple of Teika, and so his descendants have all been disciples of the Nijō family.[53] The single peculiarity of Masatsune's family is the way they write poems on poem slips[54] at official functions and the like: in three lines plus an extra five-syllable line. In all other respects their traditions are identical with those of the Nijō family.

14. When the first syllables of the first and fourth lines of a poem are the same, it is called the "ill of identical beginnings."[55] In

47. Since Masatsune was past thirty when he was selected as one of the *SKKS* compilers in 1201, Shōtetsu's characterization of him as "but a youth at the time" probably means that he was young when compared to the senior compilers—Jakuren, who died in 1202 at over sixty, Teika and Ietaka, who were around forty, and Fujiwara no Ariie, who was in his late forties. Masatsune was in fact a year older than the youngest compiler, Minamoto no Michitomo. Again, as in section 3 above, Shōtetsu's dislike for the Asukai is apparent.

48. Once more Shōtetsu's disdain for the Asukai is evident. But in this case he may have been partly correct, as reflected in the circumstances surrounding the compilation of *Shinzokukokinshū*. See n. 10 above and the introduction (pp. 26–29).

49. 1289–1372. A man of the military family (with the lay name Nikaidō Sadamune) who took the tonsure at around age twenty and went on to become one of the most important poets of his century. A Nijō adherent, he studied under Nijō Tameyo and was a colleague of Nijō Tamesada (1293–1360), after whose death he gained acceptance as the chief exponent of the Nijō school, a distinction he passed on to his heirs, the masters of the Jōkō'in, who were rivals of Shōtetsu.

50. Nijō Tameakira (1295–1364), a grandson of Tameyo.

51. "New Collection of Gleanings," nineteenth of the imperial anthologies, completed in 1364.

52. The seasonal books of the anthology were presented for imperial review in the spring of 1364, but Tameakira died the following autumn, leaving Ton'a to complete the work, which he finished just before the end of the year. As Shōtetsu suggests, Ton'a must have had access to Nijō documents in order to finish the project in the proper manner. It was partially for this reason that Ton'a's heir Gyōkō (1391–1455) was appointed librarian for the last imperial anthology, *Shinzokukokinshū*.

53. Hisamatsu points out that Masatsune was not strictly speaking a disciple of Teika, but of "equal status" with those who studied under Teika directly. In fact, the Asukai were known equally as experts at court kickball (*kemari*), and had a substantial reputation of their own. It was in later generations that the family developed close ties with the Nijō, by providing wives for Nijō heirs. It is true, however, that Masatsune acted as a messenger between Teika and his student the shogun Minamoto no Sanetomo (1192–1219) and was on good terms with the head of the Mikohidari house.

54. *Kaishi*. Literally, "pocket paper," referring to the paper upon which poems were written at gatherings and contests. The name derives from the custom of carrying the paper inside the breast pocket of one's court robe.

55. *Byōtō no yamai*. As early as the eighth century, scholars began searching for *kabyō*, or

recent times this has been no longer avoided. The so-called "ill of rhyming syllables"[56]—having the final syllables of the first and fourth lines the same—is avoided unless the verse is an acrostic.[57]

15. Teika's poem that goes

Haru no yo no	The bridge of dreams
Yume no ukihashi	Floating on the brief spring night
Todae shite	Is broken off:
Mine ni wakaruru	From the peak, a wreath of cloud
Yokogumo no sora.	Takes leave into the open sky.[58]

depicts the moment when the speaker, having awakened from his dream on a spring night, gazes out and sees a cloud taking leave of the mountain peak. The poet has skillfully given expression to the experience just as it is. The lines, "The bridge of dreams/ Floating on the brief spring night/ Is broken off," are beautifully constructed.

16. At a poetry gathering at the house of Naitō no Shirōzaemon[59] I composed the following poem on the topic "Love and a Robe":

Chigiritsutsu	Though we made our vows,
Okurishi hodo no	Years passed without a second meeting,
Toshi o heba	And now tonight,
Koyoi ya naka no	Will our robes but mark the midpoint
Koromo naramashi.	Between two equal lengths of time?[60]

uta no yamai ("poetic ills")—rhymes proscribed by Chinese poets—in Japanese poems. Most of these were ignored by the astute. At poetry contests, however, judges did occasionally rule against a poem that evinced what Shōtetsu mentions here—a situation in which the first and fourth lines of a poem begin with the same syllable.

56. Sei'in no yamai. Another poetic ill, this one prohibiting the third and fifth lines of a poem from ending with the same syllable—a more cogent proscription, as Shōtetsu notes.

57. Mono no na, literally, "the names of things." A poem in which the first syllables of the five lines form a prescribed "hidden topic" (kakushidai). Although not considered the highest articulation of the art, acrostics were often composed at gatherings and contests for amusement. For an elaborate example, see Huey 1989:37–40.

58. SKKS 38. The poem, one of Teika's most famous, alludes to the end of Genji monogatari ("The Tale of Genji," early eleventh century), the last chapter of which is titled Yume no ukihashi, "The Bridge of Dreams," and also to a Chinese legend involving a tryst between King Hsiang and a divine maiden. See II, 100, below.

59. Precise identity unknown. The Naitō were retainers (hikan) of the powerful Hosokawa clan. For a brief sketch of their literary activities, see Inoue 1984:335.

60. Source unknown.

Everyone found this puzzling and asked each other whether
there was some allusion to *Genji monogatari*.[61] I had not given the
slightest thought to *Genji* in composing the poem. It was simply
that the robe a person wears when sleeping with someone is called a
"night robe" (*yoru no koromo*) or a "middle robe" (*naka no koromo*). I
tried to treat this in a novel way, to the effect that the lovers have
had one meeting, but years have passed until tonight when they
meet again. If they must pass yet another span of years equal to the
first before their next meeting, then tonight they will be wearing
"middle robes." The idea is that since tonight is the middle point,
they are "middle robes." What a terrible age we live in when people
can no longer even understand something as simple as this!

17. Once when I was composing verse with Lord Tsukinowa[62]
in the quarters of the Yamana Senior Assistant Minister of the Trea-
sury,[63] I produced the following poem on the topic "The Morning
After a Night of Love":

Chigire kesa	Pledge me your love now!
Au mo omoi no	For this morning it is clear
Hoka nareba	That we met by chance;
Mata yukusue mo	And who can tell the future
Inochi narazu ya.	Of our uncertain lives?[64]

18. At a certain poetry gathering where the poems were being
criticized by the participants,[65] Lord Tamemasa[66] composed this
verse on "Love Promises Broken":

Kakete uki	It hurts to speak of it:
Isomatsu ga ne no	How like fickle waves that break
Adanami wa	Beneath pines on the shore

---

61. Both waka and renga poets alluded to *Genji monogatari* frequently. As Shōtetsu says,
    however, many people in his own day did not know the tale well enough to do so
    adequately. Various synopses of the tale and lists of poems excerpted from it were
    available for the benefit of those who did not have the education necessary to read it in
    its original form, but it can be imagined that such superficial understanding often
    made for lamentable results, one type of which Shōtetsu introduces here.
62. Tsukinowa was the name of a branch of the Fujiwara family. Hisamatsu suggests Tadakata
    (whose name was later changed to Motokata), son of Tsukinowa Suetada, as a possibility.
63. Yamana Ōkura no Daisuke. Identity uncertain. Hisamatsu suggests either Yamana
    Yukitomo, Yamana Tokiteru, or Yamana Mochiteru.
64. This poem appears nowhere else in Shōtetsu's works.
65. *Hōben no kai*, a gathering at which the composition of poems was followed by discussion
    and evaluation.
66. Reizei Tamemasa (also read Tametada; 1361–1417). See the introduction for his relation-
    ship with Shōtetsu and Ryōshun. For a brief sketch of his life and translations of a few
    of his poems, see Carter 1989:271–78.

Waga mi ni kaeru   You draw away, leaving harsh winds
Sode no urakaze.   To chill me through my sleeves.[67]

Everyone else emphatically declared the poem to be the loser in its round, while I alone held out, insisting on a win. "But it makes no mention of the idea of 'love promises,'" they protested.[68] "The phrase 'It hurts to speak of it' implies that love promises have been made," I retorted. "But the line 'You draw away, leaving harsh winds' is the place where the poet has taken the most trouble. If you don't understand even this much, you have no business criticizing poetry." Thus we argued, while Ryōshun sat there and listened without uttering a word. Then, with tears in his eyes, he said, "Yes, it is as Shōtetsu says." That silenced them all, and the poem was pronounced the winner.

Afterward, when the names of the poets were revealed, it turned out to be Tamemasa's poem. He was delighted by the incident and related it at every gathering he attended, I hear. A person may have penetrated near to the very marrow of the art, but unless he has arrived at the ultimate stage of understanding, he can be no judge of the poems of others.

19. Of recent poems on the topic "Snow on the Mountains at Dusk," I think this one of mine reads well:

Watarikane   Hesitant to cross,
Kumo mo yūbe o   Even the clouds feel their way along,
Nao tadoru   Searching the dusk—
Ato naki yuki no   Where the steep path over the peaks
Mine no kakehashi. Lies beneath the trackless snow.[69]

Now, it is unlikely that the clouds should be unable to cross the trackless snow in actuality, but as it is the way in poetry to attribute feelings to insentient things,[70] I have treated the clouds as if deliberately crossing the mountains at morning and evening. In the brightness of the snow piled up deep and white, they cannot tell that evening has come, making it seem as if even they are feeling their way and hesitating to cross the peaks. Such might be one's impression on gazing out at the gathering dusk on mountains deep in snow

---

67. This poem appears nowhere else in Tamemasa's works.
68. The complaint was that Tamemasa had not included the word *chigiri*, or "love promises," in his poem explicitly—or, in other words, that he had not dealt directly enough with his assigned topic (*dai*).
69. *Sōkonshū* 3986.
70. "Insentient things" translates *mushin naru mono*, things without human feeling, particularly animals and natural phenomena, which were often personified in poems.

and seeing the clouds slowly drifting across. Attributing feelings to the clouds in this way makes plausible the poetic idea that they are hesitating to cross. Also, since I say there is no sign of human footprints among the drifts, one can imagine that even the clouds have difficulty in getting across. Now, one might think that it would have been better if I had said, "There are no tracks upon the snow" (*yuki ni ato naki*), but that would have been unsuitable. The phrase "the trackless snow" has a good deal more poetic effect for the reason that since there are no such things as footprints left by clouds, my "feel their way along . . . the trackless snow" also suggests that the clouds leave no tracks. So it is more elegant to have said "the trackless snow" instead of "there are no tracks upon the snow."

Thus it is that the styles of "moving clouds" and "swirling snow"[71]—the snow blown about by the wind, or the spring haze drifting across the cherry blossoms—have an ineffable charm and elegance. A poem that has this indescribable something hovering over it is a superior poem. Such a poem has been compared to a beautiful lady who grieves over something but does so in silence. To say nothing despite one's sadness is impressive. The same thing happens when a little child of two or three brings something to a person, saying, "This, this"—knowing what it wants to say but unable to express itself clearly. The best poems are those that leave something unsaid.

20. There are poems that leave out whole lines of meaning. Narihira's[72] poem

Tsuki ya aranu	Is this not the moon?
Haru ya mukashi no	And is this not the springtime,
Haru naranu	The springtime of old?
Waga mi hitotsu wa	Only this body of mine
Moto no mi ni shite.	The same body as before.[73]

71. The styles of "moving clouds" (*kōun*) and "swirling snow" (*kaisetsu*) are treated as subcategories of *yūgen* in a number of earlier critical works, particularly in those mistakenly attributed to Teika in Shōtetsu's day: *Gukenshō* ("Notes on My Humble Opinions," in *NKGT* 4:355–56), *Guhishō* (see *NKGT* 4:293), and *Sangoki* ("Record of Three and Five," see *NKGT* 4:316). For details, see the introduction (pp. 52–54).
72. Ariwara no Narihira (d. 880), one of the "Six Poetic Immortals" (*rokkasen*).
73. *KKS* 747 (Love), by Ariwara no Narihira. (Also *Ise monogatari* ["Tales of Ise"], section 4, in *NKBT* 9:112–13 and McCullough 1968:71.) Headnote: Once, quite without premeditation, Narihira began to make love to a lady who lived in the western wing of a palace belonging to the Gojō empress. Shortly after the tenth of the first month, the lady moved away with no word to him. He learned where she had gone, but it was impossible to communicate with her. In the spring of the following year, when the plum blossoms were at their finest, memories of the preceding year drew him back to the western wing on a beautiful moonlit night. He lay on the floor of the bare room until the moon sank low in the sky. McCullough 1985:165.

seems incomprehensible unless one understands the context. The poem was composed when, thinking of his love affair with the Nijō empress the previous year, he went to the western wing of her palace.[74] What it means is, "Is the moon not there? Is the spring not the same spring as ever? I alone am the same as I always was, but tonight the one I used to meet here is gone." So it is that in the text where it says of Narihira's poetry that it "tries to express too much content in too few words, resembling a faded flower with a lingering fragrance," this poem is given as an example.[75] Narihira deliberately left out the line, "Tonight the one I used to meet here is gone" (*koyoi aitaru hito koso nakere*). Yet for this very reason the poem is also interesting.

Jakuren's[76] poem

Uramiwabi	Worn out with bitterness,
Mataji ima wa no	I vow to have an end of it
Mi naredomo	And wait no longer—
Omoinarenishi	And yet there is the evening sky
Yūgure no sora.	That always made me think of him.[77]

is incomplete. The poem implies the thought, "So then, what can I do about the sky at evening?" Thus it has left out the line, "So then, what can I do?" (*sate ika ni sen*).

21. This poem of mine on the topic "Cicadas in Late Summer" might be said to be similar to the preceding ones:

Mori no ha mo	In the forest grove
Aki ni ya awan	The leaves, too, must have their autumn:
Naku semi no	Just like the crying cicadas
Kozue no tsuyu no	Whose fragile husks must vanish
Mi o kaenu tote.	Like the dew upon the branches.[78]

The lines "In the forest grove/ The leaves, too, must have their autumn" mean that although the leaves may now have spread forth in their lush green, when autumn comes it will be their time to fall; by the lines, "Just like the crying cicadas/ Whose fragile

74. For details, see McCullough 1968:71–72.
75. The characterization of Narihira comes from the preface to *Kokinshū*, by Ki no Tsurayuki (872?–945). The poems—among them Narihira's—given as illustrations of Tsurayuki's criticisms were added later, anonymously. See McCullough 1985:7 and 11.
76. Lay name Fujiwara no Sadanaga (d. 1202). He took the tonsure in 1172, after beginning a career in the official ranks, but continued active participation in the literary life of the court.
77. *SCSS* 921 (Love).
78. This poem appears nowhere else in Shōtetsu's works.

husks must vanish/ Like the dew upon the branches," I mean that although the cicadas have shed their shells and transformed themselves, hope is vain, since in autumn they must inevitably die and become nothing. Thus I suggested the lines "Just because they have changed their shells, does that mean they have more time to live? It is futile to hope." The word "too" in the line "The leaves, too, must have their autumn" is very important. Some people will be able to comprehend the poem just on the basis of this one word, "too." I had originally thought to use the word in the last two lines, as in *tsuyu no/ Mi o kaenu tomo*, but since I had already used it in the first part of the poem, I decided to write "*kaenu tote*" instead—even though it might be easier to understand if it were *tomo* instead of *tote*.[79]

22. On the topic "Praying for Love," the poem:

Yūshide mo	Even the prayer strips
Ware ni nabikanu	Refuse to incline toward me
Tsuyu zo chiru	As dewdrops scatter.
Ta ga negigoto no	Whose orisons so stir the autumn wind,
Sue no akikaze.	Presaging the death of our love?[80]

The lines "Whose orisons stir up the autumn wind,/ Presaging the death of our love?" are somewhat obscure and may be a bit difficult to understand. They must mean that the beloved, knowing that the speaker is praying, is also making his own prayers to the gods. If the wind fails to blow toward her the sacred strips that the speaker has offered to the gods, and if the dew scatters in the wrong direction, then the beloved must be praying that they not meet again—which is what is meant by the lines, "Whose orisons stir up the autumn wind/ Presaging the death of our love?" The word "orisons" means the same as "prayers."

Now, a person might object to this kind of expression, saying that he would write instead, "Can it be that he has prayed/ Never to see me any more?" (*Ware ni awaji to/ Hito ya inorishi*) and protesting that there is no point in putting it into such difficult language. This may be very true, of course, but let such critics look at the collected poems of Teika. There is not a single flat verse[81] to be found among

---

79. In other words, he used *tote* instead of *tomo* because he had already ended a line with *mo* and wanted to avoid an unpleasant rhyme.
80. This poem appears nowhere else in Shōtetsu's works.
81. "Flat verse" translates *tada mahira naru uta*, "a dull or ordinary verse." Shōtetsu's point seems to be that poetic language should not be as straightforward as prose.

them. On the other hand, this simple poem by Tameko[82] works very well:

Kazu naranu	The cruel man
Misogi wa kami mo	Must have prayed first to the gods,
Uke so to ya	Saying, "No—forebear!"
Tsurenaki hito no	"Pay no heed to the devotions
Mazu inoriken.	Of one of so little account!"[83]

23. A novice[84] should accustom himself to composing verse freely and in a relaxed frame of mind instead of racking his brains for ingenious ideas.[85] Because his level of performance at that stage is limited, no matter how much effort he expends on a poem it will not appear remarkable to those at a higher level of accomplishment.[86] No matter how much thought he may give to it, he will be unable to produce a poem any better than is normal for the stage he has reached. Some people compose allusive variations[87] on older poems in every two out of three poems they write—a bad practice. In ancient times they considered allusive variation to be of great importance. Those who had attained a high degree of skill would change the topic of the foundation poem[88] from "Love" or "Miscellaneous" to one of the seasons, alter the arrangement of lines, and transform the conception of the older poem into something different in the new one. But when a beginner tries an allusive variation, the conception of his poem will be the same as the older one even if he does succeed in altering the arrangement of the lines. Therefore, the novice should restrain himself from composing too many allusive variations.

82. Kyōgoku Tameko (d. 1316?). Elder sister of Tamekane and major poet in the court of Retired Emperor Fushimi. For a brief sketch of her life and translations of a few of her poems, see Carter 1989:110–19.
83. *ShokuGSIS* 787 (Love). Headnote: "Praying Not to Meet a Lover."
84. "Novice" translates *shoshin*, literally "beginner." Originally the term was used to refer to young monks just beginning their course of training; later it came to be used of beginning artists as well.
85. "Racking his brains for ingenious ideas" translates *kuihoriirite anzu*, literally, "to dig into something and worry over it."
86. Imagawa Ryōshun argues a similar point in his *Ben'yōshō* ("Notes on the Fundamentals of Poetry," alternatively titled *Ryōshun isshiden*, "Ryōshun's Testament to His Heir," 1409; see *NKGT* 5:179, 185): "When one is a novice, he will write only bad poems even when he thinks they are good" and "When one is a novice, he cannot yet discriminate what is truly a good uta or renga verse."
87. *Honkadori*, the technique of borrowing words, phrases, or ideas from an older and well-known poem, with the aim of creating a new poem of great resonance. The technique can be traced to earlier times, but it was in the hands of Teika's father, Shunzei, and Teika that it reached perfection. By Shōtetsu's time *honkadori* was of course an old method, and one that had become a crutch for those of feeble imagination.
88. *Honka*. The term for the old poems that were borrowed from.

24. Some poems in *Kokinshū* are well conceived, but their language is archaic-sounding and unsuitable for the poetry of our day.[89] Just because a poem is in *Kokinshū* does not mean that it may be used as a foundation poem for an allusive variation. The poems of Narihira, Ise, Komachi, Mitsune, Tsurayuki, Henjō, and such are the most appropriate for allusive variation.[90] Even in *Kokinshū* the number of poems suitable for use as foundation poems is no more than 240 or 250, it is said.

25. A poet should not be overly concerned about learning and knowledge.[91] It is better that he have a clear understanding and grasp of the nature of poetry. To have such a clear understanding means that one's mind is enlightened.[92] A man who has a clear understanding of poetry can become a skilled poet if he wishes to. When I read over old poems I try to guess whether a given poem is in, say, the style of mystery and depth[93] or whether it ought to be classed as in the lofty style.[94] I also find myself thinking such things as, "Suppose I were to try using the words of this poem in one of my

89. *Kokin wakashū* ("Collection of Ancient and Modern Times," 905) was the first imperial anthology of Japanese poetry, compiled by Ki no Tsurayuki and three other courtiers upon the order of Emperor Daigo (885–930; r. 897–930). Because of its status as the first of the imperially commissioned collections, the anthology became a handbook for later poets, many of whom virtually memorized its contents—which they assumed set a standard in most respects. In his *Maigetsushō* ("Monthly Notes," ca. 1219), however, Teika discouraged poets from using archaic language in general, particularly proscribing indiscriminate use of words found in *Man'yōshū*. Later critics extended the caution to the *sandaishū*, or "collections of the three ages," *Kokinshū*, *Gosenshū* ("Later Collection," ca. 951), and *Shūishū* ("Collection of Gleanings," ca. 1006). *Kirihioke* ("The Paulownia Brazier," precise date unknown; see *NKGT* 4:265), another medieval text mistakenly attributed to Teika, specifically singles out *Kokinshū* as containing "words and conceptions that should no longer be used."

90. The poets listed here—Ariwara no Narihira, the court ladies Ise (fl. 870–940) and Ono no Komachi (fl. 830–850), Ōshikōchi no Mitsune (fl. 898–922), Ki no Tsurayuki, and Archbishop Henjō (816?–890)—represent the finest, and most stylistically polished, of *KKS* poets, whose works were generally devoid of the archaisms warned against by medieval critics.

91. *Utayomi wa saigaku o oboyubekarazu.* By "learning and knowledge" (*saigaku*) Shōtetsu probably means scholarly learning, and perhaps even some of the secret teachings that, while had in abundance by the heirs of the poetic houses, were not in themselves enough to produce good poetry. Tameie makes a similar comment in his *Eiga no ittei* ("The Foremost Style of Poetic Composition," ca. 1274, in *NKGT* 3:388 and Brower 1987:399).

92. The word Shōtetsu uses here is *satoru*, another term borrowed from the vocabulary of Buddhism. It implies a state of heightened, intuitive understanding beyond empirical knowledge.

93. *Yūgen tei.* For a discussion of Shōtetsu's use of this term, see the introduction (pp. 51–58).

94. *Taketakaki tei.* A formal style often involving description of grand natural scenes, rendered with archaic or pseudo-archaic diction. The style was considered particularly appropriate for poem contests and public events.

own—would I be able to produce anything as good as this? Probably not." When studying the poems of the masters one should carefully ponder each poem, and then if there are any places one does not understand, one should ask questions. Also, on more formal occasions such as poetry gatherings,[95] if a person simply leafs through the other people's papers and poem slips and lets it go at that, even though he may not understand their poems, his own level of poetic accomplishment will not advance. Again, there are those who, having had a poem explained to them by the author, think, "Well, it must be as he says," and abandon the subject even though they still fail to comprehend the poem. It is indeed difficult to admit that one does not understand a poem. Ryōshun has said that when poets gather together, the best training they can give themselves is not to compose a whole lot of poems but rather to discuss and criticize their verse together.[96] Again, to have had the experience of participating in a single poetry contest where the judgments are made by group decision[97] is far more valuable than composing verse a thousand or two thousand times by oneself. Given the fact that people are criticizing each other's poems and expressing their opinions about them, it does sometimes happen that the other person may understand a poem in one sense while that is not the way one interprets it oneself.

26. If someone should ask me what province Mount Yoshino[98] is in, I would reply that with cherry blossoms I associate Mount Yoshino, and with autumn leaves, Mount Tatsuta,[99] and that I write my poems accordingly, not caring whether these places are in the province of Ise[100] or the province of Hyūga[101] or wherever. It is of no practical value to learn and remember in which provinces these places are located. But though I make no effort to memorize such

95. *Kai*, literally, "meetings." The word implies a planned gathering, to which poets came by invitation. Many aristocratic houses held such meetings on a regular basis, usually on the same day each month—hence the term *tsukinamikai*, or "monthly meeting." Here Shōtetsu seems only to imply a formal gathering of some sort, as opposed to occasions when poems would be composed in a more informal setting—at drinking parties, for example, or at inns on the road.

96. Probably a reference to *Ben'yōshō* (see *NKGT* 5:182). See Inada 1978:169-70.

97. *Shūgihan*, a contest in which final judgments were arrived at by discussion and voting of the participants.

98. A mountainous area in central Yamato Province south of the old capital at Nara. The area was famous for its scenic beauty—most especially, as Shōtetsu notes, for its cherry blossoms.

99. A mountainous area just southwest of Nara that was famous for the beauty of its autumn leaves.

100. An ancient province; now Mie Prefecture.

101. Another ancient province; now Miyazaki Prefecture.

things, they become known to me in the course of time, so I have learned that Yoshino is in Yamato Province.[102]

27. I composed the following poem on the topic "An Autumn Evening" and requested the old retired emperor[103] to criticize it:

Ushi tote mo	Wretched it may be,
Yo mo itowareji	But I cannot say that I despise
Waga mi yo ni	The world I live in—
Aran kagiri no	Not as long as it offers me
Aki no yūgure.	The beauty of the autumn dusk.[104]

In his critique, His Majesty wrote, "How touched I am to learn that all your life your heart has been moved by the color of dusk in the autumn light," and I was told that he admired the poem exceedingly. I would not be able to write a poem as good as this any more.

28. Lord Tameshige[105] composed this poem on "An Autumn Evening":

Hitokata ni	One pathway alone
Omoishirubeki	Can lead me to understanding
Mi no usa no	Of my bitterness—
Sore ni mo aranu	And it is not the one before me now
Aki no yūgure.	In the melancholy autumn dusk.[106]

Lord Tameshige was an exceptionally ugly man. Once he seized the hand of a lady in waiting at the palace and tried to make an assignation with her for that night. "What! With your face?" she replied. He immediately responded with the following:

Sareba koso	For that very reason
Yoru to wa chigire	I ask you to meet me at night,
Kazuraki no	Feeling the same toward me
Kami mo waga mi mo	As toward the god of Kazuraki,
Onaji kokoro ni.	That paragon of ugliness.[107]

---

102. The point being that in poetry, understanding of traditional associations is more important than knowledge of the "real world."
103. Retired Emperor Go-Komatsu (1377–1433; r. 1392–1412).
104. *Sōkonshū* 1330.
105. Nijō Tameshige (1325–85). For a brief sketch of his life and translations of a few of his poems, see Carter 1989:231–38.
106. This poem appears nowhere else in Tameshige's works.
107. In his *Nigonshō* ("Notes on Two Kinds of Words," 1403, in *NKGT* 5:174), Ryōshun relates this same anecdote with Kyōgoku Tamekane as the protagonist.

29. In his critique of a hundred-poem sequence by Nagatsuna,[108] Tameie wrote, "This poem is like calling for Tarō and having him come out riding on Jirō's shoulders."[109] This was because Nagatsuna had neglected the topic and treated "the mountains all around"—a practice that Tameie abhorred. Provided the poem does not diverge from the fixed topic, it will be acceptable.[110]

30. On the topic "The Cuckoo Is Rarely Heard" someone wrote a poem treating it as singing only once. But doubts were expressed as to whether it was proper, since the topic was of the sixth month, to speak of the bird as singing just once. The decision was that the meaning of "rarely" is the same whether at the beginning of summer or the end.[111]

31. When composing a poem on a miscellaneous topic,[112] one should make an effort not to treat one of the seasons. But if a season does happen to find its way into the poem, that does not mean it must be censured.

32. With a seasonal topic there is a difference between early and late in the season, depending on the qualifying words of the topic. If one composes one's poem with this in mind, one will be able to make a clear distinction. Thus, with the topic "Moon," first comes "The Moon in the Mountains," then "The Moon on the Peaks," "The Moon on the Hills," "The Moon on the Fields," "The Moon in the Village," and so on in sequence. For the topic "The Moon in the Mountains," it is not proper to treat the moon lingering in the sky at dawn in the ninth month.[113] This is not to say that one must absolutely treat the

---

108. *Nagatsuna hyakushu* ("Nagatsuna's Hundred-Poem Sequence," 1226), a work by Fujiwara no Nagatsuna (precise dates unknown), which was actually submitted to Teika, not Tameie, in 1226. Like most such works, the sequence is organized like a small imperial anthology, with twenty poems on spring and autumn, fifteen on summer and winter, fifteen on love, and fifteen on miscellaneous topics. A printed text is available in *ZGR* 14 (item 394), part 2.

109. Teika attached short comments after most of the poems. What Shōtetsu alludes to is a comment in Teika's preface in which he criticizes Nagatsuna for including spring rain in a poem on the topic "Waiting for the Spring Moon" by reference to an anecdote in which a master calls for one servant and another comes in first. See *ZGR* 14 (item 394), part 2:861.

110. Here Shōtetsu takes a characteristically liberal attitude.

111. Here again Shōtetsu insists on the "essence" (*hon'i*) of the topic as something unchanging, regardless of specific context.

112. The rubric "miscellaneous" (*zō*) refers to poems not written on the other major topics, most especially the seasons and love. In fact, as Shōtetsu says below, seasonal imagery often did appear in such poems, although usually mixed in with other subject matter.

113. "The moon lingering in the sky at dawn in the ninth month" translates *nagatsuki no ariake*. Shōtetsu's point is that one should not substitute one topic for another, even if the two could be subsumed under one general topic.

topic as coming at the beginning of the season, but merely that one must not treat the end of the season.

33. A person who has reached a high level of skill and attainment[114] need not, when composing poems freely, have in mind any specific topics. Since each poem will of itself turn out to contain the essence of a particular topic, it makes no difference whether or not the actual words of the topic are in it.

34. In addition to the expression "eight thousand lotus stalks" (hasu no ha no yachimoto) to indicate an extremely large number, people also say "eight thousand times" (yachitabi) and "eight thousand generations"(yachiyo).[115]

35. On "The Summer Lustration":

Misogi suru	Circling round
Kono wa no uchi ni	This enclosure where I make
Megurikite	The summer lustration,
Ware yori saki ni	Autumn crosses the boundary ahead
Aki ya koyuran.	And makes its way toward me.[116]

36. On "Evening Faces":

Kakikomoru	Like the foam
Mizuno no kishi ni	That gathers on the banks at Mizuno,
Yoru awa no	The secluded land,
Kienu mo sakeru	They vanish but to bloom again—
Yūgao no hana.	The flowers of the evening faces.[117]

Sōzei[118] said of this poem, "The line 'They vanish but to bloom again' ought not to have been written that way. If I had written the poem, I would have said, 'Do they vanish but to bloom again?' (kienu ya)."[119]

37. "With a censorious look" (kakochigao) and "with a resentful look" (uramigao) are unpleasant expressions. "With a tearful look"

---

114. Jōzu tassha no kurai—in other words, one who has, with practice, arrived at the skill level (kurai) of a master.

115. All of these words are used as superlatives.

116. This poem appears nowhere else in Shōtetsu's works. Lustrations were undertaken for purification at the end of the sixth lunar month.

117. Sōkonshū 3148. Yūgao (Lagernaria siceraria) is a gourd plant that produces blossoms each evening.

118. Takayama Sōzei (d. 1455). A man of military background who became one of Shōtetsu's students. Known more now as one of the Seven Sages of linked-verse (renga shichiken) of the mid-fifteenth century, along with Shōtetsu's disciple Shinkei (1406–75) and five others.

119. Sōzei's line would seem to give the poem a more conventionally plaintive note— something that Shōtetsu seems to want to avoid.

(*nururugao*) may be used in a poem, however. Also, "with a look of feigned ignorance" (*shirazugao*) is acceptable. The poem

Oriori wa	From time to time
Omou kokoro mo	The love I hold within my heart
Miyuran o	Must show itself—
Utate ya hito no	But, alas, she gazes past me
Shirazugao naru.	With a look of feigned ignorance![120]

has been called the best poem in *Gyokuyōshū*.[121] Indeed it is very clever.

38. Such phrases as "the pathos of the waves" (*nami no aware*) and "the pathos of the water" (*mizu no aware*) should not be used in poems. To write like that makes it sound as if there were an actual thing called pathos, which is bad. One should use a phrase like "touching" or "pathetic" (*aware naru*) instead. So the old poem:

Ware yue no	If she could look upon
Namida to kore o	These tears of mine and know them
Yoso ni miba	Shed on her account,
Aware narubeki	Then surely it would seem pathetic—
Sode no ue kana.	The sight of my sodden sleeves.[122]

And another old poem:

Wasuraruru	Not for myself
Mi oba omowazu	Who am forgotten do I worry,
Chikaiteshi	But rather for him
Hito no inochi no	Who vowed he would be faithful—
Oshiku mo aru kana.	Lest the gods now take his life.[123]

This poem would seem suited to the topic "Relying on a Lover's Promise." The gist of the poem is that the lover swore to the gods that he would be faithful to the speaker, and now he has abandoned her, while she—far more than for herself who has been forgotten— worries that he may be punished by death for breaking his vow. When Genji had revealed unasked to Murasaki his affair with the Akashi lady, she had written in reply, "That you should have

120. *GYS* 1318 (Love), by Asukai Masaari (1241–1301). The fourth line in the *GYS* version reads *tsurena ya hito no*: "With a cold look on her face."
121. "Collection of Jeweled Leaves," the fourteenth imperial anthology, compiled between 1311 and 1313 by Kyōgoku Tamekane.
122. *SZS* 757 (Love), Topic Unknown, by Fujiwara no Takanobu (1142–1205), an uncle of Teika.
123. *SIS* 870 (Love), Topic Unknown, by Lady Ukon. Also noted in section 84 of *Yamato monogatari* ("Tales of Yamato," ca. 947–957). See *NKBT* 9:270 and Tahara 1980:47.

deigned to tell me a dreamlike story that you could not keep to yourself calls to mind numbers of earlier instances." And in Genji's letter had been the allusion to "the promise that I made," to which Murasaki had written, "Not for myself do I worry" (*Mi o ba omowazu*)—an allusion to this poem.[124]

39. When making an allusive variation on an older poem, the usual practice is to place material from the upper lines of the foundation poem in one's lower lines and material from the lower lines in one's upper lines. Sometimes, however, the poet will not change the position of the lines but will alter the subject matter instead. And some poems remain essentially the same as the original no matter how much the poet has altered the position of the lines. Again, there are poems based on *Man'yōshū* in which the poet has made his new verse by changing only one or two words of the original. Such a poem—by the Go-Hosshōji regent,[125] I believe—alluded to the *Man'yō* poem

Sasanami ya	The gods are sad
Kunitsu mikami no	In the land of Sasanami
Urasabite	By the rippling waves;
Furuki miyako no	And at the ancient capital,
Aremaku mo oshi.	The ruin fills my heart with grief.[126]

Keeping the first four lines down through "the ancient capital" just the same, he made his poem by composing the new line, "The moon dwells all alone" (*Tsuki hitori sumu*).[127]

40. The final *o* in the word *masurao* ("stalwart man") was long ago written with the final *wo* を of the *kana* syllabary. But nowadays

---

124. Shōtetsu seems to be confused here, lumping together two separate incidents in the *Akashi* chapter of *Genji monogatari*. The first shows Genji, still in exile in Akashi, reading a letter from Murasaki in which she gently upbraids him for his amorous wanderings; the second is set after Genji's return to the capital, when he first broaches to Murasaki the subject of his relationship with the Akashi Lady. Murasaki's reference to Ukon's famous poem serves a double purpose: to indicate to Genji that Murasaki is above berating him on his peccadillos while at the same time warning him that he too must be careful to keep his priorities straight. See *NKBZ* 13:249, 261–63 and Seidensticker 1976, I:264, 269.

125. Kujō Kanezane (1149–1207), a prominent political figure and patron of the arts. Father of Go-Kyōgoku Yoshitsune.

126. The actual *MYS* poem (33), by Takechi no Kurohito (fl. ca. 700), reads slightly differently: "The gods are sad/ In the land of Sasanami/ By the rippling waves—/ And the sight of the ruined capital/ Fills my own heart with grief!" (*Sasanami no/ kunitsu mikami no/ urasabite/ aretaru miyako/ mireba kanashi mo.*)

127. Kanezane's poem (*SZS* 981, Miscellaneous) reads: "The gods are sad/ In the land of Sasanami/ By the rippling waves—/ And in the ancient capital/ The moon dwells, all alone." (*Sasanami ya/ kunitsu mikami no/ urasabite/ furuki miyako ni/ tsuki hitori sumu.*) The *sumu* of the last line is a double entendre meaning both "to live" and "to shine clear."

everyone writes the inner syllable *o* お [128] instead. For the *o* in *mega-mi ogami* ("female gods and male gods"), it has been the custom from ancient times to write the final *wo*. That being the case, people say it ought to be acceptable to use the final *wo* in writing *masurao* as well. In the writings of Ryōshun, too, *masurao* is written with the final *wo*. [129]

41. When it comes to love poetry, many poems by court ladies strike the heart. Princess Shikishi's "If I do not live/ Then tomorrow I will not feel," [130] "Even though only I can know/ These months and days of secret love," [131] and the like are full of mystery and depth. Such others as that by Shunzei's Daughter, "Your image that I used to see/ And the vow we made," [132] or Lady Kunaikyō's "Do you not hear it?" [133] are so imbued with the very essence of poetry that one wonders whether even Michitomo [134] or the regent [135] could match them.

42. The poem by Shunzei's Daughter

Aware naru	Who else can decide
Kokoronagasa no	That at the end of my trial
Yukue to mo	Of anxious waiting
Mishi yo no yume o	I must see that our one night
Tare ka sadamen.	Was finally just a dream? [136]

is the epitome of mystery and depth. The idea of the poem is that their former night of love is unknown to anyone except herself and

---

128. *Oku no o*, the *o* of the first line of the *kana* syllabary: *a, i, u, e, o*.

129. *Hashi no o*, the *o* of the last line of the *kana* syllabary: *wa, i, u, e, (w)o*.

130. *SKKS* 1329 (Love). [Headnote: From among the poems of a hundred-poem sequence] "If I do not live/ Then tomorrow I will not feel/ His rejection—/ But if he is to visit me at all/ Oh, let him come to me tonight!" (*Ikite yomo/ asu made hito mo/ tsurakaraji/ kono yūgure o/ towaba toekashi*.)

131. *SKKS* 1035 (Love). [Headnote: On "Secret Love," from a hundred-poem sequence] "Forgetting myself,/ I begin to lament his absence/ As evening falls,/ Even though only I can know/ These months and days of secret love." (*Wasurete wa/ uchinagekaruru/ yūbe kana/ ware nomi shiritel/ suguru tsukihi o*.)

132. *SKKS* 1391 (Love). [Headnote: In the spirit of "Meeting Once, But Not Meeting Again," for a poem contest held at the Bureau of Poetry] "Can it be a dream?/ Your image that I used to see/ And the vow we made—/ I have not forgotten them, and yet/ They are no longer real to me." (*Yume ka to yo/ mishi omokage mo/ chigirishi mo/ wasurezunagara/ utsutsu naraneba*.)

133. *SKKS* 1199 (Love), by Kunaikyō (late twelfth century), one of Retired Emperor Go-Toba's ladies-in-waiting. [Headnote: On Love and the Wind] "Do you not hear it?/ Even the fickle wind that blows/ In the lofty sky/ Still makes its visit to the pines/ Who wait for word that it will come." (*Kiku ya ika ni/ uwa no sora naru/ kaze dani mo/ matsu ni oto suru/ narai ari to wa*.)

134. Minamoto no Michitomo. A favorite of Retired Emperor Go-Toba, who was chosen as one of the compilers of *Shinkokinshū*.

135. Go-Kyōgoku Yoshitsune. Another prominent poet and patron who was chosen to write the Japanese preface for *Shinkokinshū*.

136. Shunzei's Daughter (ca. 1175–1250). This poem appears nowhere else in her works.

her lover. If the lover really knew how she had been patiently waiting all this time for his visit, then she would indeed decide that the promises he made were but a dream. In the poem "If I do not live/ Then tomorrow I will not feel,"[137] too, the woman has not spoken of her distress to anyone else. She is simply there all alone, clinging to an existence that may not last until the next day, and pleading that if her lover is destined to come to her at all, then let him come tonight.

43. It is said that it was after hearing Tamehide's[138] poem,

Aware shiru	Such is this world
Tomo koso kataki	That a friend who feels its pathos
Yo narikere	Is hard to find—
Hitori ame kiku	I listen to the rain alone
Aki no yosugara.	All through the autumn night.[139]

Ryōshun became his disciple.[140] The lines "I listen to the rain alone/ All through the autumn night" actually belong in the upper part of the poem. Listening to the rain alone in the autumn night, he thinks, "Such is this world/ That a friend who feels its sadness/ Is hard to find." If he had a friend who appreciated this sad beauty, and if he were invited to go off on a ramble somewhere and they spent the night in conversation, he would not be listening to the rain like this. The fact that he does not attempt to go anywhere is particularly affecting, in my opinion. Also, if the poet had written, "I listen to the rain alone/ In the autumn midnight," the experience would have ended there. The essential thing is that by leaving it at "all through the autumn night," the experience does not end, for by saying "all through the night" the poet implies, "As I listened to the rain alone all through the autumn night, my thoughts were . . ." Thus the lines "I listen to the rain alone/ All through the autumn night" actually are the upper lines of the poem. If "I listen to the rain alone" were in the lower lines, the poem would have nothing remarkable about it.

137. See n. 130 above.
138. Reizei Tamehide (d. 1372). See the introduction (p. 7). For a brief sketch of his life and translations of a few of his poems, see Carter 1989:225–30.
139. This poem appears in Imagawa Ryōshun's *Rakusho roken* ("Anonymous Document Revealed," ca. 1412, in *NKGT* 5:202), again attributed to Tamehide. There the first line reads *nasake aru*, "Such is this world/ That a friend of true sympathy . . ." Whether Shōtetsu's memory fails him here or he has avoided *nasake aru* because it was a phrase criticized by the Nijō school is a moot point. See Araki 1977:15.
140. In *Rakusho roken* (*NKGT*:202) Ryōshun says that he became Tamehide's disciple because this poem "pierced him to the heart" (*kokoro ni shimite*).

There is a poem of Tu Fu:[141]

Hearing the rain in the cold until late in the fifth watch,
I open the gate, and see that the fallen leaves are deep.[142]

An old priest[143] who was one of my fellow monks corrected the diacritics[144] in these lines. Seeing where it had been marked traditionally to read, "Hearing it as rain" (*Ame to kiku*), he said to himself, "This is wrong," and for the first time he corrected just the one *kana* symbol, changing it to "Hearing the rain" (*Ame o kiku*). But changing just this one symbol is like the difference between heaven and earth. If it is read "Hearing it *as* rain," it means that he knew all along that it was the leaves falling, and the feeling is constricted. When it is read "Hearing the rain," it means that during the night he listened, thinking it really was rain, but toward morning when the fifth watch was over, he opened his gate and looked out to see that it had not been rain at all but falling leaves that had piled up deep in the garden. His surprise at this discovery is the whole appeal of the poem. So in Japanese poetry as well, the change of a single *kana* symbol can make a poem into something completely different.

44. On "Deep Snow in the Mountains," I wrote,

Shigure made	While the rains lasted
Kumorite fukaku	The clouds seemed to give glimpses
Mishi yama no	Of mountain depths
Yuki ni oku naki	That are not there in the snow
Kigi no shitaore.	Burdening the limbs of the trees.[145]

During the season of late autumn rains it is so cloudy that the mountains seem to have profound depth. In the snow, however, there is no depth to the mountains, and they stand out clearly before one's eyes. "Depths that are not there in the snow" is a good phrase. Also, since all the trees are bent over, there is no depth to them, either. The twist to the poem is that in the *deep* snow the mountains become *shallow*. A poem by Keiun[146]:

141. d. 770. The most famous of T'ang poets.
142. Source unknown.
143. Identity unknown.
144. *Ten*, literally "marks," which were placed in the text in order for the reader to put the words into the order of Japanese syntax.
145. *Sōkonshū* 4184.
146. Fl. ca. 1340–69. A contemporary of Ton'a. For a brief sketch of his life and translations of a few of his poems, see Carter 1989:196–202.

Kusa mo ki mo	When plants and trees
Uzumorehatsuru	Have been completely buried
Yuki ni koso	Beneath a snowfall—
Nakanaka yama wa	It is then that the mountains
Arawa narikere.	Stand out most clearly to view.[147]

But one might also write that the mountains have become deep beneath the snow.

45. A poem by Teika:

Tamashii o	I left my soul
Tsurenaki sode ni	Wrapped in her indifferent sleeve,
Todomeokite	So that in the end
Waga mi zo hate wa	I have only myself to blame
Urayamarekeru.	As a cause for jealousy.[148]

46. Lord Tsurudono[149] was the son of Lord Kōmyōbuji.[150] He is the ancestor of the present Tsukinowa family.[151] Lord Tsurudono was one of the compilers of *Shokukokinshū*.[152]

47. A poem by Lord Ietaka:

Hitozute ni	Though others say
Saku to wa kikaji	That the cherries are in bloom,
Sakurabana	I will not listen—
Yoshino no yama wa	Though it may be days before I go
Hikazu koyu tomo.	To the hills of Yoshino to see.[153]

And a poem in *Kokinshū*:

| Koenu ma wa | Unless I go there, |
| Yoshino no yama no | I can only keep on listening |

147. *Keiun hōin shū* ("Dharma-Sign Keiun's Collection," mid-fourteenth century) 168 (Winter).
148. This poem seems to be a garbled version of a poem by Teika (*SG* 72): "I left it behind/ Wrapped in the sleeve of her night robe/ At our sad parting/ And now it is my own heart/ That gives me cause for jealousy." (*Sayokoromo/ wakaruru sode ni/ todomeokite/ kokoro zo hate wa/ urayamarenuru*.)
149. Tsurudono, Fujiwara no Motoie (1203–80). He was actually a son of the regent Go-Kyōgoku Yoshitsune.
150. Kōmyōbuji-dono, Fujiwara no Michiie (1193–1252). Elder brother—not father, as Shōtetsu mistakenly notes—of Motoie (see n. 149 above).
151. Tsukinowa became the family name of those descended from Motoie (see n. 62 above).
152. "Collection of Ancient and Modern Times Continued." Eleventh of the imperial anthologies, compiled between 1259 and 1265 by Teika's son Tameie, Fujiwara no Motoie (see n. 149 above), Kujō Ieyoshi (1192–1264), Rokujō Yukiie (1223–75), Hamuro Mitsutoshi (also known by his monkish name of Shinkan; 1203–76).
153. From his personal collection, *Minishū* 612 (Spring). Headnote: Going to see the blossoms.

Sakurabana   To what others say
Hitozute ni nomi   Of the cherry flowers in bloom
Kikiwataru kana.   In the hills of Yoshino.[154]

Although Ietaka has altered the arrangement of the lines somewhat, the conception and diction of his poem are the same as in the older one. When I asked whether this was permissible, the answer was that it was all right because he changed the category of the poem from "Love" to "A Season."[155] There are many ways of making an allusive variation on an older poem. The style of leaning upon the foundation poem and the style of dialogue with the foundation poem should be understood from these examples.[156]

48. Teika and Ietaka differ somewhat in the manner and style in which they allude to older poems. Teika never takes the idea of the foundation poem for his own conception, whereas with Ietaka one can occasionally find poems with the same conception as the foundation poem.

49. In the *Sengohyaku-ban uta-awase*,[157] the person known as the Third Prince[158] was the elder brother of Retired Emperor Go-Toba.[159] He was the father of Retired Emperor Go-Horikawa.[160] Yukiyoshi[161] was the father of Yukiie.[162] Yukiie was one of the compilers of *Shokukokinshū*.

154. *KKS* 588 (Love), by Ki no Tsurayuki. Headnote: Sent to a person who lived in Yamato. The poem is found under the topic "mountain cherries" in *Kokin waka rokujō* ("The Six Books of Ancient and Modern *Waka*," ca. 976–982, in *SKT* 2:4224) but is treated as a love poem (546) in *Tsurayuki shū* ("The Tsurayuki Collection," mid-tenth century, in *SKT* 3).
155. The *KKS* poem was in the Love category; Ietaka's would be in the category Spring.
156. The "style of leaning upon the foundation poem" (*honka ni sugaritaru tei*) is mentioned in *Eiga no ittei* (NKGT 3:389 and Brower 1987:402) and Ryōshun's *Ben'yōshō* (NKGT 5:182); the "style of dialogue with the foundation poem" is mentioned by Nijō Yoshimoto (1320–88) in *Kinrai fūteishō* ("Notes on Poetic Styles of the Recent Past," 1387, in NKGT 5:144) and by Ton'a in *Gumon kenchū* ("Wise Answers to Foolish Questions," 1363, in NKGT 5:129).
157. "The Poetry Contest in Fifteen Hundred Rounds." A contest put together by Retired Emperor Go-Toba from the third of the sequences referred to as *Shōji hyakushu* ("Hundred-Poem Sequences of the Shōji Era," 1200). Participants were all the major poets of the day, including Teika, Ietaka, Yoshitsune, Jien (also known as Jichin, 1155–1225), Jakuren, and Masatsune; judgments were by Shunzei, Yoshitsune, the retired emperor, and others.
158. San no Miya. Koreakira Shinnō (1179–1221), third son of Emperor Takakura (1161–81; r. 1168–80) and older brother of Retired Emperor Go-Toba. He took the tonsure in 1211.
159. See n. 13 above.
160. See n. 23 above.
161. Fujiwara no Yukiyoshi (b. 1179). Famous poet and calligrapher.
162. Rokujō Yukiie. See n. 152 above. Here again Shōtetsu is mistaken: Yukiie was the son not of Yukiyoshi but of Rokujō Tomoie (1182–1258).

50. In the expression *tatsu miwakosuge*,[163] *miwa* means an inlet on the water, and the whole phrase means that sedges are growing around an inlet on the water. In the phrase *yabu shi wakanu*,[164] *yabu* means a thicket. *Shi* is a rhetorical particle.

51. There is a difference of opinion about the phrase *shimo no furi wa*. Some say it simply means "the fall of frost" and pronounce it *furi wa*.[165] Others say it means "the place where the frost falls," just as *takaba*[166] means "falconing ground," and they pronounce it *furiba*.[167]

52. The expression "I am overcome with awe" (*ito mo kashikoshi*) suggests a feeling of fearfulness. Such expressions as "I am filled with awe at the mention of it" (*kakemaku mo kashikoshikeredomo*) suggest the same thing.

53. A poem on the topic "Plants in the Cold" should not be about reeds because "Reeds in the Cold" and "Plants in the Cold" follow each other in the regular succession of topics.[168]

54. For the topic "The End of the Year," unless the last day of the year is specifically mentioned, the poem may also include the

---

163. A reference to a poem attributed to Hitomaro that Shōtetsu probably knew as *SSZS* 1019 (Love): "Like the deep roots/ Of the sedge growing in the inlet/ By the fields of Asaha,/ For whom else would I so deeply/ Commit myself to love?" (*Asahano ni/ tatsu miwakosuge/ ne fukamete/ tare yue ni ka wa/ waga koizaran.*) The original *Man'yōshū* version of the poem (2875), which poets of Shōtetsu's day could not understand due to their inability to interpret *man'yōgana* correctly, reads differently: "Like the stubborn roots/ Of the withered sedge that grows/ On the fields of Asaha,/ For whom else would I go on/ Persisting stubbornly in my love?" (*Asahano ni/ tachi kamusaburu/ suga no ne no/ nemokoro taga yue/ aga koinaku ni.*) Examples of the use of the phrase *miwakosuge* in later poetry exist too, e.g., *SSIS* 60 (Spring), by the Go-Koga chancellor: [Headnote: On the topic "Spring Rain in the Fields"] "Under the spring rain/ They keep changing from green to green,/ the fields of Asaha——/ But the sedge growing in the inlet/ Remains indifferent in its hue." (*Harusame mo/ furikawariyuku/ asahano ni/ tatsu miwakosuge/ iro mo tsurenashi.*)

164. A reference to a phrase that appears in *KKS* 870 (Miscellaneous), by Furu no Imamichi (fl. last half of ninth century): [Headnote: A poem sent as an expression of joy to Nanmatsu of Isonokami, who was out of court service living in seclusion at a place called Isonokami, when suddenly he was given the cap of the Fifth Rank] "The sun's splendor/ Shines into every thicket——/ So that even/ Your old home in Isonokami/ Has seen the flowers come into bloom." (*Hi no hikari/ yabu shi wakaneba/ isonokami/ furinishi sato ni/ hana mo sakikeri.*)

165. The final syllable is ambiguous and could be read either as *ha* or *ba*. Precedent for reading it *furi wa* is found in *KKS* 1072 ("Folk Music Office Songs"), a Mizuguki Song: "In our makeshift hut/ Atop the Hill of Young Plants/ My love and I/ Have kept each other warm in sleep,/ But how thick the fall of dew at dawn!" (*Mizuguki no/ oka no yakata ni/ imo to are to/ nete no asake no/ shimo no furi wa mo.*)

166. When pronounced *ba*, the final syllable implies the character 場 , or "place."

167. The situation is identical with one noted above in 166.

168. By this time, poetic topics had so proliferated that there were handbooks listing them, always in proper seasonal order. Here Shōtetsu simply notes that the somewhat broad topic "Plants in the Cold" should not be treated as including "reeds" because the latter has become a topic in itself.

next to the last day. "The End of the Ninth Month" always means the last day of the month. [169]

55. The word *saranu* comes from *sa aranu* ("it is not so"). In the expression *saranu dani* ("even if it were not so"), it means the same thing. But in the phrase *saranu wakare* ("an unavoidable parting"), the word is *saru* ("to avoid"). [170]

56. For the topic "Garden," the poem may include the eaves of the house, and for the topic "Eaves," the poem is usually about eaves. [171]

57. Among allusive variations there are any number of examples that allude to two older poems. [172]

58. In his old age, Lord Shunzei [173] continued as always to compose poetry day and night and did nothing about religious preparations for the world to come. Worried about what might become of him in the next life, [174] he undertook a retreat of seven days at the Sumiyoshi Shrine [175] and appealed to the god, vowing, "If poetry is a useless activity, I will give up this art from now on and devote myself wholeheartedly to religious preparations for the life to come." On the night of the seventh day of his retreat, the god appeared to him in a dream and said, "Japanese poetry and the Way of the Buddha are one whole, not two." [176] Concluding from this that he should not seek the path of the Buddha apart from this art, he devoted himself to poetry more fervently than ever, it is said.

169. In other words, a poet has some leeway when treating the broader topic, but none when treating the narrower one.
170. The source of the last phrase is a famous poem by Ariwara no Narihira (*KKS* 901) sent in reply to his mother, who had warned him in a letter that he must come and see her before the "unavoidable parting" of her death. "For sorrowing sons/ who would have their parents live/ a thousand long years—/ how I wish that in this world/ there were no final partings." (*Yo no naka ni/ saranu wakare no/ naku mo ga na/ chiyo mo to nageku/ hito no ko no tame.*) McCullough 1985:198.
171. Here, in contrast to his earlier statements, Shōtetsu seems to indicate that one may use a word that is itself a topic (*noki*, or "eaves") even in the context of a broader topic (*niwa*, or "garden").
172. In the earlier days of the court tradition such cases were rare, but from the Shinkokin age onward the practice of taking lines from two earlier poems and putting them together was commonplace. For example, see Carter 1989:32, poem 1 and 43, n. 1.
173. Fujiwara no Shunzei, father and teacher of Teika.
174. Because he was more dedicated to poetry than his Buddhist devotions.
175. A shrine in Settsu Province (now Osaka) whose deity had been a special patron of poets since the Heian period. The custom of going into retreat in the shrine to ask for a blessing of the god was an old one. Exactly when the retreat mentioned here took place is not known.
176. Shunzei developed this idea in full form in his famous poetic treatise, *Korai fūteishō* ("Notes on Poetic Style Throughout the Ages," 1201, in *NKBZ* 50). For a discussion, see LaFleur 1983:80–106.

Teika, too, made a retreat at Sumiyoshi,[177] timing it so that the thirteenth night of the ninth month would correspond to the seventh night of his stay,[178] and making the same appeal to the god as Shunzei had done. On the thirteenth night of the ninth month, the god appeared to him and said, "For you the moon is radiant." So he decided that the art of poetry was indeed as the god said. The work in which these and other matters are recorded is called "Record of the Full Moon."[179]

59. Ryōshun often used to say, "In my youth I used to practice composing linked verse, and thinking that instead of writing a great many bad verses I ought to try to compose five or even as few as three that satisfied me, I produced only a small number of verses. His Lordship the Regent heard about this, and when he received a paper from me containing my verses, he read it through to the end and then gave me a good scolding, saying, 'I have heard that you have recently cut down on the number of your verses in the hope of producing some good linked poetry. That is most inappropriate. Though you may polish up one or two verses and think they are extremely good linked poetry, when looked at with the eyes of an expert they are still the effort of a beginner and are not good verses at all. Therefore, while you are still a novice you should produce as many verses as possible with as little effort as you can, and eventually you will become an expert as a matter of course.'"[180]

So Ryōshun remonstrated with me in a letter at a time when I was making a deliberate effort to compose good verse. He would

---

177. In *Maigetsushō*, Teika says that this retreat took place in the Genkyū era (1204–6). See NKBT 65:136 and Brower 1985:404–5.
178. The seventh night would be the end of a full week, marking the end of the retreat, which Teika doubtless planned to coincide with the advent of the full moon.
179. The title given here by Shōtetsu is *Meigetsuki* ("Record of the Full Moon"), as is the case in *Maigetsushō* itself. The fact that the former is the title of Teika's *kanbun* journal—which says nothing about Teika's retreat at Sumiyoshi—rather than any extant poetic treatise poses a problem for scholars, many of whom have questioned the authenticity of *Maigetsushō* itself based on this fact alone. (See Brower 1985:404–5, for a summary.) Unfortunately, Shōtetsu in this section merely quotes directly from *Maigetsushō* without any notice of the problem. Later on he refers to *Maigetsushō* (see section 67 and n. 193 below) in a way that again makes it clear that he is referring to the treatise and not the journal. We have no evidence showing that Shōtetsu was aware of the existence of Teika's journal or of the title by which he might have known it.
180. The source of this comment is of uncertain origin, and perhaps dubious authenticity, since Ryōshun in his *Ben'yōshō* (NKGT 5:185) devotes a whole paragraph to why "in both *uta* and linked verse, one should not compose many verses." Inada argues that, although Shōtetsu may be trying to justify his own practice by claiming Ryōshun as an authority, one might also interpret Ryōshun's statements as meaning that composing many verses *in itself* will not guarantee excellence. See Inada 1978:168–70.

often mention His Lordship the Regent's instructions and say, "This is an example of stern kindness."

60. The work known as *Manji*[181] is a discussion by Teika of the date of *Man'yōshū*. It is very valuable. Ryōshun gave me a copy in the handwriting of Tamehide,[182] but I was coaxed into letting someone else have it who wanted it badly. It is a very concise work.

61. The poem that goes, "Evening shades into night/ On Ogura, Mount of Darkness,"[183] has puzzled people since ancient times. It has been held to be a poem on the last day of the ninth month. And the phrase "Evening shades into night" (*yūzukuyo*) has been interpreted as "a moonlit night at evening," referring to the time of the fourth or fifth day, when the moon rises at dusk. But I was uncertain about it, wondering whether this was correct. In *Man'yōshū*, where the phrase *yūzuku yo* is used, it is written in a number of different ways. Written one way (夕月夜), it means the time when the moon rises in the evening; but written another way (夕付夜), it does not mean the moon, but simply that it gets gradually darker as evening falls and shades into night.[184] The poem in *Kokinshū* means that the night follows upon the evening, and so the poet wrote, "Evening shades into night/ On Ogura, Mount of Darkness."

62. *Nage no nasake*[185] means "a slight feeling" of something or other. But the meaning of *nage no* in the poem that goes *Kurenaba nage no/ Hana no kage ka wa*[186] ("When darkness falls, will there be no shelter/ To be had beneath the blossoms?") is "How can the blossoms not be there?—Just because it has grown dark does not mean that the blossoms have disappeared."

181. *Manji*, an abbreviated title for *Man'yōshū jidai kō* ("Treatise on the Dating of *Man'yōshū*," 1195?). The work was actually written by Teika's father, Shunzei, in response to questions by Go-Kyōgoku Yoshitsune. Text in *ZGR* 16 (item 450), part 2.
182. No text in Tamehide's hand is extant.
183. *KKS* 312 (Autumn), by Ki no Tsurayuki. [Headnote: Composed at Ōi on the last day of the ninth month] "Evening shades into night/ On Ogura, Mount of Darkness,/ Where a stag cries out—/ And in his voice autumn itself/ Seems to darken to its close." (*Yūzukuyo/ Ogura no yama ni/ naku shika no/ koe no uchi ni ya/ aki wa kururamu*.)
184. Modern scholars accept Shōtetsu's interpretation.
185. The first word is written in *kana*, which leaves it ambiguous—meaning either "a slight feeling," as in Shōtetsu's first example, or "none," as in his second.
186. *KKS* 95 (Spring), by Sosei (fl. ca. 890–900). [Headnote: Sent to the Urin'in Prince when Sosei was off seeing the blossoms in the Northern Hills.] "Today I shall push on/ Deep into the recesses/ Of the spring hills./ When darkness falls, will there be no shelter/ To be had beneath the blossoms?" (*Iza kyō wa/ haru no yamabe ni/ majirinamu/ kurenaba nage no/ hana no kage ka wa*.)

63. The phrase *shika na kari so* ("do not reap like that") means the same as *sa na kari so* ("do not reap thus").[187]

64. At the Butsuji'in temple[188] they use topics like "Spring Breeze," "Spring Day," "Love in the Spring," "Spring Mountains," or "Autumn Wind," "Autumn Trees," "Autumn Grasses," and so on when composing sets of fifteen poems each on different topics. They use them when a small group of people are composing sets of ten or fifteen poems. Such topics are rather difficult to handle.[189]

65. On "Waterfowl at Night":

Yūzukuyo	As the evening moon
Mizu naki sora no	Shines down through the ice-sheet
Usugōri	Of a waterless sky,
Kudakanu toko to	Birds cry out as if in complaint
Tori ya nakuran.	Against their unyielding bed.[190]

66. *Moshio*[191] means "seaweed steeped in salt." Therefore, *moshio* may also be used in poems on the topic of "Love and Seaweed." Teika composed a poem with the phrase "pillow of salt-steeped seaweed" (*moshio no makura*).[192] If the word just meant "salt," it could not be used with "pillow."

67. *Maigetsu gohyakushu*[193] is a treatise presented by Teika to the Kamakura Minister of the Right.[194] This kind of easy instruction, with nothing particularly out of the ordinary in it, is very valuable. The kind of treatises that go into all sorts of pretentious details, such as "the meaning of *ashihiki*"[195] and the like, are all the

---

187. *Shika* is the equivalent of modern Japanese *sono yō*.
188. A cloister of Miidera, the popular name of Onjōji, an important Tendai temple located just to the northwest of the capital (modern Ōtsu City). Shōtetsu was a frequent participant in poetry gatherings held there by the priest Chōsan. See Inada 1978:102, 120.
189. The difficulty arises because the topics are so similar, thus requiring the poet to avoid using "wind" when writing about "autumn grasses," and so on.
190. This poem appears nowhere else in Shōtetsu's works.
191. Seaweed was burned to extract its salt.
192. Perhaps referring to the following poem (no. 3) on the topic "Seeing Fireflies by the Seashore" from the *Minase tsuridono rokushu uta-awase* ("Six-Poem Contest at the Fishing Pavilion of the Minase Villa"), a poem contest held in 1202 between Retired Emperor Go-Toba and Teika at the former's Minase villa. "Tell this of me:/ That I rest on my pillow/ Of salt-steeped seaweed/ Like a firefly sleeping fitfully/ On a path of vagrant dreams." (*Suma no ura ya/ moshio no makura/ tobu hotaru/ karine no yumeji/ wabu to kotaeyo.*) *SKT* 5.
193. "Critique of His Lordship's Monthly Set of One Hundred Poems." A reference to Teika's *Maigetsushō*. For a complete translation see Brower 1985.
194. Minamoto no Sanetomo, second Kamakura shogun and a student of Teika's. In fact it is not clear whether the treatise was sent to Sanetomo or perhaps to Kujō Ieyoshi or another of Teika's many students.
195. Many late medieval poetic treatises included long lists of problematic words, offering

work of other poetic houses and not the teachings of Teika. [196] This work is known as *Maigetsushō*[197] In it Teika told the Minister of the Right to "put aside the old styles of *Man'yōshū* for now."[198]

68. On "The Spring Breeze":

Iro ni fuke	Tinge it with your breath,
Kusaki mo haru o	O first breeze quickening the flower
Shiranu ma no	In the heart of man,
Hito no kokoro no	While the plants and trees still slumber,
Hana no hatsukaze.	Unaware that spring has come. [199]

The gist of the poem is that although spring has come, the branches are still wintry and unaware of spring, but the flower in the heart of man[200] quickly tells him of spring's arrival. However, being in his heart, this flower is not visible, and so the speaker asks the breeze if it might blow into it the colors of spring.

69. On "Love in Spring":

Yūmagure	In the dim twilight,
Sore ka to mieshi	I glimpsed her as in a vision
Omokage no	Scarcely seen at all:
Kasumu zo katami	An image brought back by spring haze
Ariake no tsuki.	Against the moon in the dawning sky. [201]

The idea of the poem is that at twilight, when the spring haze spreads over all, he catches a faint glimpse of someone, and thinking that it may be the woman he loves, he cherishes the image carefully in his heart. Then the sight of the moon in the sky at dawn reminds him of that vision and thus becomes a fragile keepsake of her. The imagery of thin clouds wreathing the moon and haze trailing across

definitions, sources, and so on. Shōtetsu's own comments on the meaning of *nage* in section 62 above would of course fall into this same category.

196. By "other poetic houses" Shōtetsu may be thinking of the Nijō house and its supporters such as the poets of the Jōkō'in and the Asukai, accepting only the Reizei house as Teika's legitimate heirs (see the introduction [pp. 6–14]). Alternatively, he may be insisting on a distinction between the "essays" of Teika, including *Maigetsushō*, *Kirihioke*, *Gukenshō*, etc., and the later, more pedantic works of the poetic houses of later days.

197. "Monthly Notes." See n. 193 above. Here Shōtetsu uses the accepted title.

198. In *Maigetsushō* (NKBT 65:127 and Brower 1985:410) Teika cautions to "restrain [him]self for a little while longer from composing in this [archaic] style."

199. *Sōkonshū* 2622.

200. The phrase "the flower in the heart of man" alludes to a famous *KKS* poem (797) by Ono no Komachi: [Headnote: Topic unknown] "A thing that fades/ Without showing any outward change/ In its color—/ Such is the flower in the heart of man/ In the world—the world of love." (*Iro miede/ utsurou mono wa/ yo no naka no/ hito no kokoro no/ hana ni zo arikeru.*)

201. *Sōkonshū* 4443.

the cherry blossoms is not expressed in the poem in so many words but instead is left to the atmosphere of mystery and depth and gentle elegance. Such things lie outside the words of the poem.

70. This poem in *Genji monogatari* would seem to make a good pair with mine:

Sode fureshi	He whose sleeve
Hito koso nakere	Once touched mine is here no more,
Hana no ka no	But his image hovers
Omokage kaoru	In the fragrance of plum blossoms
Haru no akebono.	Floating in the spring dawn.[202]

71. On the topic "Losing at Love," Jūa[203] was criticized for writing,

Shikamagawa	You have won out—
Hito wa kachiji . . .	Like braving your way on foot across the Shikama River . . .

This made him extremely angry. Having the other person win implied that the speaker had lost, he said.[204]

72. Poems by Yakushiji Genka, the lay priest[205]:

Samidare no	A man who knows
Furu no nakamichi	The road through ancient Furu
Shiru hito ya	Of the summer rains
Kawa to minagara	May still make his way across—
Nao wataruran.	Though the path seem a river.[206]

Yūgure no	A snowy heron
Iro naru sagi no	Colored red by the setting sun—

202. From a scene in *Tenarai* ("At Writing Practice") in which Ukifune, sequestered in a nunnery, is remembering her life and loves in the lay world (see *NKBZ* 17:343–44 and Seidensticker 1976, II:1076). The poem as it actually appears in the tale differs slightly from the one Shōtetsu quotes: "He whose sleeve/ Once touched mine is not here to see—/ Yet I catch his scent/ Floating from the blossoms/ Aglow in the spring dawn." (*Sode fureshi/ hito koso miene/ hana no ka no/ sore ka to niou/ haru no akebono.*) The change is a significant one, since Shōtetsu's version employs the word *kaoru*—a direct reference to the character of that name—while the actual poem instead refers to Kaoru's rival, Niou.

203. Perhaps identifiable with a late-fourteenth-century priest of the Konrenji, a temple of the Ji sect located on Fourth Avenue at the eastern border of Kyoto, but Inada 1978:978 argues that it may be a later figure.

204. Source unknown. Jūa's complaint is that having his poem lose implies that the energy expended by its speaker in crossing the river has been in vain.

205. Yakushiji Genka Nyūdō (b. 1308?); lay name Jirō Saemon Kinyoshi. A retainer of the warrior Kō no Moronao (d. 1351) who was active in poetic circles in the mid-fourteenth century. His personal collection, *Genka hōshi shū*, is available in *ST* 5.

206. This poem appears nowhere else in Genka's works.

Shimatsutori   Like a bright flare
Uji o yogawa to   Carried by the cormorant fishers
Kagari sasu nari.   Who make Uji the River of Night.[207]

Onajiku wa   If I had my way,
Waga kakurega no   I would ask that the mountain cherries
Yamazakura   At my hermitage
Hana mo ukiyo no   Might escape the bitter wind that blows
Kaze o nogareyo.   Through this sad, ephemeral world.[208]

These poems are in *Shingoshūishū*.[209]

73. With compound poetic topics,[210] it is the common practice to give two of the four characters their *on* pronunciations and to read the other two in *kun*. However, some topics must only be read all in *on* and others must be read all in *kun*. With the topic, "Remaining Chrysanthemums at the End of Autumn," two characters are read in *kun* and two in *on*.[211]

74. "Are we to look at cherry blossoms only in full bloom, the moon only when it is cloudless?" wrote Kenkō,[212] but apart from him, a person with this kind of sensibility is hardly to be found in the world. Such a temperament is inborn. Kaneyoshi was his name when he was a layman. He seems to have been an official retainer of the Koga or the Tokudaiji.[213] But as he had an appointment as a palace guard,[214] he used to go on duty at the imperial palace, where

207. This poem appears nowhere else in Genka's works.
208. This poem appears nowhere else in Genka's works.
209. "New Later Collection of Gleanings," the twentieth imperial anthology (1383), compiled by Nijō Tametō (1341–81) and Nijō Tameshige. None of the three poems Shōtetsu lists here actually appear in that anthology, later imperial anthologies, or Genka's personal collection.
210. *Musubidai*. Topics consisting of more than two elements: "Remaining Blossoms Seen through the Haze," "A Distant View of the Mountains in Rain," etc.
211. In other words, two are read by their Japanese readings (*kunyomi; kun ni yomu*) and two by their Chinese readings (*onyomi; koe ni yomu*). Thus the example Shōtetsu gives would be read *aki no kure no zangiku*.
212. Yoshida no Kenkō (also read Kaneyoshi; b. 1283). A major Nijō poet who is now known primarily for his *Tsurezuregusa* ("Essays in Idleness," ca. 1330), a book of essays and anecdotes that has been accepted by later generations as a quintessential statement on traditional Japanese aesthetics. The sentence Shōtetsu quotes is from section 137 (*NKBT* 30:201–5 and Keene 1967:115). For a brief sketch of Kenkō's life and translations of a few of his poems, see Carter 1989:174–83.
213. Both middle-ranking court families, the first a branch of the Murakami Genji, the second the Fujiwara. Sources indicate that Kenkō served as a retainer of the Horikawa family, an offshoot of the Koga.
214. *Takiguchi no bushi*, referring to palace guards who stood guard near the Seiryōden. They were under the direction of the Chamberlain's Office (*kurōdodokoro*), in which Kenkō served during the reign of Emperor Go-Nijō (1285–1308; r. 1301–8).

he would often have the privilege of seeing the sovereign himself.[215] He took the tonsure upon the death of Retired Emperor Go-Uda,[216] a refined and elegant reason for experiencing a religious awakening. He was a poetic genius of the first order, and together with Ton'a, Keiun, and Jōben[217] was known as one of the Four Guardian Kings[218] of poetry of his day. His *Tsurezuregusa*[219] is similar in form to Sei Shōnagon's *Makura no sōshi*.[220]

75. Whatever it may be about, a poem by a skilled poet[221] will display some special element of treatment to hold one's interest. Seeing this, the novice will feel envious and will try to compose something similar himself, only to produce a confused jumble of nonsense. So absurd is it that when others ask him, "What does this mean?" he must answer, "I'm afraid I don't understand it myself." One must be very careful about this sort of thing. While still a novice, a person should simply sit down with his fellows and compose verse that is straightforward and easy to understand. If he imitates a poetic master before reaching his level of achievement, he will produce laughable results.

76. Lord Teika wrote in one of his works, "When I asked how a poem should be composed, I was told, 'Follow the tenor of your poetic feelings.' Still today I am constantly reminded of this, a most valuable piece of instruction from my father."[222] Poetic feelings may

215. In general, only those of exceedingly high rank were allowed into the presence of the emperor. Chamberlains of the Sixth Rank (*rokui no kurōdo*), however, were given the privilege of attending on the emperor directly. Kenkō served in such a capacity under Emperor Go-Nijō before being appointed an Assistant Commander in the Military Guards (*hyōe*) of the Left, Junior Third Rank Lower, in 1307. He served in that position until the death of Emperor Go-Nijō the following year.

216. 1267–1324; r. 1274–87. Here once again Shōtetsu is mistaken. In reality it was after the death of Emperor Go-Nijō in 1308 that Kenkō retired from court service, and he took the tonsure in 1313.

217. b. 1256? Father of Keiun. For a brief sketch of his life and translations of a few of his poems, see Carter 1989:184–88.

218. *Shitennō*. Named after the demons who protected the four directions in Indian mythology. Earlier texts exclude Keiun and instead list the poet Nōyo in his place. By Shōtetsu's time, however, Nōyo had been forgotten.

219. See n. 212 above. It is worth noting that our earliest text of Kenkō's work is in Shōtetsu's hand, giving some credence to the claim that it was Imagawa Ryōshun who "discovered" the text, although the story that the latter found the contents of the book pasted in bits and pieces on the walls of Kenkō's hut as wallpaper is almost surely apocryphal (see Keene 1967:xiv–xv). Ryōshun himself says that one of his own servants had served Kenkō as a young man (*Rakusho roken*, in *NKGT* 5:209); other sources indicate that the two were acquainted, giving the traditional story some basis in fact. See Araki 1977:51–54, 91–92.

220. "The Pillow Book of Sei Shōnagon," a famous miscellany written by the mid-Heian court lady Sei Shōnagon, which was the inspiration for Kenkō's work. For a complete translation see Morris 1967.

221. *Etaru mono*, literally "one who has attained."

222. A reference to *Gukenshō* (see *NKGT* 4:354).

be either shallow or deep. While a novice, a person should compose his poem so that it suits the tenor of the poetic feelings of a beginner. For the poet of cultivated sensibility, no matter what he may write, it will be bound to suit the tenor of his poetic feelings.

77. The birch cherry (*kabazakura*) is a single-flowering cherry.[223]

78. A grape-dyed underrobe has the color of the wild grape. A deep grape color is a dark purple. This shade is called grape. You write the characters for "grape" and pronounce them "twisted vine."[224]

79. "The Kamakura Minister of the Right" refers to Sanetomo, the son of General Yoritomo.[225]

80. Henjō's lines "Surely it was not/ To tell me I should be like this"[226] have been borrowed often since ancient times. In someone's poem—I can't remember whose—on autumn leaves, they are incorporated thus: "Surely it was not/ To tell them they should be like this/ That the leaves were dyed."[227] When composing a poem that alludes to one in the imperial collections of the Three Eras[228]— if one takes, for example, the poem "Is this not the moon?/ And is this not the springtime"[229]— it is permissible to take the first line, "Is this not the moon?" and change its position by putting it into one's middle line. The ancients were very insistent that an allusion clearly show the intention to allude to a particular poem.[230]

81. Since ancient times poets have been warned never to take material from an older poem famous for certain lines and try to pass it off as their own—an older poem, that is, that contains what is called a "forbidden phrase," such as "Shining but yet clouded over" (*Utsuru mo kumoru*) or "Even though only I can know" (*Ware nomi*

---

223. An abbreviation of *kaniwazakura*, a flowering plant of the rose family.

224. "Grape-dyed" translates *ebizome*, a compound the second character of which is written with the character 葡 for vine, but pronounced *zome*, "to dye."

225. For information on Sanetomo, see n. 194 above. Minamoto no Yoritomo (1147–1199) was the founder of the Kamakura shogunate.

226. *GSS* 1240 (Miscellaneous). [Headnote: Written down and attached to something when he first shaved his head as a priest] "Surely it was not/ To tell me I should be like this/ That my dear mother/ Used to stroke my long tresses—/ As black as beads of jet." (*Tarachime wa/ kakare tote shimo/ mubatama no/ waga kurokami o/ nadezu ya ariken.*)

227. *Kakare tote shimo/ somezu ya ariken.* Source unknown.

228. *Sandaishū.* The eras of the *Kokinshū* (905), the *Gosenshū* (ca. 951), and the *Shūishū* (ca. 1006).

229. See n. 73 above.

230. A reference to *Maigetsushō*, in which Teika notes that allusion "should be done in such a way that it is clear that the older poem has been used." See *NKBT* 65:132 and Brower 1985:417.

shirite) and the like.[231] It is strictly forbidden to take such lines surreptitiously, as if one had stolen a robe, made it over into a narrow-sleeved underrobe, and worn it as one's own. When taking an older poem as a foundation for one's own, it is absolutely essential that the poet handle it in such a way as to show that he has taken it. Further, one may not take as a foundation poem a composition by a contemporary or even by someone who is dead, unless at least a hundred years have passed.[232]

82. The style of mystery and depth can perhaps be only understood by those who have actually reached that level of accomplishment. What most people seem to understand by mystery and depth is simply the style of overtones,[233] which is not mystery and depth at all. Some people call the style of the sad beauty of things[234] mystery and depth, and so on. But the style of overtones and the style of mystery and depth are completely different from each other even though everyone thinks they are the same. Lord Teika wrote, "The poet Tsurayuki, in ancient times, composed in a style of strength,[235] but he did not compose in the ultimate style of mystery and depth."[236] The style of the sad beauty of things is favored by poets.

83. By "the diversions of fisherwomen" (*ama no susami*) seems to be meant burning salt, raking seaweed, and gathering shellfish.

231. "Forbidden phrase" translates *sei no kotoba* (essentially the equivalent of *nushi aru kotoba*, "words with owners"), i.e., words from old poems that were so distinctive that poets were counseled never to use them. The examples here are *SKKS* 57 (Spring), by Minamoto no Tomochika (fl. ca. 1200–50): [Headnote: From poems presented as a hundred-poem sequence] "At the Bay of Naniwa/ Even the waves, though never hazy,/ Are veiled in haze/ In the reflection of a moon/ Shining but yet clouded over." (*Naniwagata/ kasumanu nami mo/ kasumikeri/ utsuru mo kumoru/ oborozukiyo ni*) and *SKKS* 1035 (Love), by Princess Shikishi (see n. 131 above). Both phrases are noted in Tameie's *Eiga no ittei*. (See *NKGT* 3:398–99 and Brower 1987:421, 425.)

232. Several of Teika's treatises make this same point. See *Kindai shūka* ("Superior Poems of Our Time," 1209, in *NKBT* 65:102–3; Brower and Miner 1967:345–46) and *Eiga taigai* ("An Outline for Composing Uta," ca. 1222, in *NKBT* 65:114).

233. "The style of overtones" translates *yojō no tei*. See the introduction (pp. 51–53).

234. "The style of the sad beauty of things" translates *mono aware tei*; also the "pathetic style." In both *Guhishō* (*NKGT* 4:291–92) and *Sangoki* (*NKGT* 4:315) this style is listed as a sub-category of *ushintei*—the style of "deep feeling" that Teika propounded in his later years. See Brower 1985:412–15.

235. "A style of strength" translates *mono tsuyoki tai*. The reference is to *Kindai shūka* (*NKBT* 65:100; Brower and Miner 1967: 41), in which Tsurayuki's poems are characterized in this way: " . . . a style in which the conception of the poem was clever, the loftiness of tone difficult to achieve, the diction strong, and the effect pleasing and tasteful" (*kokoro takumi ni, take oyobigataku, kotoba tsuyoku sugata omoshiroki sama*).

236. "The ultimate style of mystery and depth" translates *yūgen batsugun*. The term Teika actually uses (*Kindai shūka*, in *NKBT* 65:100; Brower and Miner 1967:41) is *yojō yōen*, or "overtones and ethereal beauty." See the introduction (pp. 51–53) for discussion.

These ordinary humble occupations are called "the diversions of fisherwomen."[237]

84. On "Love and Wind":

Sore naranu	From the heart of one
Hito no kokoro no	No longer what she used to be
Araki kaze	Blows a fierce wind—
Uki mi ni tōru	Dashing against my wretched soul
Aki no hageshisa.	The harsh autumn of her satiety.[238]

Although the violence of the woman's feelings does not blow like the wind, her harsh treatment penetrates the man's being, and his situation is pitiable. As for the five-syllable line, "No longer what she used to be" (*Sore naranu*), I tried every conceivable possibility here. One might say, "Forgetting our love" (*Wasureyuku*) or "Changed from what she was" (*Kawarite yuku*) or a thousand or ten thousand other things. But "Forgetting our love" seems weak to me. "No longer what she used to be" means that she is not even the same person. At first she was all gracious smiles, but now she is harsh and cruel—"not the same person."[239] The use of "autumn of satiety" also answers to this idea very well, since a person who has tired of another is no longer the same person.

85. When it comes to love poetry, nothing from ancient times to the present has been able to equal Teika's poems.

86. On "Love: Waiting":

| Kaze araki | A bitter wind |
| Motoara no kohagi | Blows through tangles of bush clover |

237. Medieval texts often use the word *susami*, literally "amusements" or "diversions," to refer to the arts. Here it is applied to characterize the rather uncertain occupation of women who make their living from the changeable and often dangerous sea. The only example of the phrase in the official anthologies is *Shin'yōshū* ("New Collection of Leaves," 1381; a quasi-imperial anthology compiled at the southern court) 928 (Love), by Emperor Chōkei (1343–94): [Headnote: Among some poems treating various passages from *Genji monogatari*] "Adding yet more bitterness/ To the pain of rejection, of finding/ No seaweed on this shore/ Must be this tale told unasked/ Of the diversions of fisherwomen." (*Mirume naki/ urami wa nao ya/ masaruran/ ama no susabi no/ towazugatari o.*) The emperor's poem alludes to Genji's poem sent to Murasaki along with his letter confessing his affair with the Akashi Lady (see NKBZ 13:249 and Seidensticker 1976, I:264), which also contains the phrase: "My tears rush down/ As do the tides against this shore,/ Where for a moment/ I was entangled in the seaweed/ That is the diversion of fisherwomen." (*Shioshio to/ mazu zo nakaruru/ karisome no/ mirume wa ama no/ susabi naredomo.*)
238. This poem appears nowhere else in Shōtetsu's works.
239. *Sono hito naranu*, a phrase that clarifies the meaning of the pronoun *sore* in *sore naranu* as "that person."

Sode ni mite   Mirrored in my sleeves,
Fukeyuku tsuki ni   That in the light of the sinking moon
Omoru shiratsuyu.   Grow heavy with drops of white dew.[240]

In this poem, Teika has so completely entered into the heart of the topic that even though he does not actually say it, the idea of waiting is felt implicitly. On a first hearing, one would not understand the poem at all, perhaps thinking the poet is making some sort of joke. Nevertheless, because the poet has conceived the poem after thoroughly assimilating himself to the situation of the speaker, it beautifully expresses the very essence of the topic. Gazing out upon the garden, where the bush clover are blooming in profusion, the lady waits for her lover. The wind blows roughly through the tangles of bush clover, breaking off beads of dew and dashing them to the ground. These seem to be the very tears upon her sleeve, and as the moon sinks in the advancing night, ever more tears fall upon her sleeve, which grows heavy under their weight. Thus the poet conceives the idea of the tears vying with the dew on the bush clover and imbues the poem with a profound sense of what it is for the woman to wait for her lover. One may even imagine from the style of the poem that she goes out to the edge of the veranda and sits there sadly, gazing at the garden. Truly, the effect of her experience as she sits waiting all night long in misery is conveyed in a style of gentle and evocative elegance.

87. Tametsugu[241] was the grandson of Takanobu.[242] Nobuzane[243] was Takanobu's son. Nobuzane was the one who painted

---

240. SG 858 (Love). A poem from Roppyaku-ban uta-awase ("Poetry Contest in Six-Hundred Rounds," 1193, in SKT 5:695), a contest sponsored by the regent Yoshitsune, with poems by Teika, Ietaka, the regent himself, Jien, and others; judgments by Shunzei. The first line should read Kaze tsuraki, "A cruel wind," and the fourth, Fukeyuku yowa ni, "That in the deepening night." The poem alludes to KKS 694 (Love), anonymous: "On Miyagi's fields/ Tangles of bush clover droop low/ Under heavy dew,/ Waiting for the wind to come:/ Just as I now wait for you." (Miyagino no/ motoara no kohagi/ tsuyu o omomi/ kaze o matsu goto/ kimi o koso mate.)

241. Fujiwara no Tametsugu (d. 1265). A prominent poet and painter.

242. Fujiwara no Takanobu. Son of Tametsune and Bifuku'mon'in no Kaga (d. 1193), who later married Shunzei, thus making Takanobu the latter's stepson and Teika's brother. In 1202, Takanobu took the tonsure under Hōnen (1133–1212), the founder of the Jōdo (Pure Land) sect of Buddhism. Active as a poet around the time of the compilation of Shinkokinshū, in which three of his poems are included. He was also a prominent painter whose portraits of Minamoto no Yoritomo and Taira no Shigemori (1138–79) are some of the first and finest examples of the genre.

243. Fujiwara no Nobuzane (1177–1265). Son of Takanobu. Active as a poet from around 1200, although not represented in Shinkokinshū. Gained prominence in mid-thirteenth century through contact with both Tameie and the latter's rivals of the Rokujō house.

the portrait of Hitomaro.[244] He was not a professional painter, but from Nobuzane on, the family had traditionally been skilled artists. However, the present head of the Hōjōji family neither writes poetry nor paints.[245]

88. On "Love: Forgetting":

Uki mono to	Forget about me—
Omou kokoro no	So completely that no trace remains
Ato mo naku	Of your resentment
Ware o wasureyo	In thinking me unkind to you.
Kimi wa uramiji.	Then I will hate you no more.[246]

"Love: Forgetting" means that the lover forgets the speaker time and again. It does not mean that the speaker forgets the lover. In this poem, what the lover forgets is his promises. He does not in the least forget that he thinks her cruel and hateful. If he were to completely forget that he thinks her cruel and hateful, then she would be to him as one he had never seen or heard of. If he is to forget her in this way—the poem says—let him make a thorough job of it. Then she would no longer feel any bitterness toward him. What she resents is his refusal to forget that he hates and despises her.

89. Lord Teika, on "Love: Forgetting":

Wasurenu ya	Did we not forget?
Sa wa wasurekeri	Yes, as for that, we did forget
Waga kokoro	That we told each other
Yume ni nase to zo	When we parted on that night
Iite wakareshi.	To think our love but a dream.[247]

This poem is a bit difficult to understand. During the time of Shōjō'in,[248] Kōun[249] and I were asked about the poem, and we each submitted a different interpretation. The general consensus around the capital at the time was said to be that my explanation was the

244. Like his father, Nobuzane was a famous portrait painter.
245. Nobuzane's line was called the Hōjōji. It is unclear to whom Shōtetsu refers here.
246. This poem appears nowhere else in Shōtetsu's works.
247. *SG* 268. Second line should read *sa wa wasurekeru*.
248. Ashikaga Yoshimochi (1386–1428). Fourth of the Ashikaga shoguns.
249. Lay name Kazan'in Nagachika (d. 1429). A poet and scholar of the southern court who returned to the capital after the unification of the courts in 1392 and became a prominent spokesman for the Nijō cause and thus an opponent of Shōtetsu. For a brief sketch of his life and translations of a few of his poems, see Carter 1989:259–64.

correct one. The way I explained it was that, feeling their love union to have been unreal, they told each other that they would think of it as a dream, but they forgot to remember this. They had parted, telling each other to think of their love as a dream and to forget it, but they had not forgotten their love; rather, they had forgotten their promise to forget it. Thus Teika has entered completely into the situation of the lovers, in a most moving way.

It is in his love poetry that Teika has no peer. Ietaka is scarcely less accomplished, but even he cannot match Teika when it comes to love poetry. He may have just a few poems that are up to Teika's standard, such as "Still no word from him—/ So tired he has become of me,"[250] or "Whose promises of love were they/ That bring this end?"[251] According to Kōun, the first line of Teika's poem is a question by the speaker to the beloved and means "Have you forgotten?" (*Wasuretaru ka*).[252]

90.

Yasurai ni	When you left my side,
Idenishi mama no	You seemed so hesitant to leave—
Tsuki no kage	But then you were gone.
Waga namida nomi	And now the moonlight and my tears
Sode ni matedomo.	Wait in vain upon my sleeve.[253]

This poem of Teika's is the epitome of his style of mystery and depth, like his "As we parted,/ The dew on our white hempen sleeves."[254] Such poems are difficult to understand on a quick reading.

250. *SKKS* 1316 (Love). [Headnote: From a poem contest held at the Bureau of Poetry, on the idea of "Love, Deep in the Mountains"] "Still no word from him—/ So tired he has become of me/ As he watches the wind/ Blowing clouds above Yūwa Peak/ On this evening in the mountains." (*Sate mo nao/ towarenu aki no/ yū wa yama/ kumo fuku kaze no/ mine ni miyuramu.*)

251. *SKKS* 1294 (Love). [Headnote: From *Roppyaku-ban uta-awase*] "Remember well!/ Whose promises of love were they/ That bring this end?—/ Fair clouds of yesterday blown away/ By the cold breath of the mountain wind." (*Omoiideyo/ ta ga kanegoto no/ sue naramu/ kinō no kumo no/ ato no yamakaze.*)

252. The modern scholar Kubota Jun seems to favor Kōun's interpretation. See Kubota 1985–86:47.

253. *SG* 876. Headnote: "Love and the Moon."

254. *SKKS* 1336 (Love). [Headnote: From *Fifteen-Round Poem Contest at Minase*] "As we parted,/ The dew on our white hempen sleeves/ Mingled with our tears,/ While the autumn wind struck at my heart/ With a tinge of greater cold to come." (*Shirotae no/ sode no wakare ni/ tsuyu ochite/ mi ni shimu iro no/ akikaze zo fuku.*) Teika's poem alludes to *MYS* 3182, anonymous: [Headnote: On "Sadness at Parting"] "How I dreaded it—/ That parting of the white hempen sleeves/ That covered us in bed,/ But in the tangle of my thoughts/ I allowed your hand to slip away." (*Shirotae no/ sode no wakare wa/ oshikedo mo/ omoimidarete/ yurushitsuru ka mo.*)

91. With regard to accentuation[255] in poetry, it appears that some people hold to certain practices because they are the teachings of Ietaka. As for myself, I know nothing of any teachings but those of the house of Shunzei and Teika.[256] Thus, according to Teika, the correct pronunciation of the word for Japanese paper is not *yamatogami*, but *yamatokami*, with a clear sound and a rising pitch.[257] Consequently, the word *yamatouta* ("Japanese poem") should be pronounced with a falling pitch.

92. The meaning of the lines "Where can it be/ That I shall find some rest tonight?"[258] is that the speaker will have had only a little sleep.

93. When this poem by Tameuji

Hito towaba	If someone should ask,
Mizu to ya iwan	Shall I say I did not see it—
Tamatsushima	Tamatsu Island,
Kasumu irie no	Where haze lay thick across the cove
Haru no akebono.	In the light of dawn in spring?[259]

was being considered by Tameie for inclusion in his imperial anthology, Tameuji asked whether it might perhaps be better to change the second line to "Shall I say I saw it?" (*Mitsu to ya iwan*). Since either way was agreeable to him, he thought he would leave the decision up to Tameie, who was, after all, his own father. Tameie replied that the poem had a perfectly adequate point to it as it was, and that there was nothing wrong with "Shall I say I did not see it?" So he included the poem in *Shokugosenshū*, according to the story.[260]

One may deduce from this the proper style for a poem in an imperial anthology.[261] Here, the speaker gazes out at Tamatsu

255. *Sei no koto*, literally, "voicing."
256. No specific source for the ideas expressed here is known, but it is likely that such matters would be touched upon in the "secret teachings" of the various houses.
257. "With a clear sound and a rising pitch" translates *sumite agaritaru koe.*
258. *SGSIS* 924 (Travel), by Nijō Tamesada. [Headnote: On the idea of "Going on a Journey"] "Where can it be/ That I shall find some rest tonight?/ For all around/ Here in the fields of Inami Moor/ Snow lies deep upon the reeds." (*Izuku ni ka/ koyoi wa sanen/ inami no no/ asaji ga ue mo/ yuki furinikeri.*)
259. *ShokuGSS* 41 (Spring), by Nijō Tameuji. [Headnote: On "Spring View across a Bay," for a contest between Japanese and Chinese poems in the second year of the Kenchō (1250).] The gist of the poem in Tameuji's first version is: "Since I could never describe the sight adequately in words, should I simply tell people I have not seen it?"
260. This same story is contained in Ton'a's *Seiashō* ("Notes of a Frog at the Bottom of a Well," ca. 1360–64, in *NKGT* 5:95–96). However, in Ton'a's version Tameuji's original version uses *mitsu to ya iwan* ("Shall I say I saw it?"), which his father emends to *mizu to ya iwan* ("Shall I say I did not see it?").
261. In other words, a formal poem (*hare no uta*) of the sort that could be considered for inclusion in the most prestigious of court publications.

Island at dawn, when the haze is spread all across the landscape, and wonders whether, if someone should ask him, he ought to say that he has seen it or that he has not seen it. Either way would seem to come to the same thing, but still, "Shall I say I saw it?" would be in a more realistic style.[262]

94. It says in one of Teika's writings, "In poetry there are no teachers. One makes antiquity one's teacher. Provided he steep his mind in the styles of antiquity and learn his diction from the great poets of old, who can fail to compose good poetry?"[263]

95. On formal public occasions, the lector[264] withdraws as soon as all of the poems by the courtiers have been read out loud. Not until these poems are being read does the sovereign take his own poem slip from the folds of his robe and hand it to the regent or chancellor, upon which a new lector comes in. He reads the sovereign's poem seven times. For those in the imperial entourage as well, poems by the regent and the highest court nobles are read three times. Poems by members of the shogun's family have also been read three times in recent years.

96. The topical category "Expressing a Grievance" is different in linked verse than in classical uta and may cover any feeling at all that happens to be in the poet's heart.[265] Because the topic literally means "Expressing One's Feelings,"[266] it is also permitted to include felicitations under this rubric. Thus Teika's poem, "His parent's footprints/ That he thought never to approach"[267] and the like.

262. *Jitsu naru tei. Mizu to ya iwan* might be considered superior because it involves more overtones.

263. A direct quote from the preface to Teika's *Eiga taigai* (NKBT 65:115) in which Shōtetsu has rendered the original Chinese text in Japanese. "Teacher" translates *shishō*.

264. The job of lector (*kōshi*)—who read the poems aloud before the participants at a contest or poetry gathering—was assigned to a man of experience who knew the relevant customs and precedents, which, in a highly stratified court society, were very complex. Araki Hisashi sees the influence of Ryōshun's *Gonjinshū* ("Collection of Verbal Trash," 1406; see Araki 1977:175–76) here. *Guhishō* (NKGT 4:310) presents similar information as well.

265. In waka too this topic usually elicited a lament of some sort, either concerning the loss of youth or failure to advance in court rank or office. Since *jukkai* literally means "expressing one's feelings," however, the uta poet still had the option of making a more positive statement—something the rules of linked verse, which defined the topic partly by its subtopics of reminiscence or transcience, did not allow.

266. See previous note.

267. *SG* 1495. [Headnote: On "Expressing One's Feelings," from *One-Hundred-Poem Sequence of the Chancellor and Minister of the Left*] "His parents' footprints/ That he thought never to approach/ He has now surpassed—/ This dweller on the Bay of Poetry/ Who has reached the heights of the Way." (*Tarachine no/ oyobazu tōki/ ato sugite/ michi o kiwamuru/ waka no urabito.*) This poem was written by Teika in the late spring of 1232, after he had been promoted to Middle Counselor and been appointed sole compiler of the *Shinchokusenshū*, thereby surpassing his father in honors. In spite of the usual connotations of *jukkai*, all his poems on that topic in the 1232 sequence express joy rather than sorrow.

97. When a group of poets are composing a hundred-poem sequence extemporaneously, it will sometimes happen that one of the topics will have been left out because someone has neglected to pick it up, and this will only be discovered when the poem slips are already being collected. At such a time, the missing topic is allotted to the most accomplished poet in the group, who produces his poem immediately upon receiving it. In such a situation, the poet writes his poem straight off without stopping for a moment to think it over.

Ryōshun used to say that he had seen Ton'a demonstrate such poetic mastery on two separate occasions. At a poetry gathering attended by Lord Tamesue,[268] one topic was left over for which no one had composed a poem, and this was discovered only after the poem slips were already being collected. Since Tamehide was performing the task of collecting the poem slips, he assigned the topic to Lord Ton'a to deal with. Without stopping for a moment's thought, Ton'a quickly wrote down his poem, finishing before the poem slips had been completely collected. The topic was "A Visitor Comes After the Plum Blossoms Have Fallen"—a topic that would naturally prove difficult for an ordinary person to handle. So Ryōshun, wondering what kind of verse Ton'a might have produced, listened carefully when the poems were read out, and this was what Ton'a had written:

Towaruru mo	Though unexpected,
Itodo omoi no	Your visit brings me great joy—
Hoka nareba	With consternation,
Tachie no ume wa	Since the plum blossoms on the boughs
Chirisuginikeri.	Have all fallen and passed away.[269]

Again, at another poetry gathering attended by Tamehide along with Ton'a, Keiun, Jōben, and Kenkō—celebrated poets of the day known as the Four Guardian Kings of Japanese Poetry—each of these last chose six topics on which to compose his poems, while Tamehide chose even more. The participants of lower rank who were still novices in the art chose one or two topics apiece. Now Ton'a, having glanced through his six topics, said, "I must excuse myself for a short time. I shall be back as soon as I am free." And depositing

268. Tamesue Kyō. Identity unknown. Hisamatsu hazards that an early scribe may have mistaken the character *hide* 秀 (of Reizei Tamehide, a more likely candidate) for *sue* 季.

269. This poem does not appear in Ton'a's personal anthology, but it is cited by Ryōshun in his *Rakusho roken* (NKGT 5:201), with only one slight difference in the third line, which appears there as *hoka nare ya*.

his six topic slips under a shelf at the side of the room, he went out. Thereupon, Keiun substituted his own six topic slips for those that Ton'a had left.

In due course, when everyone had composed his poems and written them down to be passed in, and people were asking what could be keeping him, Ton'a came back. Picking up the topics he had left behind, he ground some ink and prepared to write his poems, only to discover that these were not his topics, all six of them proving on examination to be different from the topics he had originally chosen. Even so, not a bit flustered, he said, "Well, someone has been playing a trick on me, I see. Who did it?" And he continued to grind his ink, dip in his brush, and quickly write down six poems, one right after the other.

After the poems had been read out loud, Keiun said, "You performed most creditably. It is at a time like this that a poet's true mastery is revealed." Ton'a replied, "What an outrageous thing to have done! You, one of the senior poets, who ought to have been warning the others not to play such tricks!" This was his poem for one of the six topics, "Frost on the Bridge":

Yamabito no	No trace remains
Michi no yukusue	Of the direction taken by the woodsman
Ato mo nashi	As he went his way,
Yo no ma no shimo no	For the jointed bridge at Mama
Mama no tsugihashi.	Is covered with the frost of night.[270]

98. At a poetry contest, the place opposite the marshal[271] is called the principal seat[272] and is occupied by the host or some other individual to whom honor is due. The place of honor above the lecturn[273] is the sovereign's seat. The other participants are packed in close together around the edges of the room next to the lector.

99. "Cherry Blossoms outside the Door at the Vesper Bell"—a good item for a hundred-poem sequence on topics from Chinese verse.[274]

270. Zoku sōanshū 285 ("Later Grass-Hut Collection," 1366?; Miscellaneous). [Headnote: Written when there was a session of "searching for topics" at the home of the regent.] In the Zoku sōanshū version—probably representing an emendation made later by the poet—the first three lines read Kesa wa mada/ Hito no yukiki no/ Ato mo nashi ("Not a trace yet/ Of people coming and going/ On this morning—"). See SKT 4.
271. Dokushi, the man who collects the poem slips, hands them to the lector, and corrects any mistakes the lector might make in reading the poems. See Guhishō (NKGT 4:310).
272. "The principal seat" translates shui, literally "the master's place."
273. The lecturn, or bundai, was a small stand upon which poems were placed.
274. Lines from the works of Po Chü-i (772–846) and other prominent Chinese poets were sometimes used as topics—referred to as kudai, or "line topics."

100. On "Early Spring in the Mountains":

Kuru haru ni	I meet springtime
Ausaka nagara	As it comes to Meeting Hill—
Shirakawa no	Where today the dawn
Seki no to akuru	Seems to break at Shirakawa Gate
Yama no yuki kana.	Over mountains of white snow.[275]

The idea is that he is striding past Meeting Hill, where he seems to greet the dawn of the New Year at the Shirakawa Gate.[276] This treatment may offer a bit of novelty, perhaps.

101. On "Praying for Love":

Aratamaru	If I could build
Chigiri ya aru to	A new shrine with cross-beamed roof
Miyazukuri	To enshrine the god,
Kami o utsushite	My prayers and purifications then
Misogi semashi o.	Might renew our vows of love.[277]

This treatment, too, is not to be found among the old poets.

102. "Spring Dawn at a Famous Place":

Akenikeri	A new day dawns.
Aramashikaba no	If only this scene might also hold
Haru no hana	Spring cherry flowers,
Nagisa ni kasumu	There where haze veils the shore
Shiga no yamamoto.	Along the mountain slopes of Shiga.[278]

In this poem, too, the line "If only this scene might also hold" is an interesting touch. How delightful it would be, says the poem, if only the cherries were blooming in profusion along the mountain slopes of Shiga where the haze spreads across the landscape at dawn.

275. *Sōkonshū* 2380. Headnote: "On 'The Arrival of Spring in the Mountains,' as my first effort on the first day of the new year Bun'an 4 [1447]."

276. Largely because of this famous poem (*GSIS* 518) by Nōin (b. 988), the topic of Shirakawa Gate was always cast in autumn setting: [Headnote: Written at Shirakawa Gate, when he was on a trip to Michinoku] "As haze spread abroad/ I set out on my journey/ From the capital,/ But now the autumn wind blows/ At Shirakawa Gate." (*Miyako o ba/ kasumi to tomo ni/ tachishikado/ akikaze zo fuku/ Shirakawa no seki.*) Here Shōtetsu departs from precedent, saying that seeing the white snow just beyond Ausaka Gate (just to the northeast of the old capital, on the border between Yamashiro and Ōmi) in early spring reminds him of Shirakawa—whose name means "White River."

277. This poem appears as no. 34 in the Notre Dame Seishin Joshi Daigaku text of *Sōkonshū*, under the title, "Praying for Love."

278. *Sōkonshū* 2874. The first word of the fourth line acts as a double entendre, *haru no hana naki*, "without spring blossoms," and *nagisa ni kasumu*, "hazy along the shore."

The idea that there are no cherry blossoms at present is buried in the phrase "veiled in haze along the shore."

103. "A Dream at Dawn":

Akatsuki no	Long past is the time
Nezame wa oi no	When I would awake at dawn—
Mukashi nite	And with increasing age,
Yoi no ma tanomu	Even those dreams have faded now
Yume mo taeniki.	That I trusted early night to bring.[279]

The time when he used to awake at dawn is now long ago, when he was forty or fifty years old and at the beginning of old age. Now he cannot sleep even in the early nighttime.

104. My first attempt at writing poetry was as a child, when I composed a verse and wrote it on the leaf of a tree as an offering to the stars in the seventh month. Every year since then until last autumn, mindful of the virtues of the stars, I have composed seven poems, written them on seven leaves, and offered them to the stars. Also, before I had actually studied how to write verse, I used to attend formal poetry gatherings and practice composition with no thought to the shame I might bring upon myself. My house was at Sanjō and Higashi no Tōin.[280] Across the street, at the house of the commissioner from the Bureau of Civil Administration,[281] there were monthly poetry gatherings attended by more than thirty persons, including Tamemasa and Tamekuni[282] of the Reizei family, the former shogunal deputy Ryōshun, and others closely associated with them.

A certain preceptor of the Ontoku'in[283] once said to me, "If you want to compose poetry, I will take you with me to the civil administrator's house across the way." At that period of my life, I was still wearing my hair long in the manner of young children, and I felt embarrassed about my extreme youth, but nevertheless I went with the preceptor to the civil administrator's house. He was at the time a lay priest of impressive appearance, more than eighty years old, and with white hair. But he came out to meet me and said, "These days, not one of the children studies poetry any more,

---

279. *Sōkonshū* 5059 gives a slightly different version of the poem, with line 3 reading *mukashi made* and the topic simply, "Dream."
280. The location of the house where Shōtetsu lived with his parents as a youth. See the introduction (p. 16).
281. *Bugyō no jibu.* Identity unknown, although Hisamatsu suggests Imagawa Ryōshun.
282. Reizei Tamekuni (precise dates unknown). Father of Tamemasa.
283. Identity unknown.

although when I, Zen'on,[284] was in the prime of youth, I used to hear of such things. It is an elegant and tasteful thing for you to do. We have a monthly poetry gathering[285] here on the twenty-fifth of every month. You are most welcome to attend. The topics for this month are thus and so." So saying, he wrote them down for me with his own hand. There were three poems to write on topics of four characters each: "Peaceful Moonlight Late at Night," "Distant Geese over the Mountains at Dusk," and "Love: No Letter since Parting."

This conversation took place toward the beginning of the eighth month. Then, when I arrived at the poetry meeting itself on the twenty-fifth, the highest places on the one side were occupied by Reizei Tamemasa and Tamekuni, and on the other side by the former shogunal deputy. Next to each of these were seated in order their close associates, together with more than thirty of Zen'on's family members, all ranged down both sides of the room according to rank. Having arrived late, I was invited to take an upper seat, which was very unexpected and embarrassing, but I took my place as directed. The shogunal deputy was at that time a lay priest of more than eighty years. He was dressed in a habit without the black overskirt and had a sash with a long fringe around his waist.

My poem on "Peaceful Moonlight Late at Night":

Itazura ni	To no avail
Fukeyuku sora no	Its radiance lights up a sky
Kage nare ya	Darkening toward dawn—
Hitori nagamuru	The moon of this autumn night
Aki no yo no tsuki.	That I gaze upon alone.[286]

My poem on "Geese" ended something like this:

Yama no ha ni	At the mountain's edge
Hitotsura miyuru	Can be seen a single line in flight—
Hatsukari no koe.	Cries of autumn's first geese.[287]

But I have forgotten the first two lines. I cannot remember my love poem, either.

284. Identity unknown, although Hisamatsu suggests that Zen'on is one of the names of Imagawa Ryōshun.
285. *Tsukinami*. It was the common thing for the poetic houses, as well as poetically inclined military men and court aristocrats, to have monthly poetry meetings at their homes, usually on the same day each month.
286. This poem appears nowhere else in Shōtetsu's works.
287. This poem appears nowhere else in Shōtetsu's works.

After this occasion, I just kept going again and again to those meetings and thus gained experience in poetic composition. I was fourteen years old at the time. Later on, while I was in the service of the abbot of Nara, and then while I was functioning as chief acolyte at the services in the lecture hall on Mount Muro, I had no leisure from my duties, and for a time composed no poetry.[288]

Afterward, following the death of my father,[289] I began to attend poetry gatherings and compose verse again. From the time of the meeting at the house of the civil administrator on down through the years, I had filled thirty-six notebooks with my compositions— more than twenty thousand poems, there must have been. All of these were destroyed in the fire at Imakumano.[290] The poems I have written since then amount to a few less than ten thousand.

105. It is a good thing when not composing poetry to look through the treatises and handbooks, but when one is going to compose a formal poem, one should resolutely put these away and ponder one's poem without them.[291] If one consults the old handbooks as one goes along, writing the poems down a piece at a time, they cannot help but be all the same, and there will be no good ones among them. When a person composes in this fashion, it becomes a habit, and he will find it impossible to write a formal poem in any other way.

Long ago, there were court ladies and such who would write their poems lying down, while others would trim the lamp to give a faint light, and having put themselves into a melancholy mood, contemplate their verse. Saigyō[292] spent his whole life traveling about composing poetry, and he would ponder his verse while on one of his religious pilgrimages, or else he would open the door on the north side of his hermitage a crack and gaze at the moonlight as he wrote. Teika used to remove the shutters on the south side of his

288. See the introduction (pp. 16–17).
289. Shōtetsu's father died in 1400.
290. See the introduction (pp. 25–26).
291. Hisamatsu here notes influence on this section of Shōtetsu's work from *Mumyōshō* ("Nameless Notes," 1211?; see *NKBT* 65:76–77 and Katō 1968:397–98) of Kamo no Chōmei (1155–1216), which describes the approach to composing formal poetry of a number of famous courtiers and court ladies, including Shunzei's Daughter, who is depicted in these terms: "When she is going to compose a formal poem, she first spends several days reading through the anthologies, and, then, after she has read enough, she puts these away, dims her lamp, finds a quiet place, and then sets to her task." Of equal importance, as Hisamatsu notes, are passages in *Guhishō* (*NKGT* 4:302–3) and the passage from *Kirihioke* noted in n. 294 below.
292. 1118–90. A monk-poet who was a friend of Shunzei and one of the major figures of the entire medieval tradition. The first part of Shōtetsu's portrait is taken from *Guhishō* (*NKGT* 4:303), where he is described as "having had the habit of chanting verse to himself while on his religious pilgrimages."

house, sit down in the exact center of the building where he could see far off to the south, and—dressed in strictly correct attire—meditate on his poems.[293] This was good practice so that his mind would not fail him when he had to compose verse on a formal occasion at places such as the imperial palace or the retired emperor's palace. Shunzei would always throw just the top part of a shabby court costume over his shoulders and ponder his verse huddled against a charcoal brazier of paulownia wood.[294] He would never, not even for a moment or two, relax and stretch out at his ease. As for the rest of us, I have found that the poems I have written on awaking from sleep and such times have invariably proved on later inspection to be no good.

106. In the old days, there used to be all manner of difficult rules about how the poem slips should be placed at the lecturn, such as, "Place your poem slip beneath the lecturn, never place it on top of the lecturn," or "The place to the right of the lecturn is the left side when viewed from the facing seats, and since this is the place of particular honor, you must place your poem at the left-hand edge of the lecturn as you face it."

In spite of such complexities, it has become the practice in recent times to keep one's poem slips in a fold of one's robe until the proceedings begin, and then pass them to the person called the inner marshal,[295] who stacks them up on the lecturn.

107. Even when it comes to the character for "poetry" in "Japanese poetry," I was told that a few generations ago it was the custom in the Nijō family to write 歌, and in the Reizei family to write 謌, but that does not mean that this distinction must necessarily be followed when writing the word. It is just that it happened to come about that in the Mikohidari family they usually write the character 謌, and in the Reizei family the character 歌. The character 倭, with the "man radical," means the same as 和. Nevertheless, anything that calls attention to itself is bad, and it is always best to do things no differently from other people.

The masters of old also said that one should keep *Kokinshū* always at hand, and should commit its poems to memory.

293. The south of the home would open onto the garden, which served as a good object of poetic meditation.

294. This portrait of Shunzei appears first in *Kirihioke* (*NKGT* 4:274–75)—the title of which is taken from the "brazier of paulownia wood" over which the aged poet is supposed to have huddled against the cold. A more lengthy version of the same scene appears later in *Sasamegoto* ("Murmured Conversations," 1463, in *NKBT* 66:147), a treatise written by Shōtetsu's student Shinkei.

295. *Uchi no dokushi.* An office that apparently developed later in the medieval period.

Part 2: Tea Talk by the Verdant Cliff
(Seigan chawa)

1. Michikaze,[296] Sukemasa,[297] and Yukinari[298] have been called the skin, the flesh, and the bones of calligraphy.[299] Michikaze wrote in a style imbued with the bones and marrow, Sukemasa in the style of the flesh, and Yukinari's style corresponds to the skin, it is said.[300] The three men lived in more or less the same period. Toward the end of Michikaze's life, Sukemasa appeared, and toward the end of Sukemasa's life, Yukinari appeared. Retired Emperor Fushimi[301]

296. Ono no Michikaze (896–966). A minor court official who went as far as Senior Fourth Lower Rank; also a poet. One of the founders of Japanese calligraphy who was famous for his cursive style. He was extremely popular during his own lifetime, enjoying especially the esteem of Emperor Daigo, at whose command he produced works for the decoration of palaces and temples.
297. Fujiwara no Sukemasa (also read Sari; 944–998). A courtier who rose as high as Third Rank in the court hierarchy. Another famous calligrapher, noted for his flowery and elegant brushwork, which is thought to display uniquely Japanese characteristics.
298. Fujiwara no Yukinari (972–1027). Another official, who rose as high as Major Counselor of the Senior Second Rank at court. In his own day he was favored by the potentate Fujiwara no Michinaga (966–1027), and his reputation continued to grow thereafter, making him the most famous of all classical calligraphers. His precise, flowing style, in contrast to the bold, masculine style of Michikaze, has long been held to represent the epitome of Japanese calligraphic art. In later ages his style was known as the Sesonji style.
299. This characterization originated in *Yūgaku ōrai* ("Instructions on Leisurely Pursuits"; text available in ZGR 13 [item 362], part 2), by Gen'e (1279–1350). Shōtetsu's source, however, was probably *Guhishō* (see NKGT 4:295), which goes on to explicate the metaphor by saying that Michikaze's style is "strong," Yukinari's "soft and pliant," and Sukemasa's somewhere in between.
300. See previous note.
301. See I, 7 and nn. 27 and 28 above.

imitated the calligraphic styles of Michikaze and Sukemasa, but for the Japanese *kana* he developed a manner entirely his own. In the few examples that still survive of Michikaze's and Yukinari's *kana*, the writing is full of gaps, like the footprints of a mouse. *Kana* with the symbols joined together in a beautiful, rounded style was the innovation of Retired Emperor Fushimi. From his time on, the whole court imitated his "palace style."[302] Retired Emperor Go-Fushimi,[303] the Hagiwara cloistered retired emperor,[304] and others all imitated Retired Emperor Fushimi's style. The calligraphy of the Rokujō palace minister, Lord Arifusa,[305] in particular, was an exact copy of Retired Emperor Fushimi's handwriting. Failing to realize this, a great many people treasure examples of his calligraphy, thinking they are by Retired Emperor Fushimi. Their *kana* is particularly alike.

Arifusa is said to have been an ancestor of the Koga family.[306] He was originally called the Zenrinji Middle Counselor. The Shimizudani and other families descended from him.[307] Michikaze and Sukemasa perpetuated the calligraphic styles of the Han dynasty, but the calligraphy of Retired Emperor Fushimi shows mastery of both Chinese and Japanese elements. When compared with examples of the handwriting of Ch'i-ang[308] and Chi-chih,[309] the character of the brushwork is exactly the same. In its blending of both Chinese and Japanese elements, Retired Emperor Fushimi's calligraphy gives an impression similar to that of a room with a set of three scrolls by a Chinese monk hanging in the alcove, together with a set of incense burner, flower vase, and candle stand in antique Chinese bronze, and Japanese folding screens covered with polished gold or silver foil. The handwriting of Shōren'in[310] is like a room

---

302. "Palace style" translates *goshomuki*, literally, the "inclination of the palace."
303. 1288–1336; r. 1298–1301. Son of Emperor Fushimi.
304. Hagiwara Hōkō—Emperor Hanazono (1297–1348; r. 1308–18). Another son of Emperor Fushimi. For a brief sketch of his life and translations of a few of his poems, see Carter 1989:203–14.
305. Rokujō Arifusa (1251–1319). Rose as high as Palace Minister of Junior First Rank. Also famous as a calligrapher.
306. A court family descended from the Murakami Genji. The actual founder of the lineage was Masazane (1059–1127).
307. Also called the Ichijō, though with no connection to the Ichijō that was one of the five regency houses (*gosekke*); Ichijō Saneaki (d. 1420) was a noted calligrapher of Shōtetsu's day. The family actually descended from the Saionji and not the Rokujō.
308. Chao ch'i-ang (1254–1322). A prominent calligrapher and painter of China's Yuan dynasty.
309. Chang chi-chih (1186–1266). A calligrapher of the Southern Sung dynasty whose work, brought back from the continent by Zen monks, was very influential in Japan.
310. Emperor Fushimi's son Son'en (d. 1356), who served as abbot of the powerful Shōren'in, one of the ruling cloisters of the Engakuji branch of the Tendai sect. His followers took Shōren'in as the name of their style.

fitted out with slatted blinds, sliding doors and folding screens of polished gold and silver, and with all of the objects and accessories entirely of Japanese origin. The handwriting of Retired Emperor Go-Kōgon[311] as seen in his letters shows an honesty without pretense, delicate and beautiful[312]; but when it is placed side by side with that of Retired Emperor Fushimi, it cannot match the latter's air of withered elegance and lofty nobility.[313] Go-Kōgon's style is like a beautiful court lady seated within her curtains. Fushimi is like a handsome man in formal court dress proceeding toward the southern pavilion in the imperial palace. When we look in upon the lady behind her curtains, she is beautiful and has a gentle elegance. But if it is a matter of appearing in public, the man in formal court dress has a more elevated dignity and splendor. Such is the character of Retired Emperor Fushimi's hand.

2. Teika wrote that a person should concentrate upon the poetry of the Kanpyō era and before,[314] and this means that one should concentrate upon poetry that is even earlier than *Kokinshū*. Judged in the light of this injunction to steep one's mind in the old poetic styles, the styles of the period of *Goshūishū* are particularly bad.[315] They are pretentious and boastful, like a funny old bronze vessel, which, although Chinese, has been fitted with a twisted spout and fins.[316] For example, on "The First Geese of Autumn":

Harauran	It will blow away
Sogai ni wataru	The tears of the first autumn geese
Hatsukari no	Crossing in a line

311. 1338–74; r. 1352–71. Son of Emperor Kōgon (1313–64; r. 1331–32) and fourth emperor of the northern court during the Nanbokuchō—the era of the southern and northern courts (1332–92).

312. "An honesty without pretense, delicate and beautiful" translates *magiruru mono naku komaka ni utsukushikeredomo.*

313. *Karabite kedakaki.* Here Shōtetsu shows his admiration less ambiguously than in section 7 above.

314. Teika makes the statement twice, once in *Kindai shūka* (NKBT 65:102; Brower and Miner 1967:44) and again in *Maigetsushō* (NKBT 65:136; Brower 1985:422). In both instances Teika refers to the mid-ninth century, or the age of the Six Poetic Immortals. See n. 90 above.

315. *Goshūishū* ("Later Collection of Gleanings," 1087), was the fourth imperial anthology, compiled by Fujiwara no Michitoshi (1047–99). The work had had a bad reputation since at least the time of Shunzei, who criticized the poems of the anthology for "concentrating solely on witty conceptions" (*Korai fūteishō*, in NKBZ 50:292). *Mumyōshō* (NKBT 65:83) offers a similar judgment: "In the age of the *Goshūishū,* poetic styles became more lax and the old styles were neglected. As one of my masters told me, 'The elders of that time apparently did not approve, for when they said a poem was in the "*Goshūishū* style," that meant that it was no good.'"

316. Here Shōtetsu seems to reveal the common medieval bias against needless decoration and adornment, although his own work was attacked by those of his own time for precisely the same faults.

Namida tsuranaru   One after another over the mountains—
Mine no matsukaze.   The wind in the pines on the peaks.[317]

The word *sogai* in this poem means the same as *oisugai*, "to follow in pursuit." The idea of flying in pursuit is conveyed by the expression, "crossing in a line/ one after another." The word *sogagiku* in the lines *Kano miyuru/ Ikebe ni tateru/ Sogagiku no* is held by the school of Toshiyori[318] and others to be the same as *shōwagiku*, and yellow chrysanthemums are called *sogagiku*, it is said. Another interpretation is that a ten-day chrysanthemum that does not last until the ninth day is called *sogagiku*. Just as the thirtieth day of the month is called *misoka*, the tenth day is called *soka*. In the house of Shunzei, *sogagiku* means that the chrysanthemums blooming by the side of the pond are somewhat bent over.[319] Or take the lines, *Sogai ni tateru/ Mine no matsu*[320] ("The pine trees on the peak/ Standing all in a row"), which mean that the pine trees are in a line, one next to the other.

The poem

Ume ga ka o   How many villagers
Iku satobito ka   Breathe in the plum tree's scent?
Kazu ōki   Many are the girls
Okute no ueme . . .   Who plant the late ripening grain . . .[321]

and so on is an amusing verse. This sort of thing would make a good simple background verse[322] in a hundred-poem sequence. The poem

317. Source unknown.
318. Minamoto no Toshiyori (also read Shunrai; 1055–1129). The poem is *SIS* 1120 (Miscellaneous: Autumn), anonymous: [Headnote: Topic unknown] *Kano miyuru/ ikebe ni tateru/ sogagiku no/ shigemi saeda no/ iro no tekorasa.* The meaning of the third and fourth lines of the poem has long been debated. Hashimoto Fumio (in his notes to the poem in *Toshiyori zuinō,* "Toshiyori's Essentials," in *NKBZ* 50:187–88) interprets *sogagiku* as 其が菊 "those chrysanthemums," and *shigami* as しが身 "the thing itself [i.e., the chrysanthemum(s)]" and *saeda* as 小枝 "the branch," arriving at this interpretation of the entire poem: "Far off over there/ Standing at the edge of the pond/ Are chrysanthemums—/ The flowers themselves and their stalks/ Of such a beautiful hue!" Toshiyori, on the other hand, takes *sogagiku* to mean "one-stalk chrysanthemum" and reads the fourth line as *shiga misaeda no* しが下枝の , interpreting it as "itself and the stalk below." Toshiyori bases his argument on a story about how Emperor Ninmyō (833-850), otherwise known as the Shōwa emperor, was so fond of "one-stalk chrysanthemums"—meaning single plants planted separately as opposed to in groups—that people began to call them *shōwagiku*, which eventually was pronounced *sowagiku* 承和菊, obscuring the word's origins. He also notes, as Shōtetsu says, that some people take *sogagiku* to mean "yellow chrysanthemum."
319. A reference to *Korai fūteishō* (*NKBZ* 50:340). Shunzei takes the *soga* in *sogagiku* to be a shortened form of *sogai,* "next to each other."
320. Source unknown.
321. Source unknown.
322. *Yariuta.* A synonym of *ji no uta,* a simple "background" verse. In the structure of poetic

Harauran	They will be swept away—
Sogai ni wataru	Those who each in turn try to ford
Nagarete no	The treacherous currents
Yo o Ujiyama . . .	Of this world, wretched as Mount Uji . . .[323]

expresses the essential truth[324] of the subject.

A good poem is one which, when recited over to oneself, somehow has a poetic feeling in its phrasing, where the flow of the melodic cadence is not constricted by the thought, and which is mysterious and gently elegant. An exceptionally fine poem lies beyond the limits of reason and thought. One cannot tell why it is so. It cannot be explained in words; it can only be felt and experienced of itself.

3. The word *hadare* means a fall of snow that is just heavy enough to make the leaves of the trees and shrubs droop a little (*hadare*).[325] Or else it means a patchy snow. In either case it refers to a light snowfall.

4. "Morning Frost":

Kusa no hara	Just ask of anyone
Tare ni tou to mo	What has become of the grassy fields,
Kono goro ya	And the reply will be:
Asashimo okite	"In this season they are dead and gone,
Karu to kotaen.	Leaving the morning frost behind."[326]

The lines "Just ask of anyone/ What has become of the grassy fields" allude to the old poem in *Sagoromo monogatari*:

Tazunubeki	Even the grassy fields
Kusa no hara sae	That might have helped me in my search
Shimogarete	Are withered by the frost;

sequences, poets were counseled to create an interesting texture by mixing in a few "design" verses (*mon no uta*, involving outstanding rhetorical effects or interesting thematic conceptions) among the more straightforward poems that made up the greater part of the whole. Teika alludes briefly to the concept in *Maigetsushō* (*NKBT* 65:131; Brower 1985:16), as do Tameie in *Eiga no ittei* (see *NKGT* 3:392 and Brower 1987:407) and Ryōshun in *Ben'yōshō* (*NKGT* 5:185, 187). It is in treatises on linked verse, however, that the terms are most clearly defined. See Carter 1987:95–100.

323. Source unknown.

324. "Essential truth" translates *hon'i*, a term encountered frequently in poetic criticism from the time of Shunzei on. The assumption behind it was that each poetic topic or image had an "essence"—often treated as inherent, but actually emerging from its definition as constituted by the tradition—which it was the task of the poet to bring out in his conception.

325. Hisamatsu notes that Shōtetsu's first suggestion here is a false etymology. In actuality, *hadare* means "patchy snow."

326. *Sōkonshū* 4172.

Tare ni towamashi   Of whom can I ask the way to her,
Michishiba no tsuyu.   Vanished like dew on the roadside?[327]

In *Genji monogatari* is the poem with the lines "Would you not search/ Among the grasses in the fields/ To find out where I had gone?"[328] And a later poem:

Shimogare wa   Withered by frost,
Soko to mo miezu   The grassy fields show not a trace
Kusa no hara   Of familiar sights;
Tare ni towamashi   Of whom can I ask the way now
Aki no nagori o.   To the memory of autumn's splendor?[329]

Thus, all of these older poems treat the idea of asking among the grassy fields. But where they all have "Of whom can I ask . . .," I have changed the wording of the foundation poem to "Just ask of anyone" in my poem.

    5. On "Love and Clouds":

Omoiwabi   If in my misery
Kiete tanabiku   I were to fade and trail away
Kumo naraba   Among the clouds,
Aware ya kaken   Would he perhaps feel pity then
Yukusue no sora. For one ending in empty sky?[330]

"Fade and trail away" means that she wishes to die forthwith, the idea being that "If he hears that she is dead, will he then feel some pity for her?"

    6. The lines

Someba zo usuki   So deeply have you dyed my heart
Iro o uramin.   That I resent the pale color of your love.[331]

are on the topic "No Love-Meeting Yet." If they had already met, then *she* might complain of the shallow color of *his* love.

327. From the first part of the second book of *Sagoromo monogatari* ("The Tale of Sagoromo," 1069–72, in *NKBT* 79:199), which describes Sagoromo's sadness after the disappearance of Asukai no Onnagimi.
328. From *Momiji no ga*, "The Festival of the Cherry Blossoms" (*NKBZ* 12:427 and Seidensticker 1976, I:152–53). The scene relates how Genji first encounters Oborozukiyo. The full text of the poem—Oborozukiyo's reply to Genji's advances—reads: "If my wretched soul/ Were to vanish from the world/ Would you not search/ Among the grasses in the fields/ To find out where I had gone?" (*Ukimi yo ni/ yagate kienaba/ tazunete mo/ kusa no hara o ba/ towaji to ya omou.*)
329. *SKKS* 617 (Winter), by Shunzei's Daughter. Headnote: Topic unknown.
330. This poem appears nowhere else in Shōtetsu's works.
331. Source unknown.

7. When I wrote the poem

Okitsukaze	The wind from the sea
Isago o aguru	Blows the sand against the shore
Hama no ishi ni	And upon the rocks—
Sonarete furuki	Its voice sighing among pines
Matsu no koe kana.	Twisted and bent down with age.[332]

I had Lord Ietaka's poem floating in the back of my mind:

Hamamatsu no	In the voice of the wind
Kozue no kaze ni	High in the pine trees on the beach—
Toshi furite	A single cry
Tsuki ni sabitaru	From a crane grown aged with the years,
Tsuru no hitokoe.	Sounding lonely beneath the moon.[333]

The effect of this poem is to make one feel as if one were looking at a scene that is not actually visible to the eyes, with moss growing on the boulders old through thousands of years of stars and frosts. The poem gives one the feeling of seeing the abode of an immortal. It is in the style of vigor and strength[334] and is not at all a poem in the style of mystery and depth.

8. The phrase "field of pines" (*matsubara*) should not be used in poetry under ordinary circumstances.[335]

9. For the topic "The Orange Tree at My Cottage Grows over the Border of Pebbles," if one uses such a phrase as "the jeweled border of pebbles" (*tama no migiri*) in one's poem, that of course takes care of it. But if one employs instead a word like "eaves," "bed," or "garden," the idea of the border of pebbles is implied.[336]

10. Following a poetic function attended by Jōkō'in,[337] the captain of the Horse Guards, the lay priest Chiun,[338] and others,

332. This poem appears nowhere else in Shōtetsu's works.
333. *Minishū* 185 (Miscellaneous). Headnote: "Crane."
334. "The style of vigor and strength" translates *futō takumashiki uta no tei*. Not one of the much-noted "ten styles," but perhaps related to the "lofty style" (*taketakaki yō*), according to Hisamatsu.
335. A confusing comment, since the phrase occurs once in Shōtetsu's own personal collection (*Sōkonshū* 573), several times in Tamemasa's personal collection (*Tamemasa senshu* 449, 839; see *SKT* 4), and in earlier poems by Retired Emperor Go-Toba, Izumi Shikibu, and others.
336. Here again, Shōtetsu gives practical counsel about the proper treatment of topics. See nn. 168, 169, and 171 above.
337. The poet Gyōkō, a great-great grandson of Ton'a and thus one of Shōtetsu's arch rivals, who had acted as librarian for the Asukai family during the compilation of *Shinzokukokinshū*. The Jōkō'in, head residence for the heir of the line since the time of Gyōkō's father Gyōjin (d. 1412), was one of the cloisters of the Ninnaji temple. For a brief sketch of Gyōkō's life and translations of a few of his poems, see Carter 1989:285–93.
338. d. 1448. Lay name Ninagawa Chikamasa. A shogunal bureaucrat and renga poet; reputed to be the author of the second part of *Shōtetsu monogatari*.

there was a debate about which poem by the old poetic immortals each would most like to have written himself, and everyone wrote his choice and handed it in. Jōkō'in submitted the poem by his great-grandfather, Ton'a:

Fukuru yo no	In the depths of night—
Kawaoto nagara	The sound of the river flowing on,
Yamashiro no	And the moonlight
Mizuno no sato ni	Shining clear above the village
Sumeru tsukikage.	Of Mizuno in Yamashiro.³³⁹

The lay priest Chiun wrote down the following poem and passed it in:

Ayashiki zo	How strange it is—
Kaesa wa tsuki no	That the moon as I go home
Kumorinishi	Has clouded over.
Mukashigatari ni	Can the night have grown so late
Yo ya fukenuran.	While we told stories of the past?³⁴⁰

The Captain of the Horse Guards submitted Shimotsuke's poem:

Wasurarenu	Though unforgotten,
Mukashi wa tōku	The past has receded far away
Narihatete	Into the distance;
Kotoshi mo fuyu wa	Yet this year, too, the winter brings
Shigure kinikeri.	Showers of cold rain and tears.³⁴¹

None of their own poems could equal these, they said. And the story goes that every time they recited these poems they were moved to tears.

---

339. Poem 544 (Autumn) in Ton'a's personal collection, Sōanshū ("Collection of the Hermit's Cottage," ca. 1359, in SKT 4). Headnote: "The Moon in a Village."
340. SKKS 1548 (Miscellaneous), by the Reverend Gyōhen (d. 1264), Major Archbishop of Ninnaji and Head Priest of Tōji. Headnote: I was with Teika on a bright, moonlit night, and he asked me when I had begun to be so devoted to poetry. I replied that it was when I was young and had for a long time been in the company of Saigyō, learning from him. After relating what Saigyō had said to me in those days, I went home, and sent Teika this poem the next morning. This same anecdote is recounted by Ryōshun (Rakusho roken, in NKGT 5:205), who mistakenly attributes the poem to Saigyō.
341. Source unknown. The "captain of the Horse Guards" (tenkyū) probably refers to Hosokawa Mochikata (also read Dōken, d. 1468), who is listed as Hosokawa Tenkyū in Shinkei's Hitorigoto ("Talking to Myself," 1468). See Inada 1978:122 and NST 23:468.

11. Once Ton'a and his son, Seal of the Law Kyōken,[342] attended a poetry party celebrating the seventh night of the seventh month. Kyōken drew the topic, "Birds on the Seventh Night," composed his poem, and showed it to Ton'a, who tossed it back to him with the comment, "I never would have expected this." So Kyōken composed a new poem and showed it to him, but again he tossed it back. Once more he composed a poem and showed it to Ton'a, and this time, too, he returned it saying, "This won't do either." "What should I do, then?" asked Kyōken. Ton'a replied, "Surely you know that for the seventh night there is a certain bird that must be treated in your poem."[343] So Kyōken composed his poem accordingly and showed it to him, and this time he made no objections.

People examined the verse while the poems were being read aloud, and the birds were magpies. His earlier poems had treated different birds, but such is the way with the Nijō family that they will not tolerate the slightest divergence from tradition. For "Birds on the Seventh Night," it must always be magpies, no matter how many times they are used. And while writing about magpies among the stars, the poet must strive to bring some novelty of treatment to his poetic conception. This is a perfectly valid way to proceed at the outset. But when one has to compose five or six poems on topics relating to the seventh night, it should be permissible to write about wild geese or other birds as well.

12. On the day of a poetry gathering for which the topics have been assigned in advance,[344] a person should not burden himself with a lot of rough drafts written on pocket paper.[345] On an occasion when the topics have been handed out ahead of time, one should on some earlier day seek out the person whom one normally consults about such matters, ask him for comments and corrections,

---

342. Kyōken Hōin (fl. ca. 1360–70). Gyōjin's father; poet of the Nijō school who was a participant in poetic circles at the time of Nijō Yoshimoto.

343. The background of this anecdote involves the ancient Chinese story of the Herdboy (Altair) and the Weaver Maiden (Vega), lovers who are kept apart all the nights of the year except for the seventh of the seventh month (*tanabata*), when they are allowed to meet on the bridge of the Milky Way. As Shōtetsu notes below, the bird Ton'a insists upon is the magpie, because of its long-standing association—based on early poems that describe the River of Heaven as a "bridge of magpie wings"—with *tanabata*. This anecdote about Ton'a appears first in Ryōshun's *Gonjinshū* (see Araki 1977:175), where it is also used as an illustration of Ton'a's rigid conservatism.

344. *Kenjitsu no kai*, a poetry gathering in preparation for which assigned topics were sent out in advance—as opposed to a meeting where topics were handed out for immediate response (see n. 37 above).

345. See n. 54 above.

rewrite one's poems in the light of his opinions, and then on the day of the party simply take these revised versions along. Poems written on pocket paper must not be crossed out or written over. This is because with these, too, one should be prepared in advance. Poem strips,[346] however, are written on extemporaneously, and they may be crossed out as much as one likes without embarrassment.

13. Stacking the poems[347] at a poetry gathering is a matter of the utmost importance. It is very difficult because they must be collected and stacked in sequence according to the participants' court rank and family standing. The stacking procedure is easy at a gathering attended solely by court nobles because their official titles and court ranks are in an established order. The procedure is difficult when the party consists of both court nobles and members of the military aristocracy. During the time of Shōjō'in, a poem by Lord Asukai,[348] who had the official title of Middle Counselor and Senior Second court rank, was placed on top of a poem by Gansei'in,[349] who was the shogunal deputy. The latter objected, saying that inasmuch as he was now the chief administrator of the realm, his poem should take precedence over Lord Asukai's. However, it was pointed out that as the office of shogunal deputy is equivalent to the imperial court position of Consultant, his poem should not be placed on top of one by a Middle Counselor, and his objection was overruled.

14. At an impromptu poetry gathering, the poem slips of the younger members of the group are written last and submitted first. When old and young are in attendance, one or two ink stones are pushed from one person to the next, with the elders and seniors writing first and the young ones in the lowest seats writing last. Notwithstanding, they must be the first to pass in their poem slips to the master of the topics. No matter how quickly they may think of their poems, the junior members must not write them down before the senior members have finished. This rule must be scrupulously observed. The elders may ponder their poems as long as

---

346. *Tanzaku*, long strips of bamboo upon which poems would be written, in the early days; later, long strips of stiff paper were used for the same purpose.

347. Poems were stacked on the dais—the order strictly prescribed by the ranks of the participants—after composition. To know the proper rules and precedents for such matters was of course of great importance to *jige* poets (commoners without court rank) such as Shōtetsu. Ryōshun discusses the same matter in *Gonjinshū* (see Araki 1977:175).

348. Probably a reference to Asukai Masayori (1358–1428), father of Masayo and a rival of Shōtetsu's who was a prominent figure of the literary coterie surrounding the shogun Ashikaga Yoshimitsu (1358–1408). For a brief sketch of his life and translations of a few of his poems, see Carter 1989:279–84.

349. Lay name Hosokawa Mitsumoto (1378–1426), shogunal deputy (*kanrei*) from 1412–21.

they like, but for the younger members in the lowest seats to take a long time over their verses and be slow in turning them in is extremely bad manners. As far as reading the poems to one another is concerned, in the old days they did not do as they do today, with everyone showing everyone else his poem written on a piece of folded paper. Instead, people sitting near one another would ask each other's opinion and offer criticisms, such as, "It should not be expressed this way in this particular place," and the like. Not like today, when there is such a hubbub all over the place that extemporaneous poetry meetings have become confused, unpleasant affairs.

15. Once, Kiyosuke[350] accompanied His Majesty on an imperial visit to Uji.[351] A poetry party was held, and everyone else had finished his poem except for Kiyosuke, who spent a long time thinking about his verse and handed it in late. Because it was Kiyosuke, the others overlooked his behavior and no one objected even though he was very slow with his composition. The poem:

Toshi henuru	So many are your years,
Uji no hashimori	O guardian of the bridge of Uji,
Koto towamu	That I must ask you:
Ikuyo ni narinu	How many ages have flowed on by
Mizu no minakami.	Since these pure waters first began?[352]

He had composed the whole of the poem from "O guardian of the bridge of Uji" to the end but was unable to think of a suitable first line and therefore took a long time trying to produce one. Finally, still perplexed after having taken far too long over the business, he

350. [Fujiwara no] Rokujō Kiyosuke. Son of Akisuke (1090–1155) and scion of the Rokujō poetic family, author of two important works of poetic criticism and lore, Ōgishō ("Notes on the Inner Secrets," 1124–44) and Fukuro sōshi. After the death of his father, he became a major contest judge and teacher, taking part in debates of the time as an opponent of Shunzei and the Mikohidari house.

351. Uji is a picturesque area south of Kyoto that has always attracted poets. The occasion of Kiyosuke's poem was not an imperial progress, as Shōtetsu mistakenly asserts, but a gathering held at the Uji Estate of [Fujiwara no] Matsudono Motofusa (1144–1230).

352. SKKS 743 (Felicitations). Headnote: Composed at Uji in the first year of Koō (1169), when the lay priest, former chancellor/prime minister, and some other people wrote poems on the topic, "The Waters of the River are Eternally Clear." The poem alludes to KKS 904 (Miscellaneous), anonymous: [Headnote: Topic unknown] "It is with you,/ O guardian of the bridge of Uji/ Of the rippling waves,/ That I feel a kind of sympathy,/ For you too have seen the ages pass." Chihayaburu/ Uji no hashimori/ nare o shi zo/ aware to wa omou/ toshi no henureba.) A different version of this anecdote is recounted in greater detail in Yakumo mishō (see NKGT supp. 3:439), according to which Kiyosuke had only come up with the last two lines by the time the party was over and had to hand it in at last in draft form. Juntoku comments that Kiyosuke had taken so long in coming up with two lines that there was no time to complete the rest of the poem. The anecdote is cited as an example of a case in which a poet pondered all day long over something and was still unable to produce a poem.

wrote the line "So many are your years" in small script as if it were a kind of note, and handed in the poem. It is indeed an unsatisfactory first line.

16. A nonsense poem[353] is one in which each and every line is about something completely different. For example, in *Man'yōshū*:

Waga koi wa	My love is like
Shōji no hikite	The hand-pull on a sliding door,
Mine no matsu	Pine trees on the peaks,
Hiuchibukuro no	The song of a warbler heard
Uguisu no koe.	In a bag of tinder tools.[354]

Waga seko ga	Broken stones
Tōsagi no o no	In the loincloth strings
Tsubureishi	Of my lover;
Kotoi no ushi no	Pimples on the saddle
Kura no ue no kasa.	Of a powerful ox.[355]

Hōshira ga	Use the stubble
Hige no sorikui	On the silly priest's chin
Uma tsunagu	to tether a horse!
Itaku na hiki so	But don't pull too hard:
Kagiri nagara mo.	There's a limit, after all![356]

17. Prince Munetaka[357] is said to have been criticized for his tendency to inject an element of "Expressing a Grievance" even into his poems on the four seasons. However, the pathetic style[358] should

353. *Mushin shojaku no uta; kokoro no tsuku tokoro nashi no uta.* A poem that makes no sense. The term comes from *Mumyōshō* (NKBT 65:87) of Kamo no Chōmei.

354. Hisamatsu notes that this poem does not appear in *MYS*, but does appear as an anonymous poem in *Kokin ikyokushū* ("Collection of Barbarian Songs, Ancient and Modern"), an early Edo-period collection of *kyōka*, or humorous uta, from previous ages.

355. This is a confusion of two nonsense poems in *MYS* (3838 and 3839, the first three lines coming from the latter and the last two from the former). The two are preceded by the headnote, "Two poems that do not make sense," and a postscript says they were composed by the imperial attendant Ahe no Kōji in response to a challenge by Prince Toneri that he would give a bag of coins to the one who could compose a poem "that could not be made sense of."

356. *MYS* 3846. Headnote: A poem making fun of priests. In the actual *MYS* version, the third line reads *uma tsunagi*, and the last line reads *hōshi wa nakamu*, "or priests will cry."

357. Munetaka Shinnō (1242–74). A son of Emperor Go-Saga (1220–72; r. 1242–46) who served as sixth of the Kamakura shoguns. In 1266 he attempted to free himself from the control of the powerful Hōjō family, but was unsuccessful. He took the tonsure with the Buddhist name Kakue in 1272. While shogun, he was active in the arts, especially kickball (*kemari*), poetry, and music.

358. See n. 234 above.

be mastered by every poet. If you write in this style in preference to the others, the results may be tolerable, but it really depends on your innate poetic inclinations. When composing in the pathetic style, if you say in your poem, "Oh, how pathetic!" in the attempt to create the effect of pathos, the result will not be the pathetic style at all. It is poems that somehow or other have a subtly pathetic feeling that are in the pathetic style. Shunzei's poems are in this style. Such poems as his

| Shimeokite | My grave is ready, |
| Ima wa to omou . . . | And I expect to go at any time . . .[359] |

or his

| Ozasahara | A drop of dew |
| Kaze matsu tsuyu no | Clinging to the bamboo grass . . .[360] |

have this subtle quality of pathos.

18. Poems by participants in the *Horikawa hyakushu*[361] may be used as foundation poems for allusive variations even though they have been only recently included in imperial anthologies. Poems by the Horikawa poets that have not been included in imperial anthologies may be used as evidence to justify poetic usage, but they may not be used as foundation poems.

19. The word *mashimizu* is the same as just *shimizu*, "pure water." It means "true pure water."

359. *SKKS* 1560 (Miscellaneous). [Headnote: Presented to the retired emperor when he was commanded to compose a sequence of one hundred poems after he was well past eighty years old] "My grave is ready,/ and I expect to go at any time/ To the autumn hills/ Where beneath the tangled wormwood/ The pine crickets cry, waiting for me." (*Shimeokite/ ima ya to omou/ akiyama no/ yomogi ga moto ni/ matsumushi no naku.*) This poem is listed in *Gukenshō* (*NKGT* 4:356) as an example of *monoaware tei*.

360. *SKKS* 1822 (Miscellaneous). [Headnote: When he was ill and thought himself near death, Shunzei sent this poem to Norimitsu, the Minister of Popular Affairs, as a petition to have Teika promoted to the office of Middle Captain] "A drop of dew clings/ To the bamboo grass,/ Waiting on the wind:/ So at this juncture I hang on,/ My thoughts concerned for my son." (*Ozasahara/ kaze matsu tsuyu no/ kieyarazu/ kono hitofushi o/ omoioku kana.*) This poem is listed in both *Gukenshō* (*NKGT* 4:356) and *Sangoki* (*NKGT* 4:318) as an example of *monoaware tei*.

361. *Horikawa hyakushu*, a collection of hundred-poem sequences by fifteen or sixteen poets—including Minamoto no Toshiyori, Fujiwara no Mototoshi (1060–1142), and Ōe no Masafusa (1041–1111)—presented to Emperor Horikawa (1079–1107; r. 1086–1107) in 1105 and 1106. Text available in *SKT* 4. Evidently the idea for the project originated with Toshiyori, with the emperor becoming involved only later as a sponsor. The topics for the sequences were chosen by Masafusa. Ton'a limits allusion in this way in *Gumon kenchū* (1363, in *NKGT* 5:131), setting a standard that both uta and renga poets repeated in their treatises for years to come. In his *Kinrai fūteishō* (*NKGT* 5:144), however, Nijō Yoshimoto makes it clear that by his day people also used poems from as late as *Shinkokinshū* as foundation poems.

20. Once when I was composing a sequence of a hundred poems as a religious offering[362]—I do not recall the occasion—it was decided that the topics should be written down in accordance with instructions from the god. Even among hundred-poem sequences there are some of inauspicious precedent, and if the topics are chosen badly they will be subject to criticism. An example of inauspicious precedent would be when the sovereign died before the hundred-poem sequences were finished.[363]

21. *Jikkinshō* was the work of Lord Tamenaga,[364] I believe. He was a poetic immortal, an authority on ancient customs and practices,[365] and a skilled calligrapher. Because he was an official at court, he considered himself to be first and foremost a man of letters. He wrote a number of interesting things in his book. I used to own a copy myself, but it was lost in the fire at Imakumano.

22. *Makura no sōshi* was written down in no particular order. It consists of three books. *Tsurezuregusa* was written in the tradition of *Makura no sōshi.*[366]

23. The lines "But if he is to visit me at all/ Oh, let him come to me tonight"[367] are a rather unpleasant way of expressing a woman's feelings. At least they would be unpleasant if they were sent in a letter to the lover, saying, "If you are to visit me at all,/ Oh, please come to me tonight." But if they are uttered while the woman is all alone, they have a pathetic beauty, or so it is written.

24. The poem by the Reverend Jichin written for the "Sets of Poems in Three Styles,"[368] with the line "Though not asleep, I am

362. *Hōraku*, referring to poems—usually sequences—presented at shrines to display gratitude or, more often, to supplicate the gods for needed favors. The practice is said to have begun in the age of *Shinkokinshū*. In Shōtetsu's day, the shrines most frequently honored in this way were the Sumiyoshi Shrine in Settsu and the Kitano Shrine just outside Kyoto to the northwest. The first volume of his own personal anthology records several hundred-poem sequences offered to temples and shrines.

363. Here Shōtetsu may be alluding to recent history, remembering that Retired Emperor Go-Komatsu had died (on the twentieth day of the tenth month of 1433) just a month after sequences had been requested (on the twenty-second day of the ninth month of the same year) in preparation for the *Shinzokukokinshū*.

364. "Ten Moral Teachings" (1252), a collection of cautionary tales; of unknown authorship. Among medieval writers, only Shōtetsu avers the poet-scholar Sugawara no Tamenaga (1158–1246) as the book's author. If the traditional date of the work is correct, however, Tamenaga obviously cannot be the author.

365. "Ancient customs and practices" translates *yusoku*. As a Doctor of Letters, Tamenaga studied ancient diaries and documents in order to serve as a consultant on proper rites and observances at court.

366. See nn. 212 and 220 above.

367. *SKKS* 1329. See n. 130 above.

368. *Santai waka* ("Poems in Three Styles," 1202, in *SKT 5*). Poems commissioned by Retired

awakened," is truly marvelous.[369] First, the expression "I am awakened" means that as he sits there awake during the evening, he is startled on hearing the cuckoo. Failing to understand this, one might say, "If he has not fallen asleep, how can he be awakened?" This may seem reasonable, but such an argument is not worth bothering about. Marvelous as this line is, could any skilled poet have conceived of it? Even supposing he had done so, such a poet would say in his first lines something like, "As evening falls,/ I gaze at the edges of the clouds" (*Yūsare no/ Kumo no hatate o/ Nagamete*) or "In the evening hours,/ I gaze up at the moon" (*Yoi no ma ni/ Tsuki o mite*). But the way this poem has it—"In the gathering dusk/ Over Mizu pasture, where they reap/ The wild grain"—is simply beyond the capacity of the average poet. This marvelous quality that transcends reason is something that no one can achieve deliberately. To be able to combine such diverse materials in this fashion is the accomplishment of a poet who has attained complete freedom in his art.

His poem on spring has an expansive quality:

Yoshinogawa	On Yoshino River,
Hana no oto shite	I seem to hear the blossoms falling
Nagarumeri	And flowing away,
Kasumi no uchi no	While concealed within a veil of haze,
Kaze mo todoro ni.	The wind echoes against the hills.[370]

Also, his poem on autumn:

Aki fukaki	Deep into autumn,
Awaji no shima no	Dawn breaks over Awaji Isle,
Ariake ni	Where the sinking moon
Katabuku tsuki o	Is seen off in a last farewell
Okuru urakaze.	By the wind from off the bay.[371]

Emperor Go-Toba from Yoshitsune, Jien, Teika, Ietaka, Jakuren, Chōmei, and Ariie (Masatsune was asked, too, but proved unequal to the task and withdrew) for a meeting at the Poetry Bureau. Each poet was required to write six poems in three major styles, according to this scheme, as given in Teika's diary: one spring and one summer, in the grand, strong style (*ōki ni futoki uta*); one autumn and one winter, in the withered style (*karabi, yase sugoki*); and one love and one travel, in the style of elegance (*en tei*).

369. *Santai waka* 894 (Summer), in *SKT* 5. "In the gathering dusk/ Of Mizu pasture, where they reap/ The wild grain,/ Though not asleep, I am awakened/ By the cuckoo's song." (*Makomo karu/ mizu no mimaki no/ yūmagure/ nenu ni mezamuru/ hototogisu kana.*)
370. *Santai waka* 13 (Spring), in *SKT* 5.
371. *Santai waka* 15 (Autumn), in *SKT* 5.

25. On "Birds in the Summer Trees" at the residence of the
Senior Assistant Minister of Palace Repairs[372]:

Hototogisu	Again the cuckoo
Mata hitokoe ni	Vouchsafes but a single song
Narinikeri	And then is silent
Ono ga satsuki no	In its hiding place amid the cedars
Sugi no kogakure.	Of the fifth month that is its own.[373]

The lines "Again the cuckoo/ Vouchsafes but a single song/ And
then is silent" are somewhat expansive. But even if I had said "a
thousand songs" or "a hundred songs," the poem might nevertheless
have had a smallness about it.

26. On "Praying for Love" for a poetry gathering at a certain
place:

Omoine no	If the god came down
Makura no chiri ni	To mingle with the dust upon the pillow
Majiwaraba	Where I lie in misery,
Ayumi o hakobu	No need would I have to turn my steps
Kami ya nakaran.	Toward his sacred shrine.[374]

The phrase "turn my steps" satisfactorily conveys the idea of walking
to a shrine to pray.

The day after writing this poem, I again drew the topic
"Praying for Love" at a gathering at the residence of the Senior
Assistant Minister of Palace Repairs. I thought of submitting a
revised version of the earlier verse, but deciding that this was a
rather weak thing to do, I composed the following:

Sono kami no	If love be the way
Megami ogami no	Established by the parent gods
Michi araba	At earth's beginning,
Koi ni misogi o	Then surely they will look with favor
Kami ya ukemashi.	On the lustrations that I do for her.[375]

---

372. *Shōsaku*, the Chinese title for *shurishiki*, the office of palace repairs. Hisamatsu suggests
the lay monk Hatakeyama Kenryō (Yoshitada; d. 1463), who appears in *Sōkonshū*.
Inada (1978:122, 93–115) makes the same identification. The name Hatakeyama
Shōsaku also appears in *Hitorigoto* (*NKST* 23:468).
373. *Sōkonshū* 3252.
374. *Sōkonshū* 4408.
375. A similar poem appears in *Sōkonshū* (4405, on "Praying for Love"): "If love be the way/
Established by the parent gods/ In ancient days,/ Then now too they will look with
favor/ On the lustrations that I do for her." (*Inishie no/ megami ogami no/ shirushi
arabal koi ni misogi o/ nao ya ukemashi.*) Inada suggests that here Shōtetsu may have
"recycled" an older poem, creating a slightly different poem for a new occasion. See
Inada 1978:367–68.

As there are a number of different occasions when ritual lustrations are performed, such as the purification of the sixth month, I used "lustrations" to suggest love. So he said.[376]

27. I have written numerous poems on the topic "Love: Returning Home From Her Gate" but have never yet written one on "Being in Love with Two Persons Equally." Also, I have never, to the best of my recollection, heard of this topic occurring at a poetry gathering. On the topic "Love: Returning Home From Her Gate," there is the poem in *Gosenshū*:

Naruto yori	Worse than a boat
Sashiidasareshi	Pushed out upon the perilous waves
Fune yori mo	From the gate of Naruto
Ware zo yorube mo	Is my plight—I who wander now,
Naki kokochi suru.	Having lost my bearings over you.[377]

28. I composed the following poem on the topic "A Love Bond on a Journey":

Yadori karu	From a passing shower
Hitomurasame o	I took refuge for just a moment—
Chigiri nite	Yet the bond was made,
Yukue mo shiboru	And now in parting I wring my sleeves,
Sode no wakareji.	Tear-drenched on the road from you.[378]

The poem was praised by Lord Asukai[379] and others.

29. The phrase "the shrike burrowing in the grass" (*mozu no kusagiku*) may be used both in a poem on "Love: Having Forgotten Where She Lives" and "A Love Bond on a Journey." "Asking an Intermediary to Convey One's Love" is a difficult topic.[380]

376. "So he said" translates *un un*. It is comments like this one that make scholars believe that *Shōtetsu monogatari* is a compendium of anecdotes and teachings written down by one of Shōtetsu's disciples.
377. GSS 651 (Love), by Fujiwara no Shigemoto (d. 931). Headnote: By the door known as the Naruto Gate in the palace of the crown prince, Shigemoto was speaking with a woman whose mother shut the door and led her inside. Shigemoto sent this poem the next morning.
378. This poem appears nowhere else in Shōtetsu's works.
379. Hisamatsu suggests Asukai Masachika (1417–90) as a candidate here. Other possibilities are Asukai Masayori (see n. 348 above) or Asukai Masayo.
380. There are various interpretations of the phrase *mozu no kusagiku*, the most common being that the disappearance of shrikes in the spring is due to their "burrowing in the grass," and thus out of sight. Shōtetsu sees the phrase as appropriate to love poems involving separation or disappearance. *Sōkonshū* records a poem (4445) by Shōtetsu on the last topic mentioned, although it does not include the phrase in question. "Please pass on to her/ This dew of tears wrung from my sleeve,/ O evening wind,/ Blowing across the field of grass/ Upon the selfsame moor as hers." (*Sode shiboru/ tsuyu o tsutaeyo/ onaji no no/ yukari no kusa no/ hara no yūkaze.*)

30. Among Keiun's children was one called Keikō. He lived at Kurodani in the Eastern Hills.[381] Once at the height of the cherry blossom season, when Reizei Tamemasa was still a consultant, his father Tamekuni, Ryōshun, and others went together to the Eastern Hills to see the blossoms, it having been agreed that they would carry the topics for their poems with them, compose their verses along the way, and read them aloud beneath the cherry blossoms at Washio.[382] "In that case," said someone, "we must invite Keikō." So they hunted out his hermitage and as he happened to be there at the time, they invited him to accompany them. Along the way they produced the topic "Seeking Out the Blossoms." This was Keikō's poem:

Sasowarete	Invited by others,
Ko no moto goto ni	I come seeking them from tree to tree—
Tazunekinu	But will the blossoms
Omoi no hoka ni	Resent it that I visit them so,
Hana ya uramin.	And not of my own free will?[383]

31. Some time ago there was a Zen priest called Sogetsu[384] who was a poet. One of his poems was included in *Shingosenshū*.[385] Though but a single poem, it was an enviable one:

Omoide no	Were I to declare,
Naki mi to iwaba	"I am one with no attachments,"
Haru goto ni	Would the blossoms—
Nareshi musoji no	My friends through sixty springs—
Hana ya uramin.	Not be angry at my treachery?

I happened to remember it in connection with the preceding verse.

32. When inscribing a poet's name on a poem slip, his rank and offices and surname are written first, and then after his given name the single character 上 in small script. This is done to show humility.

---

381. Keikō's precise dates are unknown. He lived at the Shinsho Gokuraku temple, commonly known as Shinnyōdō, a temple located at Kurodani in the Eastern Hills of Kyoto.

382. The Sōrinji, originally a Tendai temple, was converted to the Ji sect around the turn of the fifteenth century. It was famous for its cherry blossoms.

383. Source unknown.

384. A Nijō poet; fl. ca. 1350–80. Four of his poems are included in imperial anthologies.

385. "New Later Collection," thirteenth of the imperial anthologies (1303), compiled by Nijō Tameyo with the assistance of his son Tameuji and others. The poem quoted here actually comes from *Shingoshūishū* (poem 621; Miscellaneous: Spring). Headnote: Topic unknown.

33. The basic procedure in pronouncing a poetic topic is to read off the Chinese characters in Japanese. Thus, the topic *Ryoshuku kigan* ought to be read *Tabi no yado no kaeru kari*, but as this is too unwieldy, it is read *Ryoshuku no kaeru kari.*[386] However, here too, the combination *kigan* should be read *kaeru kari.* Formerly, *sanka* used to be read *yama no ie* and *denka* was read *ta no ie.*[387]

34. The poem Lord Teika wrote on "The Year's End" for the *Roppyaku-ban uta-awase*:

Tarachine ya	My dear parent—
Mada Morokoshi ni	Still awaiting in far Cathay,
Matsurabune . . .	A ship from Matsura . . .[388]

and so on—what can it be about? Of course, one can gather from the poem that someone's parent is in China waiting for him to come from Japan while the year comes to a close, and one can sense the person's loneliness and misery, but it is very difficult to understand just exactly what the situation is. I once read the text called *Matsura monogatari*,[389] which tells how the Matsura Middle Counselor goes to China as an envoy from Japan to the T'ang court, and it would seem that Teika's poem is based on this story.

Teika also composed the following poem for the same poetry contest:

Yomosugara	All night long,
Tsuki ni ureete	Grieving in the moonlight,
Ne o zo naku	I cry aloud—

386. The first case reads all the characters in Japanese; the second gives the first compound its Chinese reading and reads the second in Japanese.
387. In other words, in the past the compounds were read in Japanese, whereas in Shōtetsu's time they were evidently read in Chinese.
388. *SG* 1935. The poem is actually not from *Roppyaku-ban uta-awase* but from *Teika-kyō hyakuban jika-awase* ("Lord Teika's Personal Poem Contest in One-Hundred Rounds," 1218–32, in *SKT* 5) 194 (Round 97, Right), a "solo" contest—meaning one in which the author organizes his own poems in the format of a contest—that Teika presented to Retired Emperor Juntoku in 1218. The text of the poem there reads: "My dear parent/ Still waiting in far Cathay,/ His heart torn with grief—/ While here at Matsura Mountain/ Another year comes to an end." (*Tarachime ya/ mada Morokoshi ni/ matsurabune/ kotoshi mo kurenu/ kokorozukushi ni*.) The poem alludes either to *Hamamatsu Chūnagon monogatari* ("The Tale of Hamamatsu Chūnagon," late Heian period) or to the "Lantern Devil Legend," according to which a Japanese official sent to China is enslaved and made to serve as a living "lantern devil," standing and holding a lantern in his hand. Learning that his father is still alive, his son goes to China to rescue him. The legend is found in *Hōbutsushū* ("A Collection of Treasures," late twelfth century).
389. *Matsura no {miya} monogatari*, which scholars now accept as written by Teika himself—although, interestingly, Shōtetsu does not mention Teika as the author. For a synopsis of the plot, see Keene 1989:4–10.

> Inochi ni mukau   For my very life is forfeit
> Mono omou tote.   To the anguish of this love.[390]

The line "For my very life is forfeit" is also found in the *Matsura* text. Thus, Teika's poems sometimes allude to tales.

35. Where was it, I wonder? I remember someone wrote that with respect to *Genji monogatari* one may not use the poems themselves as the basis for allusive variation, but one may use the ideas expressed in the poems.[391] Nevertheless, people actually do borrow many of the poems, too. For example, on the lines

> Omou kata yori   Carried on the wind that comes
> Kaze ya fukuran.   From the place where my love dwells?[392]

Teika wrote:

> Sode ni fuke   Blow upon my sleeves,
> Sazo na tabine no   For thus wakeful I can have no comfort
> Yume mo miji   In a traveler's dream—
> Omou kata yori   O wind that comes to visit me
> Kayou urakaze.   From the place where my love dwells.[393]

The line "Blow upon my sleeves" is a request to the wind. Lying down for the night on his journey, he cannot sleep, and so he asks

---

390. *SG* 1375 (Love). Headnote: From a hundred-poem sequence at the palace on a spring day. *Teika-kyō hyakuban jika-awase* 135 (Round 68, Left) in *SKT* 5.

391. One of the first extant statements concerning allusions to tale literature appears in Shunzei's comments on a poem (276) by Takanobu from *Roppyaku-ban uta-awase* (Round 18, Right, Summer) in *SKT* 5, which alludes to a poem in the *Yūgao* ("Evening Faces") chapter of the tale (*NKBZ* 12:215 and Seidensticker 1976, I:61): "This flower blooming/ Under cover of the faint hues/ Of twilight—/ Would someone reveal its name/ To a traveler from afar?" (*Tasogare ni/ magaite sakeru/ hana no na o/ ochikatabito ya/ towaba kotaen.*) Shunzei's comment is, "It is not proper to have composed the poem with *Genji* so insistently in mind. It will be bad for the reputation of *Genji* as well." A similar opinion is expressed in *Go-Toba no in gokuden* ("Ex-Emperor Go-Toba's Secret Teachings"), where the retired emperor says that "Shakua [Shunzei], Jakuren, and others said . . . 'use diction from the poems in the *Genji* and other romances if you like, but do not use poetic conceptions from such works'" (*NKBT* 65:144 and Brower 1972:34). If Shōtetsu is "quoting" from these sources, however, he has it backwards. In any case, the point is academic, since by the fourteenth century the old injunctions were generally disregarded. Cf. *Kinrai fūteishō* (*NKGT* 5:144) and *Seiashō* (*NKGT* 5:44). See also Brower 1972:52–53, nn. 102, 103.

392. A reference to a poem composed by Genji as he listens to the waves at Suma, where he is in exile. The full text reads, "In longing, I listen/ To the sound of waves on the bay/ That sound so like sobs—/ Carried on the wind that comes/ From the place where my love dwells?" (*Koiwabite/ naku oto ni magau/ uranami wa/ omou kata yori/ kaze ya fukuran.*) See *NKBZ* 13:191 and Seidensticker 1976, I:236.

393. *SKKS* 980 (Travel). Headnote: At the Bureau of Poetry when the gentlemen were composing travel poems.

the wind from the place where his beloved lives to blow upon his sleeves.

36. Shunzei's house was at Gojō and Muromachi.[394] After his mother had died,[395] Lord Teika went to visit Shunzei there, only to find the autumn wind blowing desolately about the place, and Shunzei, too—whenever it was—looking sad and forlorn. So upon returning home to his own house at Ichijō and Kyōgoku,[396] Teika sent the following poem to his father:

Tamayura no	Not for a moment
Tsuyu mo namida mo	Do dewdrops or tears of grief
Todomarazu	Cease to fall
Naki hito kouru	In that garden where the autumn wind
Yado no akikaze.	Yearns for her who is no more.[397]

This poem is a most complex and deftly wrought composition,[398] whose sadness and pathos are indescribable. The word *tamayura* means "a short time." The whole poem, down to the end where he has placed the autumn wind, is pathetic and deeply moving, but where it says, "Yearns for her who is no more," it sounds particularly sad.

Shunzei's reply was:

Aki ni nari	Autumn has come,
Kaze no suzushiku	And even with the changing wind
Kawaru ni mo	As it turns cool,
Namida no tsuyu zo	The dew of my tears of grief
Shino ni chirikeru.	Goes on falling thick and fast.[399]

I find it difficult to understand why he should have written such a seemingly offhand poem.[400] For Teika's part, since the lady was his mother, it is only natural that his poem should be sad and pathetic and wring the heart. As for Shunzei, she was his wife. But because he was already old, it would not have been proper for him to say that

394. An intersection in the center of Kyoto, near what is now Gojō-Karasumaru.
395. Teika's mother, Lady Bifuku'mon'in no Kaga, died in 1193, at around age 70.
396. An intersection at the eastern end of First Avenue, near what is now Ichijō-Teramachi.
397. *SKKS* 788 (Parting). Headnote: On a stormy day in the autumn of his mother's death, he went to the house where he had once lived.
398. "Complex and deftly wrought" translates *momi ni mōdaru*. According to Hisamatsu, this may mean a style that is so full of feeling that it seems to "wring the heart." Retired Emperor Go-Toba uses a similar phrase in his teachings (*NKBT* 65:144–45; Brower 1972:35, 54 n. 107) to characterize the style of a famous poem by Minamoto no Tsunenobu (1016–97), of whom "Lord Teika thinks so highly."
399. Listed as a reply to *SKKS* 788 in *SG* 2775.
400. "Offhand" translates *sugenage ni*, "dispassionately."

he was sad and hopeless, and so he simply says that the season is autumn and the wind is cool, just as if nothing were out of the ordinary. Yet it is a fine poem all the same.

37. Among Teika's poems, a great many of those on love in particular are profoundly moving for reasons that are difficult to understand. All in all, neither Ariie nor Masatsune, nor Michitomo, nor Michimitsu[401] is a match for Teika. Only Ietaka wrote some splendid love poems that come up to his standard.

38. According to Teika, when thinking over the idea for a poem, one should always recite to oneself these lines from *Hakushi monjū*[402]:

> Back in the village,
>   my mother's tears in the autumn wind;
> At this travelers' inn,
>   no one about: the feeling of rain at dusk.[403]

Reciting this poem elevates the feelings and enables a person to compose a good poem, it is said. It is also written that one should recite the lines:

> At the Department of Ministries in the season of
>   blossoms, you gather beneath the brocade curtains;
> Upon Mount Lu in the rainy night, I sit alone in my
>   grass-thatched hut.[404]

401. Minamoto no Michimitsu (d. 1248). A younger brother of Michitomo.
402. Among the Japanese, Po Chü-i was the most popular of all Chinese poets. This was especially true of Teika, who encourages poets to study the great poet's poems in *Eiga taigai* (NKBT 65:115) and *Maigetsushō* (NKBT 65:137; Brower 1985:422 n. 77). Shōtetsu's quote probably derives from a passage in *Gukenshō* (NKGT 4:357): "Always recite some good Chinese verse to clear your mind. Because Chinese verse clears and elevates the mind, my later father used to recite the lines 'At the Department of Ministries . . . in my grass-thatched hut.' The lines 'Back in the village . . . rain at dusk' [see n. 403 below] are also spendid and the kind of thing that excites the feelings. In the *Hakushi monjū* ("The Collected Works of Master Po") there are certain crucial books. Those of old also used to say that we should peruse them constantly." See also *Guhishō* (NKGT 4:297).
403. Here Shōtetsu is repeating the mistake of Imagawa Ryōshun (see *Ben'yōshō*, in NKGT 5:182) in attributing to Po Chü-i what is actually a poem by Minamoto no Tamenori (d. 1011) from *Shinsen rōeishū* ("Anthology of Poems for Singing, Newly Selected," 1113–18?). See Kubota 1985–86, I:442.
404. *Wakan rōeishū* 555 (SKT 2), a poem by Po Chü-i. Favorite couplets from Po's poems were included in *Wakan rōeishū* ("Anthology of Japanese and Chinese Poems for Singing"), compiled by Fujiwara no Kintō (966–1041) in the early years of the twelfth century.

"At this travelers' inn, no one about: the feeling of rain at dusk," where the speaker has lain down all alone in the travelers' inn and the rain begins to patter down—this is truly sad and forlorn. The Japanese poem "In that garden where the autumn wind/ Yearns for her who is no more" suits just such a situation as this.

39. A poem by the god of Shiragi[405] is included in *Shokukokinshū*:

Karafune ni	It was well worth it:
Noritazune ni to	Embarking upon that Chinese ship,
Koshi kai wa	Sailing across the sea,
Arikeru mono o	To seek and find the True Religion,
Koko no tomari ni.	To stay in this safe anchorage.[406]

And a poem by Kōbō Daishi[407] is in *Shinchokusenshū*:

Hōshō no	The name of Muroto
Muroto to kikedo	Sounds like the uncorrupted essence
Waga sumeba	Of the Buddhist Law,
Ui no namikaze	Yet dwelling here I know no day
Tatanu hi zo naki.	When illusion's winds and waves are still.[408]

Thus, all the various gods and Buddhas have each and every one composed their poems—showing, no doubt, that Japanese poetry has a unique virtue.

40. The five-syllable lines, "Could I have thought it?" (*Omoiki ya*) and "My ardent longing" (*Waga koi wa*) have not been employed in poems for the past forty or fifty years.[409] In my opinion they are indeed unpleasant expressions. One might think that one could be a bit more indirect about who the speaker is without coming right out and saying "*My* ardent longing." And instead of "Could I have thought it?" expressions like "How unexpected" (*Omowazu yo*) and "I did not know it" (*Shirazariki*) are used.

---

405. The guardian deity of Miidera Temple. Identified with the ox-headed guardian deity and also with Susanoo no Mikoto. Originally, a god worshipped by Koreans in Japan. According to legend, the god came to Japan by ship in the guise of an old man.

406. *ShokuKKS* 691 (Shinto). Headnote: This poem is said to have been composed by Shiragi Myōjin at Miidera.

407. 774–835; also known as Kūkai. Founder of the powerful Shingon sect of Buddhism.

408. *SCSS* 574 (Buddhism). Headnote: Written at a place called Muroto in the province of Tosa.

409. Both of these expressions appear repeatedly in formal poems included in imperial anthologies from the time of *Kokinshū* onward, and there is no evidence to suggest that poets of Shōtetsu's own day had in fact discarded them in favor of phrases "more indirect."

41. The anniversary of Hitomaro's death is kept secret, so that few people anywhere know the date. It is the eighteenth day of the third month.[410] Poetry gatherings in commemoration of Hitomaro have not been held on this date. The commemorative poetry gathering sponsored by Akisue of the Rokujō house took place in summer, in the sixth month.[411]

42. It is evident from the very beginning when a person is going to become a skilled poet. Thus, Lord Ietaka composed the following verse when he was a child:

Shimozuki ni	If it makes sense
Shimo no furu koso	That in the "Frosty Month" there be
Dōri nare	Falls of frost—
Nado jūgatsu ni	Then why in the tenth month
Jū wa furanu zo.	Are there no falls of tens?[412]

Retired Emperor Go-Toba is said to have been greatly impressed by this verse, saying that it showed he was destined to become a most valuable poet.[413] When one examines the poems of skillful poets, one sees that invariably it is in the conceptions[414] of their poems that they first become adept, but that they are unable to produce with any facility the words appropriate to their turn of mind. Therefore, to have become skillful in inventing poetic ideas may prove to be a very bad thing. Good poetic language does not depend upon actually seeing the things described. On the other hand, even though a person's language is effective, if his ideas are not, he will not be able to produce a good poem. Consequently, in observation there must be understanding as well.

43. In the expression "eightfold hills where cherries bloom" (*hana no yaeyama*), "eightfold hills" is not a place-name. Although

---

410. Presumably Shōtetsu here passes on some "secret" information. The actual date of Hitomaro's death is unknown.

411. Special commemorative events held in honor of Hitomaro seem to have been held as late as the eleventh century. Shōtetsu refers to the earliest recorded instance of such services, held by Fujiwara Akisue (1055–1123) before a portrait of Hitomaro at Akisue's house on the sixteenth day of the sixth month of 1118. The poems composed at that time are recorded in *Hitomaro eigu waka* (*GR* 13 [item 283]).

412. Source unknown. The eleventh lunar month was referred to as *shimozuki*, "month of frost."

413. Hisamatsu notes that "Retired Emperor Go-Toba" is probably a mistake, since Ietaka was twenty-two years the emperor's senior. Retired Emperor Go-Shirakawa (1127–92; r. 1155–58) is a more likely possibility. A similar story is related in *Yakumo mishō* (*NKGT* supp. 3:446).

414. "Conceptions" translates *kokoro*, a term that usually refers to the "meaning," "theme," or "idea" of the poem as opposed to its *kotoba*, or vocabulary, diction, imagery, and so forth.

many poems use the word in connection with Ashigara,[415] it simply means "many mountains" (*kasanaritaru yama*).

44. Those in the beginning stages of poetic training should not compose poems on the topics used for the *Kenpō meisho hyakushu*.[416] Famous places[417] have certain expressions that have been used with them since ancient times, and poems composed today also generally conform to the tradition. They have only a slight touch of originality. It seems that beginners have a fondness for writing poems on famous places. This is because they think them easy. I, too, will write a poem on a famous place when I cannot write any other kind. By using a famous place in your poem, you can fill up two or three lines and thus save that much effort. When you use such expressions as "The Kajino Fields/ In Takashima" (*Takashima ya/ Kajino no hara*)[418] or "The pine trees on the shore/ Of Shiga in Sasanami" (*Sazanami ya/ Shiga no hamamatsu*)[419] two lines are already taken up. I have been writing poetry for some forty years now, but I have yet to compose a set of poems on the topics for those hundred-poem sequences.

415. A mountain in ancient Sagami Province (modern Kanagawa Prefecture).
416. *Kenpō meisho hyakushu* ("The Kenpō-Era One-Hundred-Poem Sequence on Famous Places"), abbreviated title for *Kenpō sannen jūgatsu nijūyokka dairi meisho hyakushu*, the name given to sequences composed by Teika, Shunzei's Daughter, Ietaka, and nine others in the tenth month of 1215, upon order of Emperor Juntoku. Text available in *SKT* 5. The topics used for these sequences, all of which involved famous place-names, were often borrowed by later poets.
417. *Meisho* or *nadokoro*, place-names made famous by earlier poems. As Shōtetsu says, most famous places were so routinely associated with particular words and/or images—Naniwa with reeds, Yoshino with cherry blossoms, and so on—that treating them in original terms was nearly impossible.
418. Famous lines deriving ultimately from *MYS* 275, by Takechi no Kurohito. [Headnote: From eight travel poems by Takechi no Kurohito] "Where shall it be/ That I find an inn tonight—/ If the sun sets/ Over the Katsuno Fields/ In Takashima?" (*Izuku ni ka/ waga yadori semu/ Takashima no/ Katsuno no hara ni/ kono hi kurenaba.*) The fact that Shōtetsu misreads Katsuno for Kajino, however, suggests that he may have had in mind *ShokuGSS* 1314 (Travel) by Ietaka. [Headnote: On "A Distant View on the Road," written for a contest of Chinese and Japanese poems at the palace in the second year of the Kenryaku era (1212)] "If I seek an inn/ In the Kachino Fields/ In Takashima,/ Then how could I reach today/ Those white clouds in the distance?" (*Takashima no/ Kachino no hara ni/ yado toeba/ kyō ya wa yukan/ ochi no shirakumo.*)
419. Even more famous lines, the most prominent source of which is *SKKS* 16 (Spring), by Shunzei. [Headnote: A poem on the New Year's Planting, presented at the Hiyoshi Shrine] "Those pines on the shore/ Of Shiga in Sasanami,/ Now grown so old:/ For what New Year's Planting/ Were they first set before the god?" (*Sazanami ya/ Shiga no hamamatsu/ furinikeri/ ta ga yo ni hikeru/ nenobi naru ramu.*) "New Year's Planting" refers to a court rite in which courtiers went out into the fields around the capital on the Day of the Rat in the first month of the year to pull up new pine saplings and other plants, which were considered symbols of longevity and good fortune. In Shunzei's poem, the intimation is that the pines on the shore near Hie Shrine had been transplanted there by suppliants.

In the old days, people used to compose poems on the topics of the *Horikawa hyakushu* for beginning practice. Even so, the Horikawa topics are a bit difficult to handle. It is best for a beginner to compose on two-word topics and the like that can be handled with smoothness and elegance. It is also good to write poems on such things as the moon or cherry blossoms, which a person happens to have right in front of him at the time. Also, one may compose on the topics used for the hundred-poem sequences of the Kōchō [1261–64], Kōan [1278–88], Kenji [1275–78], Kenkyū [1190–99], and Jōei [1232–33] eras.[420]

45. It is difficult for beginners, it would appear, to handle poetic topics in which "Love" is combined with something else, as in "Love and the Moon" or "Love and Cherry Blossoms." But it seems that topics in which two related elements are combined, as in "Love: Seeing the Beloved" or "Love Revealed," are easier to handle. For the more mature poet, topics in which "Love" is combined with another disparate element are easy, and topics such as "Love: When the Lover Has Only Heard of the Beloved" or "Love: Parting" are very difficult. On the topic "Hearing a Temple Bell in Late Spring," I wrote:

Kono yūbe	In the evening dusk,
Iriai no kane no	The booming of the vesper bell
Kasumu kana	Is muffled in haze.
Oto senu kata ni	Can it be that departing spring
Haru ya yukuran.	Goes to where there is no sound?[421]

This is the sort of easy, gentle style in which one ought to train oneself to compose. Even so, such problems as I have mentioned will occur after a poet has reached his full powers, when he goes back to the areas he covered as a beginner. It is like the reflection of the moon in the water, which looks easy to grasp but cannot by any means be taken in the hand.[422] This level of skill is impossible to attain without a great deal of effort.

46. There are two opinions about the word かひや—whether it is *kabiya* or *kaiya*. Shunzei has *kabiya* 鹿火屋, a hut where a

---

420. The sequences mentioned here all come from earlier eras, specifically from the times of *Shinkokinshū* (1206), *Shinchokusenshū* (1234), *Shokukokinshū* ("Collection of Ancient and Modern Times Continued," 1265), *Shokushūishū* ("Collection of Gleanings Continued," 1278). Conspicuously absent are works from the period of the warring poetic factions.

421. *Sōkonshū* 2674.

422. Probably a reference to the death of the Chinese poet Li Po (701–762), who drowned trying to catch the moon's reflection from the side of his boat, and/or to a famous Buddhist fable about a monkey who tried to grasp the moon's reflection in a pool, fell into the water, and drowned. The story is told in *Josuishō*. See Inada 1978:673–74.

smudge is burned to keep away the deer.[423] Kenshō[424] said the word
was *kaiya* 飼屋, a hut in which to keep silkworms.[425] The issue is
raised in his appeal against Shunzei's decisions for the *Roppyaku-ban
uta-awase.*[426]

47. At the time of the *Sengohyaku-ban uta-awase*,[427] Ietaka's
verse was not well known. On "Love and a River":

Ada ni mishi	She who proved faithless
Hito koso wasure	May well forget our time of love,
Yasukawa no	But waves of memory,
Ukise kokoro ni	Like shifting rapids on the Yasu River,
Kaeru nami kana.	Keep bringing back the misery to my heart.[428]

The two lines "Like shifting rapids on the Yasu River/ Keep bringing back the misery to my heart" are very good. The misery keeps
returning suddenly to mind over and over again.

48. On "The Moon on a Short Night":

Mizu asaku	In the shallows,
Ashima ni sudatsu	Ducks leave their nest among the reeds
Kamo no ashi no	On their short legs—
Mijikaku ukabu	For so short a time the moon's reflection
Yowa no tsukikage.	Floats upon the summer night.[429]

Ducks' legs might seem a bit farfetched for a poem, but as I wished
to emphasize the word "short," I used them in this way.

49. On "Love and Mountains":

Ausaka no	Fearful of the gales
Arashi o itami	That blow around the Hill of Meeting,
Koekanete	The drifting clouds

---

423. Probably a reference to both a comment in Shunzei's judgments for *Roppyaku-ban uta-
awase* (see n. 426 below) and to his long comment in *Korai fūteishō* (*NKBZ* 50:330–
32) on an *MYS* poem (2265) in which he interprets the word *kabiya* as a "mosquito
smudge" (*kayaribi*) burned by farmers to keep away mosquitoes—and, as a happy
coincidence, deer and other animals that might damage the crop.
424. fl. ca. 1161–1207. Famous scholar-poet adopted into the Rokujō line as the son of
Akisuke; one of Shunzei's main opponents in the contests of the late twelfth century.
425. The first character means "to raise."
426. Formally, it was Shunzei who was the judge of the contest, but Kenshō wrote an
appendix in which he quibbled with many of Shunzei's judgments, including the
latter's criticism of a poem of Kenshō's own that had used the word *kabiya* in a spring
context (poem 163 [Round 22, Left, Spring, part 2])—an appropriate season given
Kenshō's interpretation of the word, but inappropriate if Shunzei's interpretation of
the word was correct. See the judgment on the poem in *SKT* 5, and Konishi
1976:63–67.
427. See n. 157 above.
428. This poem appears nowhere else in Shōtetsu's works.
429. *Sōkonshū* 3168. Headnote: "Summer Moon."

Seki no toyama ni   Disappear in the outer hills,
Kiyuru ukigumo.   Daring not to cross the barrier.[430]

Someone is said to have remarked of this poem that it did not sound like a love poem. It seems that this was the sort of poem one would normally write on "Wind."

50. A "Moon That Has Reached the Sign of the Horse" means a moon that is in the exact middle of the sky.[431] However many days old the moon may be, if it is in the middle of the sky, it is a "Moon That Has Reached the Sign of the Horse."

51. For a poem on "Praying for Love," any of the gods may be used. And since Teika has written,

Toshi mo henu   Years have passed—
Inoru chigiri wa   Now my fruitless prayers have ceased
Hatsuseyama . . .   At Hatsuse Temple . . .[432]

it is permissible to treat prayer to the Buddhas as well.

In The Lord Regent's[433] poem,

Ikuyo ware   How many nights
Nami ni shiorete   Have I crossed Kibune River to the shrine,
Kibunegawa . . .   Drenched by the waves . . .[434]

he uses the expression "How many nights have I . . ." because he is visiting the Kibune Shrine[435] at night.

430. This poem appears nowhere else in Shōtetsu's works.
431. The "sign of the horse" was the midpoint of the ancient zodiac, at which time the moon would be directly overhead.
432. *SKKS* 1142 (Love). [Headnote: On "Praying for Love," for a contest of hundred-poem sequences at the mansion of the regent and prime minister] "Years have passed./ Now my fruitless prayers for love have ceased/ At Hatsuse Temple/ And the vesper bell atop the mountain/ Signals trysts for others than for me." (*Toshi mo henu/ inoru chigiri wa/ Hatsuseyama/ onoe no kane no/ yoso no yūgure.*) The evening bell reminds the speaker that tonight again he will be alone.
433. Gokyōgoku Yoshitsune. See n. 135 above.
434. *SKKS* 1141 (Love). [Headnote: "Praying for Love] "How many nights/ Have I crossed Kibune River to the shrine,/ Drenched by the waves/ And by the teardrops that love/ Has shed upon my sleeves?" (*Iku yo ware/ nami ni shiorete/ Kibunegawa/ sode ni tama chiru/ mono omouran.*) The poem alludes to a set of poems recorded in *GSIS* (1162–63) as an exchange between Izumi Shikibu and the god of the Kibune Shrine. 1162 [Headnote: Written upon seeing fireflies near a purification stream when she was in retreat at Kibune Shrine after being jilted by a man] "As I muse in sadness/ A firefly of the marshes rises/ As if it were my soul/ Departing from my body/ In desire for his love." (*Mono omoeba/ sawa no hotaru o/ waga mi yori/ akugareizuru/ tama ka to zo miru.*) 1163 [The Reply:] "Do not lament so—/ Shedding teardrops of love/ Flowing like the stream/ That rushes down the slope/ Here in the depths of the hills." (*Okuyama ni/ tagirite otsuru/ takitsuse ni/ tama chiru bakari/ mono na omoi so.*) Postscript: "This poem is the reply of the god of Kibune. It is said that he made himself heard to Izumi Shikibu as a man's voice."
435. A shrine located in Yamashiro Province, in the modern Kibune-machi area of Kyoto. The

52. There may possibly be a poetic source for the expression "ice cave on Mount Fuji" (*Fuji no himuro*), but I am very uncertain about it.[436] There are a number of traditional locations for ice caves, but I have never yet seen "ice cave on Mount Fuji." There is no "ice cave on Mount Fuji" in the collected poems of Retired Emperor Juntoku,[437] either. His poem that goes

> Kagiri areba   The day must come
> Fuji no miyuki no   When even Fuji's deepest snows
> Kiyuru hi . . .   Will melt away . . .[438]

is based on the poem in *Man'yōshū*:

> Fuji no yuki wa   The snows of Fuji
> Mochi ni kiete   Melt on the fifteenth day
> Mochi ni furu . . .   And fall on the fifteenth . . .[439]

which is why he wrote that the day must come when even Fuji's snows must melt. Now, his lines "But even the underbrush is cold/ Upon Mount Himuro's lower slopes"[440] show where the ice cave is actually located, although he has mentioned Fuji earlier. The idea is that even on the day when Fuji's snows are all melted, it is still cold on Mount Himuro. But none of the retired sovereign's poems say that there is an ice cave on Mount Fuji.

Again, his lines,

> Takashima ya   In Takashima,
> Atokawa yanagi . . .   Willows grow by the Ato River . . .[441]

deity of the shrine was generally worshipped as a rain god, but here Yoshitsune appeals to it to respond to a prayer of love.

436. "Ice cave" translates *himuro*, a mountain cave where ice was stored for use in summer.
437. In other words, the only poem by Retired Emperor Juntoku that might be interpreted as referring to an "ice cave on Mount Fuji" is the one following (*kagiri areba*). Those who took it as such no doubt did not pick up on Juntoku's allusion.
438. *SZKKS* 326 (Summer). Headnote: On "Ice Cave." See below for last two lines.
439. *MYS* 320. An envoy to a *chōka* by Yamabe no Akahito. The actual poem reads: "On Fuji's high peak/ The piled up drifts of winter snow/ At last are melted/ In the sixth month, on the fifteenth day—/ Only for snow to fall that same night." (*Fuji no ne ni/ furioku yuki wa/ minazuki no/ mochi ni kenureba/ sono yo furikeri.*)
440. The last two lines of *SZKKS* 326 (see n. 438 above).
441. From *Juntoku'in gohyakushu* ("Retired Emperor Juntoku's Hundred-poem Sequence," 1232), a sequence with judgments by Teika. "In Takashima/ Willows grow along the Ado River,/ And when the wind blows,/ White waves rise up to strike against/ The still unwetted lower branches." (*Takashima ya/ Adokawa yanagi/ kaze fukeba/ nurenu shizue ni/ kakaru shiranami.*) Text in ZGR (item 386) 14, part 2:732–39. That the two lines of the poem are appended to this section without comment may indicate that they were added by someone else.

53. This poem

Orifushi *yo*	This is the time:
*Mo*zu naku aki *mo*	Autumn, when the shrikes cry out,
*Fu*yugare*shi*	Is winter-withered;
*Tō*ki hajiha*ra*	And in the distant wax-tree grove,
*Mo*miji dani na*shi*.	Not even a sign of crimson leaves.[442]

is a double acrostic on the words "Although I love her, she cannot know it" (*omofu to mo yo mo shiraji*). I just dashed it off in a hurry. There are other times when no matter how hard one tries to write a verse like this, it is simply impossible. The syllables *ra, ri, ru, re*, and *ro* are especially difficult to incorporate into such a verse.

In the Tenryaku era [947–957], His Majesty[443] composed the following verse and sent it to a group of junior consorts and concubines:

Ausaka mo	On Meeting Hill,
Hate wa yukiki no	After all, there is no barrier to those
Seki mo izu	Who come and go;
Tazunete toiko	So find my place and visit me—
Kinaba kaesaji.	Come, and I will not let you go.[444]

They were all baffled by the verse, and one of the consorts, thinking that the composition was a summons because of the words "come and find and visit me," went that night to the emperor's chambers, whereas others sent back answering poems expressing their bafflement. Only one of them—the lady known as the Hirohata concubine[445]—sent His Majesty some incense, which was just what he wanted. His verse was a double acrostic on the words "a bit of blended incense, please" (*awasetakimono sukoshi*).

54. For the topic "A Fire in the Brazier," one may treat either buried embers or a burning fire, but for the topic "Buried Embers," one may not treat a fire in the brazier.[446]

---

442. This poem appears nowhere else in Shōtetsu's works.
443. Emperor Murakami (926–967; r. 946–967). This anecdote is recounted in the eleventh-century historical romance, *Eiga monogatari* ("A Tale of Flowering Fortunes," ca. 1092; see McCullough and McCullough 1980, I:77), and also in a number of poetic treatises, some of which identify the emperor as Kōkō (830–887; r. 884–887).
444. See previous note.
445. Hirohata no Kōi, a daughter of the Hirohata Middle Counselor Minamoto no Moroakira (903–955). Hirohata is the name of an area in Kyoto after which the family was named.
446. In other words, a poet is allowed to treat a particular topic from within a general category (to treat "embers" under the topic "fire") but not the other way around.

55. For the topic "Love and a Tiger," it is not correct to treat the zodiacal tiger.[447] Although the zodiacal tiger is to be sure a tiger all the same, this zodiacal tiger is written with a different character. Since the topic deals with a live tiger, it should be treated with such expressions as "the field where tigers lie," or "the arrow that pierced a rock,"[448] and the like. The Sino-Japanese reading of the character for the calendrical tiger is *in*.

The expression "the flayed pelt of a tiger" is in *Shinsen rokujō*.[449] Lord Tameie held the post of Major Counselor, and they wanted to promote his son Tameuji to Major Counselor as well, but as this was only possible if there was a vacancy, they made the father a former counselor and appointed Tameuji a new counselor. To express his chagrin, Tameie composed a verse on "the flayed pelt of a tiger."[450]

56. On "Moss on a Crag," I composed the following:

Midaretsutsu	Twisted and tangled,
Iwao ni sagaru	Shreds of moss hang from the branches
Matsu ga e no	Of pines that cling
Koke no ito naku	To a crag battered ceaselessly
Yamakaze zo fuku.	By hard blasts of mountain wind.[451]

The phrase *koke no ito naku* means "hanging moss," that is, moss that wraps itself around the branches and hangs down in shreds. Thus I

447. *Toki no tora.* According to the Chinese zodiac, the hours of the day were known by the names of animals. The hour of the tiger was the period between 3 and 5 a.m.

448. "The field where the tigers lie" comes from *SIS* 1227 (Miscellaneous: Love). [Headnote: Sent by a certain man who was pressing his attentions on a woman who already had a lover] "I might live long,/ But could I live the ages it would take/ For you to change your mind?/ Better to throw myself among the tigers/ That lie in the plains of far Cathay." (*Ari totemo/ iku yo ka wa furu/ karakuni no/ tora fusu nobe ni/ mi o nageten.*) "The arrow that pierced the rock" refers to a story in the *Shi chi* ("The Book of History," 104–91 B.C.) about Li Kwang, who shot an arrow at a rock, thinking it was a tiger, and the arrow stuck in the rock—showing that anything is possible if one tries hard enough.

449. "New Collection of Six Books," a poetry collection modeled on the late tenth-century *Kokin waka rokujō*, a compendium of some 4,500 poems from the first three imperial anthologies arranged by large topical categories (see n. 154 above). The later work, compiled between 1243 and 1244 by Fujiwara no Tameie and others, contains over 2,600 poems written by the compilers themselves on topics taken from the earlier work. Text in *SKT* 2. In actuality, there is no poem that contains the phrase Shōtetsu notes here, but he may be thinking of poem 522, on the topic "Tiger." "To have the skin/ Flayed off his back while he yet lives/ Is hard indeed—/ Even though the tiger's pelt/ Is handed down for men to see." (*Ikenagara/ wakareshi yo koso/ kanashikere/ tsutaete tora no/ kawa o miru ni mo.*)

450. Since Tameie took the tonsure in 1256, more than a decade before Tameuji became a Major Counselor (in the twenty-third day of the second month of 1267), this story can have no basis in fact.

451. This poem appears nowhere else in Shōtetsu's works.

used the term "shreds of moss." But *ito naku*, as in *ashi no ito naku* and other such expressions, also means "ceaselessly."

57. Women and girls, when they write poems on pocket paper, should not leave a blank space at the bottom. It is all right to leave any amount of blank space at the top.

58. "Wisteria in Early Summer":

Natsu kite mo	Summer is here,
Niou fujinami	But still the swaying wisteria is bright
Aratae no	Against the mountain,
Koromogae senu	Looking as if it had not changed
Yama ka to zo miru.	From rough hempen robes.[452]

The phrase *Aratae no/ Fujie* ("Fujie Cove/ Of the coarse hempen cloth") is used in *Man'yōshū*.[453] Because sprays of wisteria blossoms are coarse and yet lovely, it is called "rough hempen wisteria" or "rough yet lovely wisteria." The expression *aratae no koromo* ("rough hempen garb" or "lovely hempen garb") also refers to a robe that is white and beautiful, and so I think there can be no objection to employing the phrase *aratae no koromo* in my poem.

59. On "Waiting for the Cuckoo":

Toshi mo henu	Years have passed,
Matsu ni kokoro wa	And although my patience has been short
Mijikakute	In anxious waiting,
Tama no o nagaki	The cord of my life has been lengthened,
Hototogisu kana.	Listening for the cuckoo's song.[454]

"The cord of my life has lengthened" refers to myself. Since I have lived to the age of seventy, "the cord of my life is long." And because I have waited for the song of the cuckoo every year, I said "years have passed." To treat the topic in this way may be rather trivial, I realize, but in trying to compose verse different from what has already been written by others, I sometimes get lost among the mountains and thickets.

60. On "Love and a Dream":

Namida sae	Even my tears
Hito no tamoto ni	Seemed to sink into her sleeve

452. *Sōkonshū* 3264; also *Shōtetsu senshu* 206 (*SKT* 4).
453. *MYS* 252. [Headnote: From a group of eight travel poems by Kakinomoto Hitomaro] "As a fisherman/ Catching sea bass in the waters/ Of Fujie Cove/ Of the coarse hempen cloth—/ Is that how they see me, a traveler?" (*Aratae no/ Fujie no ura ni/ suzukitsuru/ ama to ka miran/ tabi yuku ware o.*)
454. *Sōkonshū* 3202.

Iru to mishi	As I looked on—
Tama todomaranu	But a dream gives no assurance
Yume zo ukitaru.	If my soul cannot stay with her.[455]

In the "Lavender" chapter, I believe, when Genji comes to take Murasaki away with him even though she is still but a child, the nurse Shōnagon recites the following poem:

Yoru nami no	Not yet knowing
Kokoro mo shirazu	The intentions of the waves advancing
Waka no ura ni	Upon the Bay of Youth,
Tamamo nabikan	The seaweed lacks the assurance
Hodo zo ukitaru.	To yield to the pull of the waves.[456]

For Genji to come and fetch the child away when she is still young and install her in his household with no assurance as to whether he will always keep her by him or quickly grow tired of her is indeed an undependable arrangement. That is why Shōnagon says in her poem, "The seaweed lacks the assurance/ To yield to the pull of the waves." So in my poem, too, "a dream gives no assurance" means that although his soul enters into the beloved's sleeve, it cannot remain there indefinitely and must soon return to his body. Hence I said, "My soul cannot stay with her." When he awakes from the dream in which he saw his soul enter the beloved's sleeve, the soul returns to him. In a poem about a dream, if one uses words like "see" and "awake," it becomes «text garbled here»[457] and this is bad. In my phrase "As I looked on," it is implied that he had the dream, and therefore without explicitly saying that he wakes up, the phrase "my soul cannot stay" implies that he has awakened. Although he sees his soul enter her sleeve, it does not stay there, and so the dream gives no assurance.

61. On the topic "The Cuckoo in the Fourth Month":

Hototogisu	O cuckoo,
Ono ga satsuki o	As you wait for your month of June,
Matsu kai no	You may well shed

---

455. This poem appears nowhere else in Shōtetsu's works.
456. From the *Wakamurasaki* ("Lavender") chapter of *Genji monogatari* (NKBZ 12:316 and Seidensticker 1976, I:103). Genji's poem, to which Shōnagon's is a reply, is as follows: "At the Bay of Waka/ It may be hard to find the seaweed/ Hidden among the reeds./ But why should the admiring waves/ Tamely halt and go back out to sea?" (*Ashiwaka no/ ura ni mirume wa/ kataku tomo/ ko wa tachinagara/ kaeru nami ka wa.*)
457. The NKBT text has *akō narite waroki* here, which makes no sense. NKGT 5:259 has *akatsuki naru nari* ("it has become dawn"), which does not fit the context very well either.

Namida no taki mo   A waterfall of futile tears—
Koe zo sukunaki.   But even so your cries are few.[458]

In *Ise monogatari* is the poem composed by Yukihira[459] on seeing the
Tsuzumi Waterfall:

Waga yo o ba   Which is the greater:
Kyō ka asu ka to   This waterfall, or the waterfall
Matsu kai no   Of my futile tears
Namida no taki to   As I wait for today or tomorrow
Izure takaken.   To bring me a better time?[460]

I simply altered it a little to a waterfall of the cuckoo's tears and thus
gave it a touch of novelty. Without changing older poems around a
little bit in this fashion, it would be impossible to compose poetry.
The phrase *matsu kai* means "as I wait." The character for *kai* is 間.

62. *Amagiru* means "to become cloudy." *Me kirite* ("eyes cloud
over"), *namida kirite* ("clouded with tears"), and the like come from
the same word.

63. In poetry one must be extremely careful about fancy
phrases. Teika deals with the subject of fancy phrases in his *Miraiki*.[461] Lines such as Masatsune's "The Bay of Karaka/ Where they
burn the bitter salt"[462] and the like are fancy phrases.

---

458. This poem appears nowhere else in Shōtetsu's works.

459. Ariwara no Yukihira (818–893), older brother of Narihira. Less successful at poetry than
    at court, where he rose as high as Middle Counselor of the Senior Third Rank.

460. From section 87 of *Ise monogatari*, in which Yukihira laments his lack of advancement in
    court office; also *SKKS* 1649. See *NKBT* 9:163–64 and McCullough 1968:130–32.
    In actuality, it was Nunobiki Waterfall in Yamashiro (modern day Kōbe City).
    Tsuzumi Waterfall is located in Higo (modern Kumamoto Prefecture).

461. *Miraiki* ("A Record of the Future"). A collection of fifty poems presented as examples of
    bad poetry—i.e., too full of fancy phrases, wordplay, etc. The book bears the
    fictitious name of Kakinomoto Tsurami (a combination of *Kakinomoto* Hitomaro, Ki
    no *Tsura*yuki, and Mibu no Tada*mi*) as its author, but poets of Shōtetsu's day at-
    tributed it to Teika, and modern scholars attribute it to Abutsu the Nun or someone
    of her day. Text available in *NKGT* 4. In his *Kensai zōdan* ("Kensai's Notes about This
    and That," late fifteenth century), the linked-verse poet Kensai (1452–1510) repeats
    a familiar attack against Shōtetsu by saying that "of all the poems that he wrote
    during his lifetime there are scarcely ten that succeed in eluding the examples of the
    Miraiki" (*NKGT* 5:393).

462. *ShokuGSS* 212 (Summer), by Asukai Masatsune; originally from an imperial poem
    contest (*Dairi hyaku-ban uta-awase*) held in 1216 (and not from one in 1214, as the
    headnote to the poem in *ShokuGSS* says; see poem 76 [Round 38], in *SKT* 5 [item
    213]). "Upon the isle/ Of Karaka, the tide flows in/ Where the fisher folk/ Gather
    seaweed in the summer rains/ That fall with no sign of clearing." (*Mitsu shio no/
    Karaka no shima ni/ tamamo karu/ amama mo mienu/ samidare no koro.*) Teika, the judge
    for the contest, awarded it the win, praising it, however, for the pivot word em-
    ployed in lines three and four—*tamamo karu/ amama mo mienu* (*ama* functioning
    as both "fisher folk" in the first phrase and "rain" in the second)—and not for the
    first two lines, as Shōtetsu suggests. It is important, nevertheless, to note that Shō-
    tetsu here seems to endorse "fancy phrases" as legitimate, calling on Teika as his
    authority. Masatsune's poem alludes to *MYS* 943, an envoy to a *chōka* by Yamabe no

64. People often misunderstand the meaning of the topic "Lingering Moonlight Crossing the Barrier." When composing a poem on this topic, it is a mistake to interpret it as the moon crossing the barrier. It is a person who crosses the barrier in the moonlight. Therefore it is to be treated as "in the lingering moonlight" (*nokoru tsuki ni*).

65. In poetry there are many vexations. Winding up loose ends and thinking of the future—I must conclude that things never turn out as one had intended. If one continues to compose poems of the sort that everyone else considers good, one must remain forever at that ordinary level. On the other hand, when one writes poems whose essence is profound and difficult,[463] others fail to understand them, and this is frustrating. No doubt what is generally called good would seem to be good enough, I suppose.

66. Everyone says that the poem

Yoshinogawa	At Yoshino,
Kōrite nami no	The river is overcome with ice:
Hana dani mo	Even the blossoms
Nashi . . .	Of the waves are gone . . .[464]

is a fine poem, but I used to write poems just as good all the time.

67. Sometimes on awaking from sleep I happen to think of one of Teika's poems and feel as if I were about to lose my mind. When it comes to composing in a polished and ingenious style,[465] there are no poems equal to Teika's.

68. The poems of an accomplished artist have an atmosphere apart from the words and somehow impart a feeling of sad beauty when one recites them over to oneself. In the *Roppyaku-ban uta-awase*, on the topic "Love and a Wild Boar":

Urayamazu	I do not envy him:
Fusu i no toko wa	For while the wild boar may lie down
Yasuku to mo	Upon a carefree bed,
Nageki mo katami	My anguish is as a reminder—
Nenu mo chigiri o.	My sleeplessness, as a sign of love.[466]

Akahito. "Upon the isle/ Of Karani, where they gather seaweed,/ I wander, musing/ That if only I were a cormorant,/ I would not long so for my home." (*Tamamo karu/ Karani no shima ni/ shimami suru/ u ni shi mo are ya/ ie omowazaramu*.) Karaka no Shima is a famous place-name that came from a misreading of the characters for Karani in *MYS*. The place is located on the coast in modern Hyōgo Prefecture.

463. *Yūen*, literally, "obscure and distant."
464. Source and author unknown.
465. *Mōdarutei*. Probably related to *momi ni mōdaru* (see n. 398 above).
466. *SG* 889; originally from *Roppyaku-ban uta-awase* 1061 (Love; Round 21, Left), in *SKT* 5.

The idea is that all day long he yearns sadly for the beloved, but even though he suffers, his suffering is a reminder of her, and all night long he is unable to sleep and is afflicted with painful longing. But this, too, is the effect of a bond of love through many lives. So he says he does not envy the sleeping boar his easy rest. Truly an affecting idea.

The poem

Tomochidori	O friendly plovers,
Sode no minato ni	Come visit me on the bay of tears
Tomeko kashi	Within my sleeve—
Morokoshibune no	Wave-tossed like a Chinese ship
Yoru no nezame ni.	Heaved to port this sleepless night.[467]

is based on the poem in *Ise monogatari*:

Omōezu	All unexpected,
Sode ni minato no	A flood of tears has made a bay
Sawagu kana	Within my sleeve,
Morokoshibune no	Wave-tossed as if a Chinese ship
Yorishi bakari ni.	Had come heaving in to port.[468]

69. The topic "Love: In Hiding" means that the other person is hiding from the speaker. Her whereabouts is being concealed from him. "Love: Dislike" and "Love: Forgotten" also mean that the speaker is disliked or forgotten by the other person. Topics of this type ought all to be construed as having the character 被, indicating the passive voice.[469]

70. When composing only a few verses, such as a set of twenty or thirty, it is good to select compound topics[470] that will give you something to think about.

71. The topic "Love: Seducing a Man's Wife" means that the speaker seduces another man's wife. Women like Utsusemi and Ukifune in *Genji monogatari* would be suitable for this situation.[471] I once composed the following poem on this topic at a poetry gathering:

Mi o Uji to	Wretch that I am,
Tanomi Kohata no	To court the Uji lady I have crossed

467. *SG* 3121; originally from *Sengohyaku-ban uta-awase* 1959 (Round 980, Right), in *SKT* 5. The first line should read *naku chidori*, "O crying plovers."
468. From section 26 of *Ise monogatari* (*NKBT* 9:129 and McCullough 1968:91) and also *SKKS* 1358 (Love), Anonymous.
469. This character was used to indicate the passive voice in Sino-Japanese, or *hentai kanbun*.
470. *Musubidai*. See n. 210 above.
471. Utsusemi ("The Lady of the Locust Shell"), the wife of the governor of Iyo, was pursued by Genji in his youth; Ukifune, on the other hand, was pursued by both Kaoru and Niou.

Yama koete	Kohata Mountain,
Shiranami no na o	Only to earn a bandit's name
Chigiri ni zo karu.	For this vagrant bond of love.[472]

72.

Uguisu no	Seeking the song
Koe no nioi o	Of the warbler's fragrant tones,
Tomekureba	I reach a mountain
Ume saku yama ni	Where the spring breeze brings to me
Harukaze zo fuku.	The scent of blossoming plums.[473]

73. "Late Summer" is treated in the same manner as "The End of Spring" or "The End of Autumn." It means the last of summer.

74. On "Rice Seedlings":

Tabi yukeba	Making a journey
Saori no tauta	To other places, other provinces,
Kuni ni yori	I hear different songs,
Tokoro ni tsukete	All to celebrate the planting
Koe zo kawareru.	Of seedlings in the paddy fields.[474]

The festival of transplanting the rice seedlings falls in the fifth month.[475] I used the phrase "making a journey" for no particular reason, but as the words do occur in older poetry, there is no objection to them.

75. With respect to alluding to older poetry, one need hardly mention that *Genji monogatari* is one of the acceptable works. But allusions are also made to the older tales. Everyone alludes to *Sumiyoshi*,[476] *Shōsammi*,[477] *Taketori*,[478] and *Ise monogatari*—both to

---

472. *Sōkonshū* 4543. The poem involves a play on the place-name Uji and *ushi*, to "feel wretched." It alludes to the story of Ukifune in *Genji monogatari*, which relates how Niou the interloper secretly visits Ukifune at Uji, where her lover Kaoru has hidden her away.

473. This poem appears nowhere else in Shōtetsu's works. It may be a garbled version of, or perhaps an allusion to, a poem by Go-Kyōgoku Yoshitsune (*SKT* 3:107). "The warbler's song/ Becomes a heady fragrance/ On the spring breeze/ That wafts through the plum tree/ Where the bird makes his nest." (*Uguisu no/ koe no nioi to/ naru mono wa/ ono ga negura no/ ume no harukaze.*)

474. *Sōkonshū* 3450; also *Shōtetsu senshu* 44 (*SKT* 4).

475. *Saori*, the festival of the first day of rice planting. Also referred to as *sabiraki* or *naetate*.

476. *Sumiyoshi monogatari* ("The Tale of Sumiyoshi"). A story of a child persecuted by a cruel stepmother. Present text is a Kamakura-period version of an earlier original.

477. *Shōsammi monogatari* ("The Tale of Shōsammi"). A romance of the Kamakura period. Said by some to be another name for *Iwashimizu monogatari*.

478. *Taketori monogatari* ("The Tale of the Bamboo Cutter"). The earliest of Japanese tales, which recounts the story of an old bamboo cutter who finds a moon maiden in the forest, raises her, and enters marriage negotiations with a number of suitors only for her to fly back to the moon in the end.

the poems and to the prose text. In addition to poems by poets who participated in the *Horikawa hyakushu*, it is permissible to allude to any of the poems by poets of that same period. Because Saigyō was a member of Retired Emperor Toba's palace guard, many of his poems must have been written during the reign of the former emperor Horikawa.[479] Therefore it is permissible to use Saigyō's poems for allusive variations.

76. During the early stages, a novice ought to practice constantly. I used to dash off a hundred verses in an evening, or a thousand verses in a day. At the same time, one should sometimes spend five or six days mulling over a mere five poems or even two poems. In this fashion, when a person writes some verses at a gallop and others for which he pulls in on the reins, he will become adept at both slow and rapid composition and will develop into a skilled poet. If he is determined from the outset to write a fine poem, he will be unable to compose even one or two verses, and in the end will fail to make any progress. "Snow amid the Solitude," "Cherry Blossoms at their Peak," "The Sacred Tree," "The Upper Branches."[480]

77. "Falling Cherry Blossoms":

Sakeba chiru	No sooner do they bloom,
Yo no ma no hana no	Than the cherry blossoms scatter—
Yume no uchi ni	The fleeting dream
Yagate magirenu	Of a night that takes away all doubt
Mine no shirakumo.	About the white clouds on the peak.[481]

This is a poem in the style of mystery and depth. Mystery and depth is something that is in the heart but is not expressed in words. The moon veiled in thin clouds, or the bright foliage on the mountains concealed by autumn mists—such poetic conceptions are regarded as having the effect of mystery and depth. But if one asks in which particular feature the mystery and depth are to be found, it is difficult to specify exactly. A person who failed to comprehend this fact would argue that the moon is at its most enchanting when it is glittering brightly in a clear sky with not a cloud in sight. But with

479. Saigyō was appointed a samurai in the *hokumen*, or personal guards, of Emperor Toba (1103–56; r. 1107–23) in 1140, at age twenty-three. However, since Horikawa died ten years before Saigyō was born, the latter could hardly have written many of his poems during that reign.

480. These last are perhaps suggested as topics for practice.

481. *Sōkonshū* 3098.

mystery and depth it is impossible to say just what it is that is enchanting or lovely.[482]

The lines "The fleeting dream/ Of a night that takes away all doubt/" allude to a poem in *Genji monogatari*. Meeting with Fujitsubo, Genji recites:

Mite mo mata	Though now we meet,
Au yo mare naru	Few have been our nights of love,
Yume no uchi ni	Few our trysts to come—
Yagate magiruru	Would I might make my wretched being
Uki mi to mo ga na.	Melt into this fleeting dream![483]

This poem, too, is in the style of mystery and depth. By the lines "Though now we meet,/ Few have been our nights of love,/ Few our trysts to come—" he means that it has been extremely difficult for them to meet from the very beginning, and in the future it will be almost impossible. So he says, "Few have been our nights of love,/ Few our trysts to come." If instead of awaking from this dream it were to remain a dream forever, then he would simply melt away into the dream. By "dream" he means their present meeting. So he says he wishes he might simply melt away into this dream in which he has seen his beloved.

Fujitsubo's reply:

Yogatari ni	Out in the world
Hito ya tsutaen	Still they would talk of my shame—
Tagui naku	Even if I myself,
Uki mi o samenu	Wretched beyond all compare,
Yume ni nashite mo.	Should vanish in an endless dream.[484]

Fujitsubo is Genji's stepmother. Nevertheless, this love affair has come about between them, and so she says that even if her wretched being vanished away in a dream, her shameful name would remain behind, to be bandied about in the gossip of the court. She has composed her poem skillfully, picking up the lines in Genji's poem, "Would I might make my wretched being/ Melt into this fleeting dream!" In my poem, by the lines "No sooner do they bloom/ Than the cherry blossoms scatter—/ The fleeting dream" I mean that no

---

482. Here Shōtetsu alludes to concepts developed by Kamo no Chōmei and Yoshida no Kenkō. See the introduction (pp. 54–57).
483. From the *Wakamurasaki* ("Lavender") chapter of *Genji monogatari*. NKBZ 12:306 and Seidensticker 1976, 1:98.
484. Ibid.

sooner do the cherry blossoms seem to come into bloom than in a single night they are already scattered and gone. When one gazes out the next morning, no longer can the clouds be mistaken for cherry blossoms, and so I said, "Of a night that takes away all doubt/ About the white clouds on the peak." By "the fleeting dream" I mean the time it takes for the blossoms to bloom and fall.

78. "Frogs in Rice Paddies":

Yuku mizu ni	Is it to write
Kawazu no uta o	On moving water, or keep count
Kazu kaku ya	Of the songs of frogs—
Onaji yamada ni	Is that why birds come and alight upon
Tori mo iruran.	The same mountain paddy fields?[485]

The birds are snipe.[486] Snipe are associated with autumn, and so saying simply "birds" is sufficient to indicate what kind of birds they are. When the rice paddies are newly planted, all sorts of birds come and alight upon them.

79. There is nothing more delightful than the time when the cicadas cry in the shadow of mountains touched by the last lingering light of the evening sun. It is a fine thing to take such a conception and turn it, as in "The fringed pinks/ Upon the mountains where in evening's glow/ The cicadas are crying."[487] Because of the phrase "where in evening's glow the cicadas are crying," one might expect the words "clouds" or "sunlight" in the latter part of the poem, and to have turned it to "fringed pinks" may be a bit difficult to grasp, but it is an interesting twist nonetheless.

Teika's poem

Ransei no	Against the image
Hana no nishiki no	Of brocade-curtained splendor
Omokage ni	At the flowery court,
Iori kanashiki	Sad is this lonely hermitage
Aki no murasame.	In a shower of autumn rain.[488]

485. This poem appears nowhere else in Shōtetsu's works. An allusive variation on *KKS* 522 (Love), Anonymous. "More futile is it/ To write words on the water/ Of a flowing stream/ Than to have love for someone/ Who does not love you in return." (*Yuku mizu ni/ kazu kaku yori mo/ hakanaki wa/ omowanu hito o/ omou narikeri.*)

486. *Shigi*, a small variety of waterfowl; a longbill.

487. Probably a reference to *KKS* 244 (Autumn), by Sosei. "Am I the only one/ To be moved by their beauty?/ The fringed pinks/ On mountains where crickets cry/ In the light of evening's glow." (*Ware nomi ya/ aware to omowamu/ kirigirisu/ naku yūkage no/ yamatonadeshiko.*) The original has *kirigirisu*, "crickets," instead of Shōtetsu's *higurashi*—no doubt because he felt that the latter, a double entendre that means both cicada and "end of daylight," was more fitting in context.

488. *SG* 3121, from a set of thirty poems dated 1196. The "brocade curtains" refer to the surroundings of those currently acting as officials in the court.

makes a skillful turn with the original materials. The conception comes from the Chinese poem:

> At the Department of Ministries in the season of
>   blossoms, you gather beneath the brocade curtains;
> Upon Mount Lu in the rainy night, I sit alone in my
>   grass-thatched hut.[489]

The words "flowery court" and "brocade curtains" refer to the imperial palace.

80. In the phrase *shio no yaoai*, the word *yaoai* is written with the characters 八百合 , meaning "eight hundred joinings."[490] An area where the rising tide flows in from all directions to reach the high point is called *yaoai* or "eight hundred joinings."

81. Such expressions as *so yo sara ni*[491] ("verily, never") and *soso ya kogare*[492] ("behold, the withered trees") are too self-consciously artistic and should be avoided. They make an unpleasant impression.

82. On the topic "Awaking from a Dream in the Depths of Night," someone wrote:

Aki no yo wa	Somehow I had thought
Nagara ni tsukuru	That the autumn night would be as long
Tameshi made	As Nagara's span,
Omoinezame no	Until I awoke from my yearning sleep
Yume no ukihashi.	To a floating bridge of dreams.[493]

But I pointed out that there was no such thing as awaking to a dream—that he should have written of awaking *from* a dream instead.[494] So he corrected the poem accordingly.

---

489. By Po Chü-i. See nn. 402–4 above.

490. The phrase is found in *Nihongi* ("Chronicles of Japan," 720) and in the following poem from the "Akashi" chapter of *Genji monogatari* in which Genji attributes his salvation from a storm to the intervention of the god of the sea. "Had it not been/ For the saving grace of the gods/ Who dwell in the sea,/ I would have been swept away/ By the eight-hundred joinings of the tide." (*Umi ni masu/ kami no tasuke ni/ kakarazuba/ shio no yaoai ni/ sasuraenamashi.*) NKBZ 13:218 and Seidensticker 1976, I:249–50.

491. An example of this phrase appears in Teika's *SG* 2234. "Autumn has come!/ The wind blows, sighing across the reeds/ And lo! never once/ Does it allow the dew to rest/ Upon the fields of Miyagino." (*Aki kinu na/ ogi fuku kaze no/ soyo sara ni/ shibashi mo tamenu/ miyagino no tsuyu.*)

492. There are no extant examples of *soso ya kogare*, but *soso ya* appears in *SKS* 108 (Autumn), by Ōe no Yoshitoki (precise dates unknown): [Headnote: Topic unknown] "Behold, it seems/ The autumn wind has blown upon/ The leaves of reeds:/ Will the white beads of dew/ Have been scattered to the ground?" (*Ogi no ha ni/ soso ya akikaze/ fukinu nari/ kobore ya shinuru/ tsuyu no shiratama.*)

493. Source unknown.

494. That is, Shōtetsu would substitute *nezamuru yume* for *nezame no yume*.

83. On a poem slip for a single verse, the topic should be written under the words "Composed on . . ." in this fashion: "Composed on 'The Pine Trees Have Spring Color,' a Poem." The poem itself is written in three full lines plus a fourth of three syllables. It looks unsightly to leave a large amount of empty space at the end. It is also bad to write so that it fills up the whole paper. It is best to leave the same amount of empty space at the end of the poem as has been left before the words "Composed on." It is bad to leave too wide a space between the lines of the poem. At the same time, it is also bad to have the lines as close together as they are when there are three poems on the slip. One should leave a little space between them. Laymen write the headnote in a single line on the paper, thus: "On a spring day under the same circumstances. Composed on . . ." Priests write only "Composed on . . ." Writing "On a summer day," "On an autumn day," or "On a winter day," is called "superscription" (*hashizukuri*).

84. So long as a person composes his poems with intense seriousness, his art will not deviate from the Way. Nevertheless, that is but one of the styles to be found in the imperial anthologies. It may be difficult for a man to be called a skilled poet if he deviates from it, but this sort of thing only came about after the division into poetic factions. Throughout his life Tamekane preferred poetry of so eccentric a kind that in the end no one ventured to follow him. At the same time, Tameyo composed primarily in the style of intense seriousness, and as a result Ton'a, Keiun, Jōben, Kenkō, and all the other important poets adopted the style of his house. Thus everyone composed in this style of intense seriousness,[495] believing it alone to be the epitome of the art, and from this period on poetry began to suffer. Prior to this division into poetic schools, all three generations[496] seem to have written poems in many different styles.

85. "The Cuckoo in the Village":

Ayanaku mo	How thoughtless!
Yūbe no sato no	As evening falls the village echoes
Toyomu kana	With shouts and noise,
Matsu ni wa sumaji	So the mountain cuckoo will not stay
Yamahototogisu.	Among these pine trees where I wait.[497]

---

495. "Style of intense seriousness" translates *kyokushin no tei*, presumably meaning the conservative *ushin* style of the Nijō school and its adherents.

496. *Sandai*. The three patriarchs of the Mikohidari line, Shunzei, Teika, and Tameie.

497. This poem appears nowhere else in Shōtetsu's works.

The poem declares that as evening closes in, the village becomes noisy. If this were linked verse, unless people were overtly mentioned it would be necessary to specify what it is that is noisy.[498]

86. "Love and Smoke":

Kou tote mo	So senseless is my love
Kai nashi Muro no	That the guardian gods of smouldering
Yashima moru	Muro in Yashima
Kami dani shiranu	Cannot see the smoke of passion
Mune no keburi wa.	Rising from within my breast.[499]

The phrase *Muro no Yashima moru* ("the guardian gods of smouldering/ Muro in Yashima") is in a somewhat unusual position, and this gives the poem a touch of novelty. But even so I do not think I would use this expression a second time. In middle antiquity[500] it was thought to be disgraceful for anyone to copy and reuse such expressions as *Ike ni sumu/ Oshiakegata* ("Dawn where the mallards/ Dwell in the pond") or *Tsuyu no nuki/ Yowa no yamakaze* ("The warp of dew/ Is fragile, O mountain wind/ Rising in the night").[501]

87. The bishop of Jissō'in,[502] intending to make a retreat deep in the mountains, stopped over at the Sonshō'in[503] in Nara and

498. What Shōtetsu means here is unclear. Perhaps he is reasoning that since in linked verse the first half of the poem would constitute a complete statement, some word indicating the source of the noise would have to be made to make the meaning of the verse clear. However, just the opposite is generally true in linked verse, where ambiguity is necessary to the whole process of "linking" verse to verse.

499. *Sōkonshū* 4643. First line there reads *tatsu tote mo*, "It rises uselessly." Muro no Yashima is identified as a place in either Shimōsa or Shimotsuke where vapor rises from pools of water in the fields (perhaps hot springs?), looking like smoke. Many poems using it compare the smoke of passion to Muro no Yashima's vapors.

500. The era of Teika and Ietaka.

501. The source of *ike ni sumu* . . . is *SCSS* 969 (Love), by Ietaka. [Headnote: A poem on love, from a set of twenty poems submitted to his Majesty in the second year of Kenryaku (1212)] "The moon in the sky/ Shines upon the pond at dawn/ Where mallards dwell,/ And gazing at ice on my sleeve/ I see its reflection in my frozen tears." (*Ike ni sumu/ oshiakegata no/ sora no tsuki/ sode no kōri ni/ naku naku zo miru.*) The other lines, also by Ietaka, come from poem 6160 of *Fuboku wakashō* ("The Japan Collection," in *SKT* 2), a large collection of famous poems not appearing in imperial anthologies put together by Fujiwara no Nagakiyo with the consultation of Reizei Tamesuke. [Headnote: On autumn foliage for a gathering at the Tsukinowa Palace] "The warp of dew/ Is fragile, O mountain wind/ Rising in the night——/ Have pity, then, and blow gently/ On the rich brocade of Tatsuta." (*Tsuyu no nuki/ yowa no yamakaze/ konogoro wa/ Tatsuta no nishiki/ kokoro shite fuke.*) Both poems qualify as *shūku*, or "ornate verses," by virtue of their use of pivot words and elaborate metaphors.

502. Giun (b. 1386), son of Ashikaga Mitsuaki (d. 1418). Jissō'in was one of the *monzeki*, or cloisters, of the Miidera branch of the Tendai sect located in Iwakura village, Atago district, Yamashiro Province.

503. Hisamatsu places this temple in Nara, perhaps following Nagashima Fukutarō, who identifies it as a sub-temple of Tōdaiji. However, neither scholar gives any proof, and the location and affiliation of the temple remains unclear. See Inada 1978:37.

spent the night. When he set out again the following morning, the abbot offered him a cup of wine with his own hand to wish him an auspicious journey. Thereupon the bishop took out a poem slip and handed it to me, saying, "Let me have a good poem to send me on my way." The suddenness of the request threw me into confusion, but as there was no way I could decently refuse, I calmly ground some ink and wrote down the following poem, which I presented to him:

Kono tabi wa	This time your journey
Yasuku zo koen	Will be easy as you make your way
Suzu wakete	Through bamboo thickets,
Moto fuminareshi	Treading the same path among the crags
Iwa no kakemichi.	That you have walked in days gone by.[504]

This was the second time he had made such a retreat into the mountains, and therefore I wrote, "Treading the same path . . ./ That you have walked in days gone by."

88. The younger brother[505] of the Reverend Jichin used to reside at the Ichijō'in[506] in Nara. On the fifteenth night of the eighth month, when, true to its reputation, the moon was shining brightly, he happened to be strolling about in the vicinity of the central gate, where a number of temple laborers were sweeping the courtyard. "What about it, lads?" said one, "His Reverence Jien must be composing poems on a night like this!"

The next morning the brother sent a long letter to the Reverend Jichin, remonstrating with him as follows:

"I fear to give offence by what I have to say, but I dare not keep it to myself. As the leader of all the temples on Mount Hiei[507] and the sustaining power for three thousand priests, you ought to be advocating and practicing the teachings of both the sect of the True Words[508] and the sect of Concentration and Insight.[509] That you spend your days and nights amusing yourself with elegant verses on the wind and the moon violates the principles of the Buddhist religion and degrades you to the level of a common layman. It is sacrilegious. The coarse laborers in the service of this temple were making remarks about you last night in the moonlight. You may

---

504. This poem appears nowhere else in Shōtetsu's works.
505. Believed to be Shin'en, an older brother of Jichin who served as abbot of the Ichijō'in, one of the cloisters of Kōfukuji in Nara, from 1224 on.
506. Jichin served four times as *Tendai zasu*, the highest of all Tendai offices.
507. Site of the great Tendai monastery northeast of Kyoto.
508. Shingon. The esoteric sect of Buddhism, as opposed to exoteric teachings of Tendai. Both traditions were maintained in the great Tendai enclave on Mt. Hiei.
509. *Shikan*, another name for the Tendai sect.

imagine how much more you must be the subject of common gossip all over the country. I beg of you to give up this art of poetry forthwith."

The Reverend Jichin, who was at that time abbot of Tennōji,[510] was in residence at that temple, and when the letter was brought to him, he wrote the brief reply, "I was delighted to receive your message," and added the following verse:

Minahito ni	Every human being
Hitotsu no kuse wa	Is said to have a single vice,
Aru zo to yo	And so I beg you:
Kore oba yuruse	Allow me to sing these songs of mine
Shikishima no michi.	On the Path of the Many Isles.[511]

On receiving this, the abbot of Ichijō'in was scandalized and gave up the whole thing as a bad business.

89. On "Love: When There Is Familiarity but No Intimacy":

Yo no tsune no	Though I pretend
Hito ni mono iu	To speak with her as if she were
Yoshi nagara	Just anyone at all,
Omou kokoro no	It seems that my yearning heart
Iro ya miyuran.	Betrays the color of my love.[512]

The expression "To speak with her as if she were/ Just anyone at all" may sound vulgar, but would it not be natural under the circumstances?

90. On "Lamps at an Old Temple":

Nori zo kore	This, then, is the Law:
Hotoke no tame ni	To the lamps that are lighted
Tomosu hi ni	For the Buddha's sake,
Hikari o soeyo	Add the sparkling radiance
Koto no ha no tama.	Of a string of gemlike Words.[513]

When the topic is treated in this fashion, the "old temple" is implied. It is ridiculous to insist one must have the actual word "temple" in a poem on the topic, "An Old Temple." "Old" is also merely an ancillary element. The phrase means simply "temple."[514]

---

510. Jichin is known to have lived at Shitennōji (in modern day Osaka) twice: the first time for most of the year 1208, and the second time from 1213 until 1225.

511. Source unknown.

512. *Sōkonshū* 4403. The topic implies that the couple are acquainted but have never had a love meeting.

513. This poem appears nowhere else in Shōtetsu's works.

514. In other words, since most temples are old, Shōtetsu sees no need to insist on explicit use of the word in one's poem.

91. "Auspicious Words at a Shrine":

Iohara ni	True, this Mio
Arazu Nagara no	Is the one in Nagara
Miyama moru	And not Iohara,
Mio no kami matsu	But still the gods protect this holy hill,
Urakaze zo fuku.	Bay breezes blow through sacred pines.[515]

The place known as the "Bay of Mio in Iohara" is in the province of Suruga.[516] The pine trees of that place, too, are treated in poetry. Now this place is also called Mio, but because it is not in Iohara, I said, "True, this Mio/ Is the one in Nagara/ And not Iohara." By saying "the gods protect . . ." the idea of "auspicious words" is conveyed. And because here, too, the wind must blow in off the bay, I wrote "Bay breezes blow . . . ."

92. Among amateurs of poetry there are a number of different kinds, just as there are various types among the amateurs of tea.[517] First among the amateurs of tea are those who possess beautiful tea utensils, who take pleasure in collecting China cups, T'ien-mu bowls, tea kettles, water jars, and all manner of tea articles.[518] In Japanese poetry their equivalent are those who are provided with elegant ink stones, desks, poem slips, and pocket paper, who always compose a complete set of verses, who choose places for their poetry meetings that are proper and well regulated—such men are like the amateurs of tea.[519]

Then again, those who are called tea drinkers are not particularly concerned about their utensils, but no matter where they are, they are always ready to engage in a bout of tea tasting.[520] If it is Uji

515. This poem appears nowhere else in Shōtetsu's works.
516. A famous place located on the coast in what is now Shizuoka Prefecture. The Iohara of Shōtetsu's poem is another place, located near Nagara Mountain in Ōmi (modern Shiga Prefecture).
517. Tea and the tea ceremony were very popular in his day, especially among the warriors who were Shōtetsu's primary patrons.
518. "China cups" refers specifically to cups made of Fu Kien porcelain, produced from the period of the Sung dynasty (960–1127) on; T'ien-mu (J *tenmoku*) tea bowls, noted for the beauty of their black- or persimmon-colored glaze, were produced at temples on Mount T'ien-mu in Chekiang. Along with other vessels and utensils, both were brought back from the continent by Zen monks and became popular for use in the tea ceremony.
519. *Chasuki*, literally, "connoisseurs of tea." Obviously, these were people of wealth, usually lords of the warrior class, who could afford to collect such wares and sponsor tea gatherings.
520. "Bout of tea tasting" translates *jippukucha*, an elegant competition in which participants would try to identify the highly valued *kōcha* ("red tea") in a tasting involving three kinds of tea, with three swallows each, and then one swallow of another kind of tea altogether.

tea, they will sip it and say, "This is the tea of the third picking," or "This tea was produced around the first of the third month."[521] Or with Toganō tea,[522] they will be able to tell by tasting whether it is from the tea gardens of Tobata[523] or the tea gardens of the Saga[524] area. Those who are able to recognize where a tea is from by tasting it, in the manner of Yamana, the former officer of the imperial guards,[525] are called tea drinkers. The equivalent of such men in poetry are those who are able to tell the good from the bad, who know whether a given word may or may not be used in a poem, who understand whether a given poetic conception is correct or incorrect, who can accurately rate people's poems as of high or low quality. Such men may be understood to be thoroughly versed in the very essence of poetry and should be ranked in a class with the tea drinkers previously mentioned.

Next are the tea guzzlers.[526] So long as it is tea, it means nothing to them whether it is crude and coarse or the best quality— they just go on swilling it down by the bowlful with no notion of whether it is good or bad. Such men who drink great quantities of tea are the tea guzzlers. Their equivalent in poetry are those who have no discrimination in diction and no regard for the good or bad in poetic ideas, who are not at all particular whether they associate with skilled poets or unskilled ones but go on forever pouring out verse simply because they like to write it. These men are the same sort as the tea guzzlers. So long as a person belongs to one of these three types of amateurs, no matter which one, he may take his proper place at a gathering.

Chiun used to say, "I am one of the tea guzzlers."[527]

93. In the early stages of learning, the very best form of practice is to compose poems in the company of many other people.

521. Uji, a rich farming region south of the capital, was famous for the quality of its tea, but the taste differed according to when the tea was picked—tea from the third picking (sanbancha; corresponding to August in the modern calendar) being most bitter and tea from the first picking (ichibancha; corresponding to May) being of highest quality.

522. Toganoo is an area just west of Kyoto. The monk Eisai (1141–1215), a Zen monk who is traditionally credited with being the first to bring tea to Japan, sent seeds to his friend Myōe (1173–1232) at his temple in the Toganoo, which ever after was famous for its tea gardens.

523. Presumably a reference to the Toba area, located just south of the capital.

524. Another farm district, just to the west of the capital.

525. Yamana Kingo. Identity uncertain. Hisamatsu suggests Yamana Tokihiro (d. 1435), who was a vice-commander of the imperial guards and father of Yamana Sōzen (lay name Mochitoyo; 1402–73).

526. Chakurai, those who simply gulp their tea down without the formalities.

527. Chiun. A samurai in the service of the shogun Ashikaga Yoshinori. Chiun was also an active poet who studied under Shōtetsu.

Later on there is no objection to composing by oneself. But if a person starts composing poems by himself from the beginning, his verses will be largely incomprehensible and lacking in interest.

94. When composing a large number of poems at one sitting, a person should persist with the first idea he has conceived and not give it up for something else. If he starts picking and choosing, using this and rejecting that, he will find it impossible to compose his poems.

95. The word *amabiko* ("prince of heaven") refers to the sun. The prince star, *hikoboshi*, also appears in poems as *ama tsu hikoboshi* ("prince star of heaven").[528] The element *tsu* is merely a filler.[529] The expression simply means "heavenly prince."

96. By "the day of no cutting or sewing" (*tachinuwanu hi*) is meant that only on the seventh day of the seventh month does the Weaver Maiden do no weaving or sewing of cloth. At other times she weaves on and on incessantly.[530]

97. The phrase *koromode no tanabata* ("the seventh night like the sleeve") is strung together simply to introduce the syllable *ta*, "hand," in *tanabata*. Wondering whether that was the way it ought to be, I figured it out for myself. It is on the same order as *koromode no Tanakami*. If only it were put together simply as *koromode no ta*, it might be possible in one way or another to work it into a poem.[531]

98. The phrase *tegai no inu* ("hand-reared dog") refers to the Herd Boy Star having a dog. It is found in a poem in *Man'yōshū*.[532] The Bridge of Magpies (*kasasagi no hashi*) refers to the magpies on opposite sides of the River of Heaven stretching out their wings from each side so that the Weaver Maid can cross. The Bridge of Autumn Leaves (*momiji no hashi*) also refers to the Bridge of Magpies.

528. The element *hi* in *hiko* means "sun," with *ko* meaning "child." Thus originally the word meant "child of the sun," later being used as an honorific applied to the gods and, still later, to male names. *Hikoboshi* is Altair, the Herd Boy of the Tanabata legend. See n. 343 above.

529. *Yasumeji*, literally a "resting word." A syllable added simply to produce the right syllable count.

530. See n. 343 above. It was because she failed to do any sewing for a long period after her marriage to the Herd Boy that the Weaver Maiden was separated from her husband and allowed to meet him only once a year. "On and on incessantly" translates *sanze jōju*, a Buddhist term meaning "residing forever, for three generations," which is a more emphatic way of saying "constantly."

531. There are no extant examples of *koromode no tanabata*, no doubt because the phrase involves nine syllables, an awkward number to work into a 5–7–5–7–7 poem. *Koromode no Tanakami*, however, does appear occasionally, the first part acting as a "pillow word" (*makura kotoba*) introducing the place-name Tanakami Mountain.

532. There are several poems in *MYS* in which dogs appear, but none of them in this phrase. Hisamatsu suggests that Shōtetsu might have in mind the word *hikuboshi*, another word for *hikoboshi* which appears in *Wamyō ruijūshō* ("A Categorized List of Japanese Readings," 938).

It does not mean the trees with their autumn foliage. It is called the Bridge of Autumn Leaves because the tears of blood shed in the grief of parting by the Herd Boy and Weaver Maid fall on the magpies' wings, which turn crimson and look like autumn leaves.[533]

99. *Yamabumi* means "tramping through the mountains." The word *yamabumi* is found in only one place in *Genji monogatari*. When Ukon goes to Hatsuse and meets Tamakazura and then comes back and tells Genji about it, she says, "Tramping through the mountains I happened to come upon a person who would move your heart."[534]

100. How can one define the style of mystery and depth? It is not something that can be described exactly, either in words or in terms of what one feels in one's heart so as to say, "This is the style of mystery and depth." Because the styles of moving clouds and swirling snow are also known by this name, perhaps the poetic effect of clouds trailing in the sky or of snow floating on the wind may be called the style of mystery and depth.

In the work known as *Guhi{shō}*,[535] or something of the sort, written by Teika, it says, "If the style of mystery and depth were to be defined by means of a comparison, in China there once lived a sovereign called King Hsiang. Taking his midday nap one day, he had dropped off to sleep, when a divine maiden came down from heaven and, in such a way that he could not tell whether it was dream or reality, gave herself to him with a pledge of love. Loath to part from her, King Hsiang begged her to remain, but the divine creature said, 'I am a heavenly maiden from the world above. Because of a bond from a previous life, I have come here at this time and given myself to you in love. But I cannot remain in this land.' So saying, she was about to fly away, when the king, overcome with longing, said, 'Then at least leave me some keepsake.' The divine maiden replied, 'Let this be a keepsake of me: there is a mountain near the royal palace called Mount Wu. Gaze out upon the clouds that trail away from this Mount Wu in the morning and the rain that falls on it in the evening.' And she disappeared. After this, filled with love and longing for the divine maiden, King Hsiang would gaze out upon the clouds that trailed away from Mount Wu in the morning and the rain that fell in the evening as a reminder of

533. See n. 343 above. The idea of a bridge of leaves appears in many poems, the first and most famous of which is *KKS* 175 (Autumn), Anonymous. [Headnote: Topic unknown] "Is it because/ She uses the bright foliage/ As a bridge to cross/ That the Weaver Maid of Heaven/ Waits so eagerly for autumn?" (*Ama no Kawa/ momiji o hashi ni/ wataseba ya/ Tanabatatsume no/ aki o shi mo matsu.*)

534. *NKBZ* 14:112–13 and Seidensticker 1976, I:401.

535. *Guhishō*, one of the forged texts that Shōtetsu regarded as the work of Teika. See the introduction (pp. 51–56).

her. His attitude in gazing at the morning clouds and the evening rain may be called the style of mystery and depth."[536]

So it is written. But here, too, just where the mystery is to be found depends upon the inner feelings of each individual. No doubt it is something that cannot possibly be explained in words or distinguished clearly in the mind. Perhaps one can only say that the style of mystery and depth conveys an effect of hazy, shimmering delicacy. Should one call the style of mystery and depth the poetic conception of four or five court ladies clad in silken trousers, gazing out upon the blossoms in full bloom in the southern palace? When it is asked just what there is about such a scene that is mysterious and deep, it is impossible to single out any particular element.

101. Having heard that Teika had said of him, "When Takasuke was young his poetry was not a bit inferior to that of his lordship his father, and I was quite confident of his future. But as he grew older, his poetry deteriorated badly," Takasuke is said to have retorted angrily, "Very well then, never mind about the poetry of my older age. Why doesn't he pick some poems of my youth for his imperial anthology?"[537]

As for Lord Ietaka's poetry, Lord Teika thought it frightening because it had, he said, some slight qualities of a style that presaged the extinction of his house.[538] And indeed it is strange that Ietaka's family line continued only from him to Takasuke, and thence to Ietaka's grandson Takahiro, and then died out.[539]

536. The relevant passage from *Guhishō* (see Hisamatsu's supplementary note 35, *NKBT* 65:284) is as follows: "The style of mystery and depth, too, is not a single style, but among the poems that are grouped together as poems of mystery and depth are the effects of moving clouds and swirling snow. Mystery and depth is the general term for these. Moving clouds and swirling snow are metaphors for charming, elegant women. In this respect, a poem that is gently elegant and elevated in tone and gives a feeling of the moon veiled in clouds may be said to be in the style of moving clouds. Again, a poem that is gentle and elegant, has an unusual air about it, and gives the feeling of fine snow dancing in the air and swirling about in a not too strong wind may be said to be in the style of swirling snow." The treatise then quotes from the original source of Teika's story, a rhyme-prose poem (*fu*) titled the *Kao-t'ang fu* (Rhyme-prose on Kao-t'ang), from the *Wen hsuan* ("Selections of Fine Writing"), a famous Chinese compendium of poetry and prose. See also *Gukenshō* (*NKGT* 4:355–56). For a thorough treatment of King Hsiang and the divine maidens of the Chinese tradition, see Schafer 1973.

537. Takasuke (d. ca. 1255) was the son and heir of Ietaka. His verse was praised by Teika, although the latter chose only two of Takasuke's poems for *Shinchokusenshū*. His work was also praised by Retired Emperor Go-Toba. After the latter's death, however, Takasuke became estranged from poetic circles and died an unhappy man. His personal collection of 342 poems is found in *SKT* 4.

538. See n. 15 above.

539. Takahiro (dates unknown) was actually of the Kujō family and not a son of Takasuke, but rather of Yukiie. Furthermore, it is not true that Ietaka's line died out so soon, since Takahiro's grandson Fuyutaka was a poet represented in *Gyokuyōshū*.

102. "Appreciating the Cherry Blossoms":

Hitoeda no	I adorn my cap
Hana no iroka o	With a single sprig of blossoms,
Kazasu yue	But their freshness
Itodo yatsururu	Only makes the sleeves of old age
Oi no sode kana.	Seem all the more faded and worn.[540]

During the snowy weather he had dressed in worn-out old clothes, but they look particularly bad here.

103. Ietaka did gain a name as a poet only after the age of forty. Prior to that he had composed quite a number of poems, but it was only after he turned forty that he was accorded any honor or praise.[541] Ton'a was over sixty before he achieved a reputation in the art.[542] Thus the masters of old did not have fame and honor from the time they were novices. Name and reputation are won by dint of constant practice and accumulated achievements. It is absurd how the men of the present day, having thus far produced only one or two hundred poems, think they can quickly become just like Teika or Ietaka. It was Teika himself who wrote, "Unless a man keeps walking, he will never reach his distant destination."[543] It is, they say, like going to the eastern provinces or to Kyushu: one can expect to arrive after a requisite number of days, but instead they try to get there by a single step as soon as they have decided to go.[544] If a man is deeply devoted to this art, if he pursues it unremittingly day and night, if he composes one poem after another lightly and easily but always pressing forward to the next one, he is bound to arrive at some interesting results sooner or later, quite naturally and without deliberately striving for success. On the other hand, His Lordship the Go-Kyōgoku regent[545] died at the age of thirty-seven, but being by nature a skilled poet, he wrote some compositions of the highest

540. This poem appears nowhere else in Shōtetsu's works.
541. Here Shōtetsu is influenced by a passage in Go-Toba no in go-kuden (NKBT 65:147 and Brower 1972:37). It was when he was around forty that he gained the support of Retired Emperor Go-Toba.
542. It was with the decline in talent of the Nijō house in the 1360s that Ton'a rose to greatest prominence.
543. A reference to a passage from Gukenshō (NKGT 4:358): "If a person is really intent upon this art, he should forget about eating and sleeping and set his heart upon composing poems day and night. On a long journey, one can never succeed in reaching his objective unless one puts one foot in front of the other. What example is there of a man becoming a skilled poet without composing poems?" This agrees with Shōtetsu's own idea about the necessity for constant practice.
544. The eastern provinces (the Kanto) and Kyushu, the two most important population centers outside of the capital area, were both treated as "distant" from the capital.
545. Go-Kyōgoku Yoshitsune (see n. 18 above).

excellence. If he had lived to the advanced age of eighty or ninety, how many even more valuable poetic treasures he would have produced! people said. Lady Kunaikyō died in her twentieth year, and one would have expected that in the course of time she would have benefited from continued practice and discipline, but the reason she already had fame and honor was because she was a natural born poet. When it comes to skill and talent that are inborn, from the very beginning stages of the novitiate such people immediately achieve accuracy and precision, so that it is not necessary to wait for the improving effects of discipline. But for the rest of humanity who are not like these few, provided they spend months and years spurring themselves on with unremitting discipline, in the end the time will come when they will naturally attain understanding and enlightenment. Above all there is nothing more precious and essential than dedication to the Art. In ancient times as well, men who were devoted to poetry were indulged in matters of unprecedented importance, and had their verses included in imperial anthologies. So long as a man is truly devoted to this Art, how can the time of enlightenment fail to come for him?[546]

* * * * * * * * * * *

This preceding volume is a copy by Tō no Sosan[547] of the manuscript in the author's hand.

546. In this final passage, Shōtetsu uses Buddhist terminology, thus ending his treatise the way it began—with a characterization of his art as a religious "way" of life that demands total dedication. His final sentence is reminiscent of the sentence that ends Teika's *Eiga taigai* in both tone and syntax (*NKBT* 65:234), which Shōtetsu quoted above in I, 94.
547. A nephew of Shōtetsu's student Tō no Tsuneyori (1401–84). See the introduction (pp. 40–42).

LIST OF CHARACTERS FOR NAMES AND TERMS

Characters from *Shōtetsu monogatari* are rendered in archaic form (*kyūkanji*), as in the *NKBT* edition; contemporary forms (*shinkanji*) have been used in all other cases.

Abutsu Ni 阿佛尼

Ahe no Ōji 安部祖父

Akamatsu Norisada 赤松教貞

aki no kure no zangiku 秋暮殘菊

Amida Butsu 阿彌陀佛

Ankamon'in no Shijō 安嘉門院四條

ari no mama ありのまま

Ariwara no Narihira 在原業平

Ariwara no Yukihira 在原行平

Asayama Bontō 朝山梵燈

Ashikaga Mitsuaki 足利満詮

Ashikaga Yoshiakira 足利義詮

Ashikaga Yoshimasa 足利義政

Ashikaga Yoshimitsu 足利義満

Ashikaga Yoshimochi 足利義持

Ashikaga Yoshinori 足利義教

Asukai Masaari 飛鳥井政有

Asukai Masachika 飛鳥井政親

Asukai Masatsune 飛鳥井政經

Asukai Masayo 飛鳥井政世

Asukai Masayori 飛鳥井政縁

Ausaka 逢坂

Awa no Kuni 阿波の國

aware no tei 哀れの躰

Ben'yōshō 弁要抄

Bifuku'mon'in no Kaga 美福門院の加賀

Bitchū 備中

bosatsu 菩薩

bōshitsu no tei 亡室の躰

bugyō 奉行

Bugyō no Jibu 奉行の治部

buke kadan 武家歌壇

bundai 文臺

butsudō 佛道

Butsuji'in 佛地院

byōtō no yamai 平頭の病

chakurai 茶くらひ

Chang chi-chih 張卽之

Chao ch'i-ang 趙子昂

chazuki 茶數寄

Chi-chih 卽之

chigiri 契

Chinzei 鎮西

Chiun 智蘊

chōka 長歌

Chōkei Tennō 長慶天皇

chokusenshū 勅撰集

Chōsan 長算

chū 中

dai 題

Daigo Tennō 醍醐天皇

Daikyō'in 大教院

dai o saguru 題を探る

denju 伝授

dokushi 讀師

ebizome ゑび染

Eiga no ittei 詠歌一躰

Eiga monogatari 栄花物語

Eiga taigai 詠歌大概

Eisai 栄西

Eishō-bon 永正本

Emperor Chōkei → see Chōkei Tennō

Emperor Go-Nijō → see Go-Nijō Tennō

Emperor Go-Saga → see Go-Saga Tennō

Emperor Horikawa → see Horikawa Tennō

Emperor Murakami → see Murakami Tennō

Emperor Ninmyō → see Ninmyō Tennō

Emperor Toba → see Toba Tennō

en 艶

engaku 縁覚

en no tei 艶体

etaru mono 得たる者

fu 賦

Fubokushō 夫木抄

Fūgashū 風雅集

Fuji 富士

Fujiwara Motoyasu 藤原元康

Fujiwara no Akisue 藤原顕季

Fujiwara no Ariie 藤原有家

Fujiwara no Ietaka 藤原家隆

Fujiwara no Michiie 藤原道家

Fujiwara no Michinaga 藤原道長

Fujiwara no Motoie 藤原基家

Fujiwara no Mototoshi 藤原基俊

Fujiwara no Nobuzane 藤原信實

Fujiwara no Sadanaga 藤原定長

Fujiwara no Shigemoto 藤原滋幹

Fujiwara no Shunzei 藤原俊成

Fujiwara no Sukemasa 藤原佐理

Fujiwara no Takanobu 藤原隆信

Fujiwara no Takasuke 藤原隆祐

Fujiwara no Tameie 藤原爲家

Fujiwara no Tametsugu 藤原爲繼

Fujiwara no Tametsune 藤原爲經

Fujiwara no Teika 藤原定家

Fujiwara no Yukinari 藤原行成

Fujiwara no Yukiyoshi 藤原行能

Fujiwara [Saitō] Toshinaga → see Saitō Toshinaga

fūkotsu 風骨

Fukurō sōshi 袋草紙

furiha ふりは

Furu no Imamichi 布留今道

Fushimi no In 伏見院

futō takumashiku no tei ふとうたくましき哥の躰

Gansei'in 岩栖院

Gen'e 玄恵

Genji monogatari 源氏物語

Genka 元可

Genshō 源承

Gen'yōshū 現葉集

Giun　義運

Go-Fushimi no In　後伏見院

Go-Horikawa no In　後堀河院

Go-Hosshōji Regent　後法性寺攝政

Gojō no Sanbon　五條三品

Go-Kōgon no In　後光嚴院

Go-Komatsu no In　後小松院

Go-Kyōgoku Sesshō　後京極攝政

Go-Kyōgoku Yoshitsune　後京極良經

Go-Nijō Tennō　後二条天皇

Gonjinshū　言塵集

Go-Shirakawa no In　後白河院

Go-Saga Tennō　後嵯峨天皇

gosekke　五摂家

Gosenshū　後撰集

goshomuki　御所むき

Goshūishū　後拾遺集

Go-Toba no In　後鳥羽院

Go-Toba no in gokuden　後鳥羽院御口伝

Go-Uda no In　後宇多院

Guhishō　愚秘抄

Gukenshō 愚見抄

Gumon kenchū 愚問賢註

Gusai 救済

Gyōgetsu (Reizei Tamemori) 曉月

Gyōhen 行遍

Gyōjin 堯尋

Gyōkō 堯孝

Gyokuyōshū 玉葉集

hadare はだれ

Hagiwara Hōkō 萩原法皇

Hakushi monjū 白氏文集

Hamamatsu chūnagon monogatari 浜松中納言物語

Hamuro Mitsutoshi 葉室光俊

Hanazono no In 花園院

hanka 反歌

hare no uta 晴の歌

Harima no Kuni 播磨の國

hashi no o はしのを

Hatakeyama Kenryō 畠山賢良

Hatakeyama Mochizumi 畠山持統

Hatakeyama Yoshitada 畠山義忠

Henjō 遍昭

hentai kanbun 変体漢文

hie sabi 冷えさび

Higashiyama 東山

Higo 肥後

higurashi 日ぐらし

hikan 被官

hikoboshi 彦星

himuro 氷室

Hino Katsumitsu 日野勝光

Hirohata no Kōi 廣幡の更衣

Hitomaro 人丸

Hitomaro eigu waka 人麿影供和歌

Hitorigoto ひとりごと

Hiyoshi 日吉

Hōbutsushū 宝物集

hōhen no kai 褒貶の會

Hōjō 北條

Hōjōji 法性寺

hokumen 北面

Hōnen 法然

hon'i 本意

honka 本哥

honkadori 本哥取

honka ni sugaritaru tei 本哥にすがりたる躰

hōraku 法樂

Horikawa no In 堀川院

Horikawa hyakushu 堀川百首

Horikawa Tennō 堀川天皇

Hosokawa Dōken 細川道賢

Hosokawa Katsumoto 細川勝元

Hosokawa Mitsumoto 細川満元

Hosokawa Mochikata 細川持賢

Hosokawa no Shō 細川庄

Hsiang-Ō 襄王

hyakushu 百首

hyakushu no tsugiuta 百首の續歌

hyōe 兵衞

Hyūga no Kuni 日向の國

ichibancha 一番茶

Ichijō'in 一條院

Ichijō Kaneyoshi 一条兼良

Ichijō Saneaki 一条実秋

Imagawa Ryōshun 今川了俊

Imagawa Sadayo 今川貞世

Imakumano 今熊野

Inawashiro Kensai 猪苗代兼載

Iohara いほはら

Ise no Kuni 伊勢の國

Ise monogatari 伊勢物語

Isshiki Norichika 一色教親

Iwami no Kuni 石見の國

Iwashimizu monogatari 石清水物語

Izayoi nikki 十六夜日記

Izumi Shikibu 和泉式部

Jakuren 寂蓮

Jibu Nyūdō 治部入道

Jichin 慈鎮

Jien 滋圓

jige 地下

Jikkinshō 拾訓抄

jippukucha 十服茶

Ji Shū 時宗

Jissō 實增

Jissō'in 實相院

jitsu naru tei 實なる躰

Jōben 淨辨

Jōdo Shū 淨土宗

Jōkō'in 常光院

Josuishō 除睡鈔

Jūa 重阿

jukkai 述懷

Juntoku'in gohyakushu 順德院御百首

Juntoku no In 順德院

kabazakura かば櫻

kabiya かびや/鹿火屋

kabyō 歌病

kai 會

Kai'inji 海印寺

kaisetsu no tei 廻雪躰

kaishi 懐帋

Kakinomoto no Hitomaro 柿本人麻呂

Kakinomoto Tsurami 柿本貫躬

Kakue 覚恵

kakushidai 隠題

Kamakura 鎌倉

Kamakura no Udaijin 鎌倉右大臣

kami no ku 上の句

Kamo no Chōmei 鴨長明

kana 假名

kaniwazakura かにはざくら

Kanpyō 寛平

kanrei 管領

Kantō 関東

Kao-t'ang fu 高唐賦

Karaka no Shima からかのしま

kasen 哥仙

kayaribi 蚊遣火

Kazan'in Nagachika 花山院長親

Kazuraki no Kami かづらきの神

ke 假

keiko 稽古

Keikō 慶孝

Keiun 慶運

Keiun hōin shū 慶運法印集

kemari 蹴鞠

kenjitsu no kai 兼日の會

Kenpō meisho hyakushu 健保名所百首

Kenpō sannen jūgatsu nijūyokka dairi meisho hyakushu
健保三年十月二十四日内裏名所百首

Kensai zōdan 兼載雑談

Kenshō 顯昭

Kibune 貴船

Kindai shūka 近代秀歌

King Hsiang → see Hsiang Ō

Ki no Tsurayuki 紀貫之

Kinrai fūteishō 近来風躰抄

kirigirisu きりぎりす

Kirihioke 桐火桶

Kitano 北野

Kiyosu 清洲

Kōbō Daishi 弘法大師

kōcha 紅茶

koe ni yomu 聲に讀む

Kōfukuji 興福寺

Koga Masazane 久我雅実

Kōgon Tennō 光嚴天皇

Kokin denju 古今伝授

Kokin ikyokyushū 古今夷曲集

Kokin wakashū 古今和歌集

Kokin waka rokujō 古今和歌六帖

kokoro 心

Kōkyō 広経

Komatsu Hidekiyo 小松秀清

Komatsu Masakiyo 小松正清

Komatsu Yasukiyo 小松康清

Kōmyōbuji Dono 光明峯寺殿

Kō no Moronao 高師直

Konrenji 金蓮寺

Korai fūteishō 古来風体抄

Koreakira Shinnō 惟明親王

kōshi 講師

kotoba 詞

Kōun 耕雲

kōun kaisetsu no tei　行雲廻雪の体

kōun no tai　行雪躰

kū　空

kudai　句題

kuihoriirite anzu　くひほり入りて案ず

Kujō Ieyoshi　九条家良

Kujō Kanezane　九条兼実

Kujō Michiie　九条道家

Kujō Takahiro　九条隆博

Kūkai　空海

kun　訓

Kunaikyō　宮內卿

kun ni yomu　訓に讀む

kunyomi　訓讀み

kurai　位

Kuroda　黑田

Kurodani　黑谷

Kurōdodokoro　藏人所

Kyōgetsu　敎月

Kyōgoku Tamekane　京極爲兼

Kyōgoku Tameko　京極爲子

Kyōgoku Tamemoto 京極為基

Kyōgoku Tamenori 京極為教

Kyōken Hōin 經賢法印

kyokushin no tei 極信体

Kyoto 京都

Kyushu 九州

Kyūshū Tandai 九州探題

Li Po 李白

Maigetsu gohyakushu 毎月御百首

Maigetsushō 毎月抄

Makeishura 摩醯首羅

makura kotoba 枕詞

Makura no sōshi 枕の草子

Manji 萬時

man'yōgana 万葉仮名

Man'yōshū 萬葉集

Man'yōshū chūshaku 萬葉集注釋

Man'yōshū jidai kō 萬葉集時代考

Masakiyo 正清

mashimizu 眞清水

masurao ますらを

Matsudono Motofusa　松殿基房

Matsura no Miya monogatari 松浦宮物語

Meigetsuki 明月記

meisho 名所

mezuraka めずらか

Mibu no Tadami　壬生忠見

Miidera　三井寺

Mikohidari　御子左

Minamoto no Chikayuki　源親行

Minamoto no Michimitsu　源通光

Minamoto no Michitomo　源通具

Minamoto no Moroaki　源庶明

Minamoto no Sanetomo　源實朝

Minamoto no Tamenori　源爲憲

Minamoto no Tomochika　源具親

Minamoto no Toshiyori　源俊頼

Minamoto no Tsunenobu　源経信

Minamoto no Yoritomo　源頼朝

Minase tsuridono rokushu uta-awase　水無瀬釣殿六首歌合

Minbukyō　民部卿

Minishū　壬二集

Mino no Kuni　美濃の國

Miraiki　未來記

mōdaru tei　もふだる躰

momi ni mōdaru　もみにもうだる

mono aware tei　物哀れの躰

mono no na　物の名

mono tsuyoki tei　物つよき躰

monzeki　門跡

Mumyōshō　無名抄

Munetaka Shinnō　宗尊親王

Murakami Genji　村上源氏

Murakami Tennō　村上天皇

Muro no Yashima　室の八島

Muroyama　むろ山

mushin naru mono　無心なる物

musubidai　結題

Myōe　明恵

Myōkōji　妙行寺

nadokoro　名所

naetate　苗立

Nagarayama　ながらやま

nagatsuki no ariake　長月の在明

Nagatsuna　長綱

Nagatsuna hyakushu　長綱百首

nage no nasake　なげの情

Nagusamegusa　なぐさめ草

Naitō no Shirōzaemon　內藤四郎左衞門

naka no koromo　中の衣

Nara　奈良

Nigonshō　二言抄

Nihongi　日本記

Nijō Tameakira　二条爲明

Nijō Tamemigi　二条為右

Nijō Tamesada　二条為定

Nijō Tameshige　二条爲重

Nijō Tametō　二条為遠

Nijō Tameuji　二条爲氏

Nijō Tameyo　二条爲世

Nijō Yoshimoto 二条良基

Nikaidō Sadamune 二階堂貞宗

Ninagawa Chikamasa 蜷川親当

Ninmyō Tennō 仁明天皇

Ninnaji 仁和寺

Nishi no Kisaki 西の后

Nōin 能因

nōsho 能書

Nōyo 能与

Nunobiki no Taki 布引の滝

nushi aru kotoba 主ある詞

Oda no Shō 小田庄

Ōe no Masafusa 大江匡房

Ōe no Yoshitoki 大江嘉言

Ogasawara 小笠原

Ōgishō 奥儀抄

oku no o 奥のお

Ōmi 近江

omoshiroki tei 面白き躰

omoshiroshi 面白し

Ōnin no Ran 応仁の乱

Onjōji　園城寺

Ono no Komachi　小野小町

Ono no Michikaze　小野道風

Ono no Shō　小野の庄

Ontoku'in　恩徳院

onyomi　音讀

Ōshikōchi no Mitsune　凡河内躬恆

Ōtomo no Yakamochi　大伴家持

Owari no Kuni　尾張の國

Po Chü-i　白居易

Rakusho roken　落書露顕

Reizei Mochitame　冷泉持為

Reizei Tamehide　冷泉爲秀

Reizei Tamekuni　冷泉爲邦

Reizei Tamemasa　冷泉爲尹

Reizei Tamemori　冷泉爲守

Reizei Tamesuke　冷泉爲相

Reizei Tameyuki　冷泉為之

renga　連歌

renga shichiken 連歌七賢

Retired Emperor Fushimi → see Fushimi no In

Retired Emperor Go-Fushimi → see Go-Fushimi no In

Retired Emperor Go-Horikawa → see Go-Horikawa no In

Retired Emperor Go-Kōgon → see Go-Kōgon no In

Retired Emperor Go-Komatsu → see Go-Komatsu no In

Retired Emperor Go-Shirakawa → see Go-Shirakawa no In

Retired Emperor Go-Toba → see Go-Toba no In

Retired Emperor Go-Uda → see Go-Uda no In

Retired Emperor Hanazono → see Hanazono no In

Retired Emperor Juntoku → see Juntoku no In

Retired Emperor Takakura → see Takakura no In

Retired Emperor Uda → see Uda no In

Retired Empress Ankamon → see Ankamon'in no Shijō

Retired Shōgun Shōjō'in → see Shōjō'in

Rinzai Zen 臨済禅

rokkasen 六歌仙

rokui no kurōdo 六位蔵人

Rokujō Akisue 六條顯季

Rokujō Akisuke 六条顯輔

Rokujō Arifusa 六條有房

Rokujō Ariie 六条有家

Rokujō Kiyosuke 六条清輔

Rokujō Tomoie 六条具家

Rokujō Yukiie 六条行家

Roppyaku-ban uta-awase 六百番歌合

Ryōshun isshiden 了俊一子伝

Saga 嵯峨

Sagoromo monogatari 狭衣物語

sahiraki 早開

saigaku 才覺

Saigyō 西行

Saitō Toshinaga 斎藤利永

Saki no sesshō-ke uta-awase 前撰政家歌合

samuraidokoro 侍所

sanbancha 三番茶

Sanbō'in 三宝院

sandai 三代

sandaishū 三代集

Sangoki 三五記

sanjōdō 三乗道

San no Miya 三の宮

Santai waka 三躰和歌

sanze jōju 三世常住

saori さをり

Sari 左理

satoru 悟る

Seal of the Law Kyōken → see Kyōken

Seiashō 井蛙抄

Seigan chawa 清巖茶話

sei'in no yamai 聲韻の病

sei no koto 聲の事

sei no kotoba 制のこと葉

Sei Shōnagon 清少納言

Sengaku 仙覺

Sengohyaku-ban uta-awase 千五百番歌合

Senjun 專順

sen wakadokoro 撰和歌所

Sesonji-ryū 世尊寺流

Settsu 攝津

Shakua 釋阿

Shiba 斯波

shigi 鴫

shika しか

shikan 止観

Shikishi Naishinnō 式子內親王

shimizu 清水

Shimizudani 清水谷

shimo no ku 下の句

shimozuki 霜月

Shinchokusenshū 新勅撰集

Shin'en 信円

Shingon Shū 眞言宗

Shingosenshū 新後撰集

Shingoshūishū 新後拾遺集

Shinkan 真観

Shinkei 心敬

Shinkokinshū 新古今集

Shinnyōdō 真如堂

Shinsen rōeishū 新撰朗詠集

Shinsen waka rokujō 新撰和歌六帖

Shinshō Gokurakuji 真正極楽寺

Shinshūishū 新拾遺集

Shin'yōshū　新葉集

Shinzokukokinshū　新続古今集

Shiragi Myōjin　新羅明神

Shirakawa no Seki　白川の關

Shirin saiyōshū　詞林採葉集

Shisetsu jikenshū　師説自見集

shishō　師匠

shitennō　四天王

Shitennōji　四天王寺

Shōgetsu　招月

Shōgetsu seigan wakashō　招月清巖和歌抄

shōgun　將軍

Shōji hyakushu　正治百首

Shōjō　正清

Shōjō'in　勝定院

Shōjōkōji　清浄光寺

shōka　證哥

shoki　書記

Shōkō　正広

Shōkō nikki　正広日記

Shoku gen'yōshū　続現葉集

Shokugosenshū 續後撰集

Shokugoshūishū 続後拾遺集

Shokukokinshū 續古今集

Shokushūishū 続拾遺集

shōmon 声聞

Shōmyōji 称名寺

Shōren'in 青蓮院

shōsaku 匠作

Shōsammi monogatari 正三位物語

shoshin 初心

Shōtetsu 正徹

Shōtetsu monogatari 正徹物語

Shōtetsu nikki 正徹日記

Shōtetsu senshu 正徹千首

Shōwa Tennō 承和天皇

shūgihan 衆議判

shugo 守護

shui 主位

Shūishū 拾遺集

shūku 秀句

Shunzei no Musume 俊成の女

shuri daibu 修理大夫

shurishiki 修理職

Sōanshū 草庵集

Sochin 素珍

Sōga 宋雅

Sogetsu 素月

Sōgi 宗祇

Sōkonshū 草根集

Son'en Hōshinnō 尊円法親王

Sonmyōmaru 尊命(明)丸

Sonshō'in 尊勝院

Sōrinji 双林寺

Sosei 素性

Sugawara no Tamenaga 菅原爲長

Sugiwara 杉原

Sumiyoshi 住吉

Sumiyoshi monogatari 住吉物語

Suruga 駿河

susami すさみ

Susanoo no Mikoto 須佐の男の命

Tachibana no Noritaka 橘範隆

tada mahira naru uta ただまひらなる哥

Taira no Shigemori 平重盛

Takakura no In 高倉院

Takatsu 高津

Takayama Sōzei 高山宗砌

Takechi no Kurohito 高市黒人

Takeda 武田家

Takeda Shinken 武田信賢

taketakaki tei 長高躰

taketakaki yō 長高様

Taketori monogatari 竹取物語

takiguchi no bushi 瀧口の武士

Tamemasa senshu 為尹千首

Tamesue-kyō 爲季卿

tanabata 七夕

tandai 探題

tanzaku 短冊

Tatsuta 立田

Teika-kyō hyakuban jika-awase 定家卿百番自歌合

Teika sūhai　定家崇拝

ten　點

Tendai　天台

Tendai zasu　天台座主

tenkyū　典厩

tenmoku　典目

Tesshoki　徹書記

Tesshoki monogatari　徹書記物語

t'ien mu → see *tenmoku*

Toba　とば

Toba Tennō　鳥羽天皇

Tōdaiji　東大寺

Tōfukuji　東福寺

Toganoo　栂尾

Tōji　東寺

toki no tora　時の寅

Tokudaiji　德大寺

Ton'a　頓阿

Toneri　舎人

Tō no Sosan　東素珊

Tō no Tsuneyori　東常縁

Tō no Ujikazu　東氏数

Tosa nikki 土佐日記

Toshiyori zuinō 俊頼髄脳

Tōtomi 遠江

Tōyashū kikigaki 東野州聞書

tsugiuta 續歌

tsukinamikai 月次会

Tsukinowa Dono 月輪殿

Tsukinowa Motokata 月輪基賢

Tsukinowa Suekata 月輪季尹

Tsukinowa Tadakata 月輪尹賢

Tsurayuki shū 貫之集

Tsurezuregusa つれづれ草

Tsurudono 鶴殿

Tsuzumi no Taki つづみの瀧

uchigiki 打聞

uchi no dokushi 內の讀師

Uji 宇治

Ukon 右近

ushin tei 有心躰

utamakura 歌枕

uta no yamai 歌の病

utayomi 哥讀

waka 和歌

wakadokoro 和哥所

Wakan rōeishū 和漢朗詠集

Wamyō ruijūshō 倭名類聚抄

Wen hsuan 文選

Wu shan 巫山

Yakumo mishō 八雲御抄

Yakushiji Genka Nyūdō 藥師寺元可入道

Yakushiji Jirō Saemon Kinyoshi 藥師寺次郎左衛門公義

Yamabe no Akahito 山部赤人

Yamana Hirotaka 山名熙貴

Yamana Mochiteru 山名持照

Yamana Mochitoyo 山名持豊

Yamana Noritoyo 山名教豊

Yamana Noriyuki 山名教之

Yamana Ōkura no Daisuke 山名大藏大輔

Yamana Sōzen 山名宗全

Yamana Tokihiro 山名時熙

Yamana Tsuneteru 山名常照

Yamana Yukitomo 山名之朝

Yamashiro 山城

Yamato 大和

Yamato monogatari 大和物語

yariuta やり哥

yasumeji やすめ字

yōen tei 妖艶躰

yojō tei 餘情躰

yojō yōen no tei 餘情妖艶躰

yokoshima 邪

Yoshida no Kenkō 吉田兼好

Yoshino 吉野

yūen 幽遠

Yūgaku ōrai 遊学往来

yūgen batsugun 幽玄抜郡

yūgen tei 幽玄躰

yusoku 有職

yūzukuyo 夕づくよ

Zen'on 禪薀

Zenrinji Chūnagon 禪林寺中納言

Zen Shū 禪宗

zō 雑

Zoku sōanshū 続草庵集

BIBLIOGRAPHY

Works identified by abbreviation in the notes and works appearing in anthologies cited by abbreviation are not listed here. See "List of Abbreviations."

Araki Hisashi. 1977. *Imagawa Ryōshun no kenkyū*. Tokyo: Kasama Shoin.

Brower, Robert H. 1972. "Ex-Emperor Go-Toba's Secret Teachings: *Go-Toba no In Gokuden*." *Harvard Journal of Asiatic Studies* 32:5–70.

————. 1981. "The Reizei Family Documents." *Monumenta Nipponica* 36.4:445–61.

————. 1985. "Fujiwara Teika's *Maigetsushō*." *Monumenta Nipponica* 40.4:399–425.

————. 1987. "The Foremost Style of Poetic Composition: Fujiwara Tameie's *Eiga no Ittei*." *Monumenta Nipponica* 42.4:391–429.

Brower, Robert H. and Earl Miner. 1967. *Fujiwara Teika's Superior Poems of Our Time: A Thirteenth Century Poetic Treatise and Sequence*. Stanford: Stanford University Press.

Carter, Steven D. 1983. *Three Poets at Yuyama*. Japan Research Monographs 4. Berkeley: Institute of Asian Studies.

————. 1987. *The Road to Komatsubara: A Classical Reading of the Renga Hyakuin*. Harvard East Asian Monographs 124. Cambridge: Harvard University Press.

————. 1989. *Waiting for the Wind: Thirty-six Poets of Japan's Late Medieval Age*. New York: Columbia University Press.

Fujiwara no Ietaka. *Minishū. SKT* 3.

Fujiwara no Shunzei. *Korai fūteishō. NKBZ* 50.

————. *Man'yōshū jidai kō. ZGR* 16, part 2.

Fujiwara no Tameie. *Eiga no ittei. NKGT* 3.

Fujiwara no Teika. *Eiga taigai. NKBT* 65.

————. *Kindai shūka. NKBT* 65.

————. *Maigetsushō. NKBT* 65.

Fukuda Hideichi. 1976. "*Shōtetsu monogatari*," in *Chūsei hyōronshū. Kanshō nihon koten bungaku* 24. Tokyo: Kadokawa Shoten.

Gen'e. *Yūgaku ōrai. ZGR* 13, part 2.

Genji monogatari. 6 vols. *NKBZ* 12–17.

Go-Toba no In. *Go-Toba no In gokuden. NKBT* 65.

Guhishō. NKGT 4.

Gukenshō. NKGT 4.

Hitomaro eigu waka. GR 13.

Horikawa hyakushu. SKT 4.

Hosoya Naoki. 1976. *Chūsei karon no kenkyū*. Tokyo: Kasama Shoin.

Huey, Robert N. 1989. *Kyōgoku Tamekane: Poetry and Politics in Late Kamakura Japan*. Stanford: Stanford University Press.

Imagawa Ryōshun. *Ben'yōshō*. *NKGT* 5.

————. *Nigonshō*. *NKGT* 5.

————. *Rakusho roken*. *NKGT* 5.

————. *Shisetsu jikenshū*. *NKGT* 5.

Inada Toshinori. 1978. *Shōtetsu no kenkyū: chūsei kajin no kenkyū*. Tokyo: Kasama Shoin.

Inoue Muneo. 1984. *Chūsei kadan-shi no kenkyū, Muromachi zenki*, rev. ed. Tokyo: Kazama Shobō.

Ise monogatari. *NKBT* 9.

Juntoku no In. *Juntoku'in onhyakushu*. *ZGR* 14, part 2.

————. *Yakumo mishō*. *NKGT* suppl. vol. 3.

Kamo no Chōmei. *Mumyōshō*. *NKBT* 65.

Katō, Hilda. 1968. "The *Mumyōshō* of Kamo no Chōmei and Its Significance in Japanese Literature." *Monumenta Nipponica* 33.3–4:321–430.

Kawazoe Shōji. 1964. *Imagawa Ryōshun*. Vol. 117 of *Jinbutsu sōsho*. Tokyo: Yoshikawa Kobundan.

Keene, Donald, trans. 1967. *Essays in Idleness: The Tsurezuregusa of Kenkō*. New York: Columbia University Press.

————. 1989. "A Neglected Chapter." *Monumenta Nipponica* 44.1:1–30.

Keiun. *Keiun hōin shū*. *ST* 5.

Kennaiki. 2d ed. 10 vols. *Dai Nihon kokiroku* series. Iwanami Shoten, 1987.

Kenpō meisho hyakushu. SKT 5.

Kensai. *Kensai zōdan. NKGT* 5.

Kidō Saizō, ed. 1985. *Rengaronshū 3. Chūsei no bungaku* 12. Tokyo: Miyai Shoten.

Ki no Tsurayuki. *Tsurayuki shū. SKT* 3.

Kirihioke. NKGT 4.

Kokin waka rokujō. SKT 2.

Konishi Jin'ichi. 1976. *Shinkō roppyaku-ban uta-awase.* Tokyo: Yūseidō.

Kubota Jun, ed. 1985–86. *{Shakuchū} Fujiwara Teika zenkashū.* 2 vols. Tokyo: Kawade Shōbo Shinsha.

LaFleur, William R. 1983. *The Karma of Words: Buddhism and the Literary Arts in Medieval Japan.* Berkeley: University of California Press.

Levy, Ian Hideo. 1981. *The Ten Thousand Leaves: A Translation of Man'yōshū, Japan's Premier Anthology of Classical Poetry.* Vol. 1. Princeton: Princeton University Press.

McCullough, Helen Craig. 1968. *Tales of Ise: Lyrical Episodes from Tenth-Century Japan.* Stanford: Stanford University Press.

————, trans. 1985. *Kokin Wakashū: The First Imperial Anthology of Japanese Poetry.* Stanford: Stanford University Press.

———— and William H. McCullough. 1980. *A Tale of Flowering Fortunes: Annals of Japanese Aristocratic Life in the Heian Period.* 2 vols. Stanford: Stanford University Press.

Minamoto no Toshiyori. *Toshiyori zuinō*. *NKBZ* 50.

Miraiki. *NKGT* 4.

Miura Mitsuo. 1976. "Shōtetsu," in *Chūsei kinsei no kajin*, vol. 7 of *Waka bungaku kōza*. Tokyo: Ōfūsha.

Morris, Ivan. 1967. *The Pillow Book of Sei Shōnagon*. 2 vols. New York: Columbia University Press.

Nagatsuna hyakushu. *ZGR* 14, part 2.

Nihon koten bungaku daijiten. 1984. Comp. Ichiko Teiji et al. 6 vols. Tokyo: Iwanami Shoten.

Nijō Yoshimoto. *Kinrai fūteishō*. *NKGT* 5.

Reizei Tamemasa. *Tamemasa senshu*. *SKT* 4.

Roppyaku-ban uta-awase. *SKT* 5.

Sagoromo monogatari. *NKBT* 79.

Saki no sesshō-ke uta-awase. *SKT* 5.

Sangoki. *NKGT* 4.

Santai waka. *SKT* 5.

Schafer, Edward H. 1973. *The Divine Woman: Dragon Ladies and Rain Maidens in T'ang Literature*. Berkeley: The University of California Press.

Seidensticker, Edward G. 1976. *The Tale of Genji*. 2 vols. New York: Alfred A. Knopf.

Sei Shōnagon. *Makura no sōshi*. *NKBT* 19.

Sengohyaku-ban uta-awase. *SKT* 5.

Shinkei. *Hitorigoto*. NST 23.

_____. *Oi no kurigoto*. In Kidō Saizō, ed., 1985 above.

_____. *Sasamegoto*. NKBT 66.

_____. *Tokorodokoro hentō*. In Kidō Saizō, ed., 1985 above.

Shinsen rōeishū. SKT 2.

Shoku gen'yōshū. GR 7.

Shōtetsu. *Eikyō kunen shōtetsu eisō*. ST 5.

_____. *Kika jukkai waka*. In Inada 1978 above.

_____. *Koi uta ichijuku*. In *Koten sōshō sōkonshū*. Notoru Damu Joshi Seishin Daigaku, 1973.

_____. *Nagusamegusa*. In *Zoku-zoku kikō bunshū*. Nihon Tosho Senta, 1977.

_____. *Seigan chawa*. NKGT 5.

_____. *Shōtetsu eiga*. ST 5.

_____. *Shōtetsu eisō*. ST 7.

_____. *Shōtetsu monogatari*. NKBT 65.

_____. *Shōtetsu senshu*. SKT 4.

_____. *Sōkonshū*. ST 5.

_____. [Kurokawa-bon] *Sōkonshū*. In *Koten sōshō*. Notoru Damu Seishin Joshi Daigaku, 1973.

_____. *Tesshoki monogatari*. NKGT 5.

_____. *Tsukikusa*. ST 5.

Sōgi. *Azuma mondō. NKBT* 66.

Tahara, Mildred. 1980. *Tales of Yamato: A Tenth-Century Poem-Tale.* Honolulu: The University Press of Hawaii.

Teika-kyō hyakuban jika-awase. SKT 5.

Ton'a. *Gumon kenchū. NKGT* 5.

―――. *Seiashō. NKGT* 5.

―――. *Sōanshū. SKT* 4.

―――. *Zoku sōanshū. SKT* 4.

Tō no Tsuneyori. *Tōyashū kikigaki. NKGT* 5.

Waka bungaku daijiten. 1962. Comp. Kubota Utsuho et al. Tokyo: Meiji Shoin.

Waka bungaku jiten. 1982. Comp. Ariyoshi Tamotsu. Tokyo: Ōfūsha.

Waka kanshō jiten. 1970. Comp. Fujihira Haruo, Kubota Shōichirō, and Yamaji Heishirō. Tokyo: Tōkyōdō.

Waka no kaishaku to kanshō jiten. 1979. Comp. Inoue Muneo et al. Tokyo: Ōbunsha.

Wakan rōeishū. SKT 2.

Yakushiji Genka. *Genka hōshi shū. ST* 5.

Yamato monogatari. NKBT 9.

Yoshida no Kenkō. *Tsurezuregusa. NKBT* 30.

INDEX

ABOUT THE AUTHORS

Robert H. Brower, one of the founders of the study of Japanese literature in the United States, was Professor Emeritus of Japanese Language and Literature at the University of Michigan. His career spanned four decades, during which time he published numerous articles and monographs on traditional Japanese poetry and poetic criticism, as well as the classic study, *Japanese Court Poetry* (with Earl Miner, 1962).

Steven D. Carter is Professor of Japanese in the Department of East Asian Languages and Literatures at the University of California, Irvine. His works include *Traditional Poetry of Japan* (1991), an anthology of translations of Japanese poems; *Waiting for the Wind: Thirty-Six Poets of Japan's Late Medieval Age* (1989); and *The Road to Komatsubara: A Classical Reading of the* Renga Hyakuin (1987).

Printed and bound by CPI Group (UK) Ltd, Croydon, CR0 4YY

13/04/2025

14656508-0002